D1625946

THE VICTORIANS

THE VICTORIANS

Twelve Titans
Who Forged
Britain

JACOB REES-MOGG

WH
ALLEN

3 5 7 9 10 8 6 4 2

WH Allen, an imprint of Ebury Publishing,
20 Vauxhall Bridge Road,
London SW1V 2SA

WH Allen is part of the Penguin Random House group
of companies whose addresses can be found at global.
penguinrandomhouse.com

Copyright © Jacob Rees-Mogg 2019

Jacob Rees-Mogg has asserted his right to be identified as the
author of this work in accordance with the Copyright, Designs
and Patents Act 1988

First published by WH Allen in 2019

www.penguin.co.uk

A CIP catalogue record for this book is available from the British
Library

Hardback ISBN 9780753548523

Typeset in 11/16 pt Clarendon Lt Bt
by Integra Software Services Pvt. Ltd, Pondicherry

Printed and bound in Great Britain by Clays Ltd, Elcograf S.p.A.

Pengu   future for
our bu   made from

My mother on her 80th birthday, without whom this book could not have been written.

Contents

Introduction: The Eminent Victorians

Early in 1895, Queen Victoria's private secretary Sir Henry Ponsonby attended on Her Majesty for the last time. Ponsonby had served the Queen in this role since 1870 but he had suffered a stroke in the previous year. He was no longer able to fulfil his duties and now he was calling on the Queen at Osborne to say his farewells. It is recorded that he looked at Victoria and said slowly, 'What a funny little old woman you are.' The Queen's response was 'Sir Henry, you cannot be well' and she swiftly rang the bell for him to be removed from the Royal presence.

In a peculiar way, this unorthodox comment issued by a loyal courtier has become something of the standard view of the entire Victorian age. It is a very strange view or summation of a time of truly transformational, revolutionary change in Britain, an age when life expectancy was increasing, material wealth rising year by year and the Constitution evolving gloriously into a settled and stable state. All of it reduced to the figure of this littlest of little old ladies, of rather an excessive fusspot, who is never amused. At a stroke, the gilding of the Victorian period becomes scraped and damaged.

In his famous book *Eminent Victorians*, published in 1918, the Bloomsburyite Lytton Strachey did his bit to scratch at this gilding. His book took a blow torch to the heroes of the British nineteenth century while the abiding cynicism of our age has tended to accept his assessment. This too seems counter-intuitive because the briefest glance at the history of Victorian Britain reveals its abiding achievements and the parade of significant public figures from whom so much can be learned. Sadly, society these days, which has so little faith in anything, is understandably nervous of those Victorians who believed in so much, who embraced a sense of purpose and destiny so glaringly lacking both in their Hanoverian predecessors and in the beau monde of our contemporary world. In *Eminent Victorians*, Strachey mocked the weaknesses where they could be found but ignored the 'great image, whose brightness was excellent ... This image's head was of fine gold, his breast and his arms of silver, his belly and thighs of brass.' Such beautiful and resonant language comes from the Book of Daniel, as it described a glorious and gleaming figure. Only its feet were wrought of clay. Yet Strachey focused on the clay alone.

Perhaps it is natural to mock the recent past. We do so in order to ignore the failures of our own world so it is little surprise that the twentieth century should laugh at the Victorians. The twentieth century was a new age when, as Bloomsbury promised, tea would be taken at different and exciting times of the day but it was a period which embraced war and destruction on a scale unprecedented in world history. No wonder the new century should seek instead to laugh at the era just passed while a century of growing cynicism and of decline should glance enviously back to a period of moral certainty, of success. It could hardly have been any other way.

Nonetheless, I owe a debt to Strachey and his mean-minded book because when I had leafed through *Eminent Victorians* I was struck by its unfairness and its cynicism. It occurred to me that it was time to look again at some of these eminent Victorians and to reassess their effect upon and contribution to their world and to our own. Now is the time to reconsider and marvel at how remarkable the Victorian period was and to study the luminaries who led it and who invested in the condition of the people. After all, good leadership matters. Historians quarrel about the importance of individuals in the development of history and argue about how much would have happened anyway. However, the drive and industry of certain people cannot be ignored and the effects of their lives and their decisions can in fact be discerned and something of their impact glimpsed. Indeed, such was the quality of leadership in Victoria's reign that it is more difficult to decide whom to exclude than to include as so many figures dominated their own fields. It is thus a reasonable complaint to say that any selection is essentially arbitrary.

Hence I have chosen a dozen such leaders in this book. A dozen who share certain common characteristics but who would not by any means have agreed with each other on everything. They come from throughout the 'long Victorian century', which stretches from the birth of Lord Palmerston in 1784 to the death of Albert Venn Dicey in 1922. Two elder statesmen, in the figures of Palmerston and Sir Robert Peel; two later, and rival, politicians, in the form of William Gladstone and Benjamin Disraeli; two military men, in the shapes of Sir Charles Napier and Charles Gordon; the architect Augustus Pugin and the legal authority Dicey; the great cricketer W. G. Grace and the administrator William Sleeman. Finally, Victoria herself and her consort Albert.

Each was patriotic but in a positive rather than an aggressive sense. Napier saw faults with England, especially in its relationship with Ireland but he also realised that the law was a force for good and would help people in India as much as it did at home. Gordon, like Napier, had a strong belief in the equality of all people. Each life was valuable to him and when he was victorious in battle he was generous. Similarly, he believed that spreading British civilisation, and specifically stifling the slave trade, was an intrinsic good in its own right. Victoria, as she presided over an age and a culture, embraced a vision of equality for all of her subjects and was in no doubt that her rule was essentially benign. Indeed, her treatment of her non-British servants maddened her Court but it was a crucial part of her understanding of her imperial role.

Disraeli also understood the importance of a collective vision. His political drive was to improve the condition of the people and to make two nations one. Palmerston's patriotism was the most muscular but the main point of his vision, encapsulated in his famous *Civis Romanus sum* speech, was that it included all British subjects. Sleeman is in some ways the most thoroughly conventional of the individuals collected in this book, for he was an arch-bureaucrat convinced that British administrative processes could use British law to counter and stop a great evil. Dicey saw with clarity how the law worked and how it related to the unique British constitutional settlement and his legal thinking developed a new orthodoxy. This remarkable man ensured that a true understanding of the Constitution is an absolute subject for romanticism which is of continuing benefit to the nation.

Each figure, whether it be Grace wielding a cricket bat or Gladstone with a moral vision in defence of the Christians in Bulgaria, had confidence in the positive nature of their home nation. The origins of this moral vision predate the age: the early nineteenth-century Prime Minister George Canning, although he died before Victoria came to the throne, was a strong influence on both Palmerston and Peel. Canning declared resoundingly, 'We avow ourselves to be partial to the COUNTRY in which we live notwithstanding the daily panegyrics we read and hear on the superior virtues and endowments of its rival and hostile neighbours. We are prejudiced in favour of her Establishments, civil and religious; though without claiming for either that ideal perfection, which philosophy today professes to discover in the more luminous systems that are arising on all sides of us.' These words epitomise the wise confidence that the Victorians placed in their nation.

All of these heroes possessed a practical patriotism. They recognised the civilising effect of their own nation and understood the good fortune of Britain, as a nation blessed by being the first to receive the benefit of a good Constitution and the rule of law. They also had the self-confidence to say that civilisation was a good thing and that it is reasonable to export it to other countries to remove such hardships as exist there. Pugin particularly wanted to reassert the Gothic beauty of England, an aspect of life that he felt had been lost because of the effects of the Reformation. He believed that all types of people benefited from the beauty of holiness and that it was a truly universal gift. Peel was also absorbed by domestic concerns and was determined to advance the prosperity of factory workers by offering cheaper bread.

This is by no means to argue that all the policies of these figures coincided. Disraeli vigorously opposed Peel and later Gladstone. Indeed, their clashes and debates are the stuff of political history yet it is important to note that they shared common philosophical ground. All three clearly wanted to improve the condition of the people and help them to enjoy the fruits of a modern society. None of our figures was a socialist, aiming to cut back prosperity for all in a hopeless quest for a phoney equality. Even Napier, whom we could describe as the most Blairite figure in this book, wanted the great social movement of Chartism to succeed within the *existing* structure, because he wished the northern city dweller to be as well-to-do as the southern farmer.

Perhaps the strongest believer in the civilising effect of modernity was Prince Albert. The Great Exhibition was a monument, almost a temple, to the latest productive methods. It was created not only as a patriotic effort to show the best of British enterprise but also as part of a global vision to demonstrate that all the world could prosper from these advances. Such an unabashed desire to spread civilisation at home and abroad meant having confidence in the British system and it was this faith that made each of these figures true patriots. This Victorian self-assurance is anathema to the present-day politically correct elite but it had the effect of improving people's lives enormously.

In addition to their belief in progress and their wish to see its benefits spread across the world, they all had a determination and drive to succeed. They knew, or at least believed, that what they were doing was good, with the result that they put tremendous energy into turning a vision into reality. Perhaps Grace symbolises this determination most potently. He possessed enough energy for two men and devoted this vitality to ensuring he was the best in the world. He was a tough and brave competitor who was keen to win because he knew he was good. As for Gladstone's energy, it meant that when properly channelled he was unstoppable and has since gone down in legend.

Even Disraeli, certainly not as physically strong as Gladstone, was hugely driven. Sometimes this had negative effects, such as the case of his vicious parliamentary attacks on Peel. At other times, however, it was tremendously positive, particularly in his successful twenty-eight-year campaign to make the Conservatives electable again. He was driven by a sense of destiny, he had a clear view of his ultimate vision and spent a lifetime travelling towards it.

Albert shared such a tremendous drive, so much so that it was commonly thought that he worked himself to death. Even on his deathbed, feebly writing with a pencil, he was drafting memos to improve Britain's relationship with the United States. These figures were not interested in 'chillaxing'. Instead, they embraced the most thoroughgoing work ethic. Perhaps Albert took it too far. Perhaps Pugin did too, for his work literally drove him into an asylum and an early death. Others managed better and more quietly, Sleeman for example, the remote imperial administrator, who achieved what he did by mastering a grand filing system and combining it with remorseless and exhausting travel. This is hardly a romantic vision of Empire but it was truly one of the great works on the nineteenth century.

Sleeman's innate ordinariness, his position as a competent bureaucrat, in fact symbolises something about the Victorians. They were devoted to the everyday and they made it transformational. The efforts of both Palmerston and Disraeli to improve public health, especially water supplies, Peel's drive to lower the cost of food and reform the penal system or Gladstone's desire to reform Ireland: these were all schemes to improve the daily conditions of the people. They were practical schemes and they were essentially *mundane*. These people were so committed that they drafted and delivered those dull, essential details of implementation.

Their belief in progress was an aspect of their religion for many, though not all. Gordon and Gladstone are the two with the most immediately evident faith and confidence that they were carrying out God's work. It was part of their tragedy that God was asking them to do conflicting things. For Pugin his religious drive was set within a clear historic context. He saw his work as a grand scheme to be completed over generations and imagined that the beauty of holiness would help guide people in the right direction. Pugin's religious fervour equalled that of Gordon and the fervently High Anglican Gladstone but it was rooted in a more Catholic perspective of time, which meant he understood that all of his endeavours need not be completed before lunch.

This religiosity connected with a more general belief in *duty*, a belief that encompassed those who were not especially religious. The slaughter of the First World War made duty an unfashionable concept to later generations but surely a true patriot must value dutifulness above other virtues. Victoria herself was the exemplar. She knew of the dissipation of her Hanoverian predecessors and was determined to live a better life. Although she found being Sovereign sometimes very demanding, she persevered with her work just the same.

The Victorians had confidence in their civilising effort, a belief in the goodness of their own nation and the drive necessary to finish the job. How favourably this compares with the contemporary nervousness about the country where moral relativism accepts an equivalence between good and bad and with a tangible feeling that all we can do is manage decline. This is where we today can and must learn from our ancestors. After all, is it not still true that the British Constitution is a model that works better than those in other nations? That is why it has been so widely copied. Democracy, the rule of law, the rights of property and freedom of speech led, for the Victorians and for us, to a stable and prosperous state. From that bedrock, the conditions of the people improved for the Victorians and continue to improve now.

Other systems are simply less good and they harm the lives of the least well-off, because they rob them of the political voice that democracy and free speech grant to them. The rights of property ensure that investors can be made confident of a return and that democracy will not be abused to steal from the minority to the short-term benefit of the majority. All of this is underpinned by the rule of law. The Victorians were proud of the system they created and we should be too. They created it and we must reinvigorate it.

Moral relativism is not a 'good thing'. To give one example, it was not 'culturally inappropriate' for Sleeman to intervene to stop Thugee. In fact it was wholly beneficial and an advantage to all mankind. Likewise, Gordon's desire to extirpate the slave trade in the Nile valley was honourable while Napier's desire to advance the livelihoods of the people of Sindh was noble in its aims, even if less successful in practical terms. Each of these figures understood the power of sensible and moral intervention. Perhaps Tony Blair is more of a Victorian in his vision and ambition than either he or I would like to admit. Gladstone's moral outrage and Palmerston's defence of British interests were similarly noble. As we shall see, the Balkans debate is one of the real blots on Disraeli's reputation. The lesson is that great nations may not always be able to intervene directly but they *must* invariably support the moral standard which they believe in. The great Victorians understood this and were willing to do so.

The work ethic of our forebears is also deeply admirable. It is not that people are lazier today, rather that leisure has come to be seen as a right rather than as a reward for work. There was a true nobility in such figures as Albert and Sleeman who really gave their lives to their understanding of duty. Elizabeth II, Victoria's great-great-granddaughter, is one of the last surviving individuals whose whole life has been about duty but for Victorians it was a mainstay of their society.

Clearly none of these figures thought that managing the decline of Britain was sufficient. This is not to blow the trumpet for imperial expansion, for they were by no means all keen to expand the Empire. Rather it is to assert that they all were committed to improving the lot of mankind. They had confidence that society's ills, so much more pressing in their time than in ours, would be ameliorated and eradicated through human ingenuity. Theirs was not an age that believed in stopping new ideas or processes. Inevitably, not all of their schemes worked and the patent office is full of failed inventions. Crucially, they did not operate a precautionary principle that slowed progress to the benefit of the inefficient and the indolent.

The British today have even more opportunity than the Victorians did to be successful. The basic standard of living of the people is better and the knowledge of what works is far advanced. Yet if we cannot share the inner belief and self-confidence that propelled the Victorians we will stand still, petrified as other nations overtake us. Margaret Thatcher showed how the new Victorian spirit can work and reinvigorate a failing nation. Since she left office, the forces of stagnation, trepidation and hesitation have returned. These heroes of old who possessed belief and patriotism, a sense of duty, a confidence in progress and knowledge of civilisation have shown us what can be done, even if the Lytton Stracheys of this world disbelieved and mocked them. He was wrong. The truth is that Victorian Britain was not the society of a funny little old woman but one of greatness, nobility and good sense.

Peel: People Before Party

Sir Robert Peel (5 February 1788–2 July 1850) was the son of a Lancastrian mill owner who rose to the highest elected office in the land and his is one of the most fascinating of early Victorian lives. From stout defence of the status quo to advocate of change and reform, he undertook one of the great journeys in British politics. Yet Peel remained at heart a conservative, weighing up what change must be embraced in order to maintain the structures and values he held dear. He was a true Conservative, the founder of today's Conservative Party and the man whose actions caused the party to split from top to toe. Add to these ironies and contradictions a quiet, blameless and honourable private life so we have all the ingredients for an absorbing Victorian history.

This chapter focuses on Peel's status as essentially a self-made man, able to use his intrinsic talents and gifts that came his way, in order to better himself in the true Victorian style. It is also to show how change, radical change, is sometimes absolutely necessary, how it can

1

work and how it can serve the national interest in the most fundamental ways.

*

'There seems to me to be very few facts, at least ascertainable facts, in politics.' So remarked Sir Robert Peel, reflecting on the views accumulated in the course of a lifetime seated behind the most important desks in the land. No shortage of facts exists about this gentleman but nor, from his day forward, has there been an end to the disputes which surround any discussion of Peel. Did he, for example, betray the very Conservative Party he founded? Did he put principle before politics? Was he, in every sense, representative of his age or was this a man apart, both from his peers and from today's world?

Peel enjoyed a very long career in the front rank of British politics yet his greatness was achieved relatively late in life. His personal life was a virtuous contrast to the dissolute world of Regency grandees, a self-improving Harrovian and, upon death, a symbol of his age and an argument never to be finished about his role in shaping it.

Above all else, Peel is remembered for his decision, as Prime Minister, to dismantle the economic rules that had kept the price of food artificially high in Britain and led to disaffection in our cities. There is so much more to contemplate in the history of arguably our greatest male peacetime Prime Minister, but in this chapter the case will be made that the central fact of cheaper food for the British population was indeed the great achievement of Peel's life. The stability that Britain in the nineteenth

2

century enjoyed, in stark contrast to Europe and the Americas, rested on many things, among them providence and faith, an industrious head of state, a robust yet flexible parliamentary system, the ever-increasing productivity of British industry and finance, the humane relationship between the aristocracy and the masses and the equitable legal order to which all were subject. Yet at the very core of this stability was the truth that, thanks to the reforms instituted by Peel, her people could be fed.

*

Robert Peel was born on 5 February 1788 in the family home at Chamber Hall in Bury, Lancashire. His father, Sir Robert Peel, was one of the first great figures to epitomise the wealth and power of the burgeoning Industrial Revolution in Britain. The Peels were emphatically self-made, members of the Lancastrian yeomanry who in two generations rose from the land to a baronetcy, 15,000 employees and, as the nineteenth century progressed, the full Victorian flush of generals, a Speaker, a winner of the Victoria Cross, an India Secretary, a Derby winner and aristocratic marriage.

Above all, there was a Prime Minister. Legend tells that the first Sir Robert Peel told his son, 'Bob, you dog, if you do not become Prime Minister one day, I'm disinheriting you.' This was not a threat to be taken lightly, for the first Sir Robert was a man of his word and a driven man in all aspects of his life. In his youth he had worked with his own hands in the family's mills before becoming an MP for Tamworth, a 'pocket' or family-controlled borough which had come his way after he bought some Staffordshire lands which had fallen out of the dissolute hands of the then Earl of Bath. An improving, paternalistic mill owner, he used his position in Parliament to introduce such reforms as the Health and Morals of Apprentices Act, which limited the hours children could work in mills and obliged mill owners to provide them with a basic education. In doing so, this Anglican 'Church and King' Tory stood out against the Nonconformist, radical stereotype of the northern industrialist, forever fighting such statist restrictions on the free exercise of commerce and individual liberty. He was made a Baronet in 1800. The younger Robert Peel was born not only into a world of considerable wealth and stability but also into a family with a strong sense of obligation to those less fortunate than themselves. It seems important to underline this point for it acts as an early indicator of the general moral and political texture of Peel's later life.

The elder Sir Robert liked to put his son through his paces, for example requiring the young Robert to precis sermons on a Sunday after church to test his piety, attention, memory and the workings of his mind. Education was of high importance in such a family and after various local Lancashire grammars, the young Peel was despatched to Harrow. The school in Peel's generation was to establish a near monopoly on future premiers, with Peel himself, Goderich, Aberdeen and Palmerston all appearing one by one on its rolls. From Harrow to Oxford, specifically Christ Church, where Peel was an academic triumph, earning a double first in Mathematics and Classics with large audiences turning up to hear his public examinations. University was followed by a

brief stint at Lincoln's Inn before Sir Robert arranged a
parliamentary seat for his son.

The influence of Peel the father can be clearly tracked
throughout the life of Peel the son. The opinions of the
son were firmly shaped by those of the father. The elder
Peel excoriated the French Revolution, the memory of
which was to haunt Britons for half a century and more.
His cause was emphatically that of John Bull, his values
those of liberty, order and property. Nonetheless, in due
course, the son became his own man. Douglas Hurd notes
that the older Sir Robert had 'a good life, well sustained
by family pleasures, worldly success, orthodox Christian
faith and a strong practical mind'. In all these qualities
his eldest son certainly shared but he added his own set
of interests and characteristics too.

The younger Peel became a man of taste, in his case
afforded not so much by leisure as by learning, discern-
ment and sensibility. His private collection of pictures
figured in guidebooks, becoming an attraction that distinguished visitors to London made certain to see. In addition, he threw himself into the wider world of the arts.
From 1824, he served as a trustee of the newly formed
National Gallery and he commissioned likenesses of his
contemporaries from Sir Thomas Lawrence, one of the
most distinguished painters of the day. So close, indeed,
was the relationship with the great painter that Peel
was to be the last man Lawrence dined with and acted
as pallbearer at Lawrence's funeral at St Paul's on 21
January 1830.

He was a moving force in the Royal Commission on
Fine Art, charged with the internal decoration of the new
Palace of Westminster which began to take shape from

1840 after its predecessor was destroyed in the famous fire of 1834. In this task, Peel was joined by Prince Albert, who headed the Commission. The two men became friends while Augustus Pugin's vision for the building proved to be a lasting masterpiece of Gothic design. Peel was also a defender of the Royal Academy against parliamentary radicals who wanted to dismember it, a champion at the end of his life of the scheme for a Great Exhibition and a personally generous patron of the Artists' Benevolent Fund. He was, in other words, sensitive and informed about the visual arts, his one true passion away from governing. He was also wonderfully practical too. As a trustee of the British Museum, he was insistent on the provision of both affordable guidebooks and plentiful 'conveniences'.

Peel's public manner could be offputtingly cool, if not cold, and in this sense he lacked any overt common touch. Conversely his private life was stable and warm. He was a devoted and constant husband to his wife Julia, as well as an attentive and loving father to their five children, and he enjoyed the comforts of family life to the full. Some were to sneer in hatefully snobbish terms at his modest antecedents. Queen Victoria thought he was not a gentleman because he parted his tailcoat when he sat down but the man himself never questioned his place in the social order he had spent his political youth defending. If his offspring were to have the life befitting those who counted among their godparents the Duke of York that was all to the good.

A well-rounded individual, with aspirations for his future and for his nation and family and the good sense never to lose touch with the needs of society: such was

Peel the man. Most importantly, he was the scion of a self-made family and he remained true to and aware of his roots and antecedents. This stood him in good stead.

*

As is the case with all successful political careers, the young Peel's was marked by good fortune. His first parliamentary seat in 1809 was the rotten borough of Cashel, County Tipperary in Ireland and as soon as he was elected the Prime Minister, Spencer Perceval, chose him to second the reply to the King's speech which opened the new session of Parliament. Peel took the opportunity to make his mark and his maiden speech was acclaimed as the best and most powerful since that of Pitt the Younger in 1781. Soon he was a member of government. His first ministerial office was as under-secretary for War and Colonies, answering to Lord Liverpool as Secretary of State. Here he had responsibility for the secret service, a role he drily disclaimed to his successor: '[it] gave me very little trouble as I am no great advocate of sending people to the Continent to collect information which generally reaches us in the papers before it arrives from the spy.' Following Perceval's assassination in May 1812, Liverpool became Prime Minister and now another change beckoned.

The young Peel enjoyed the patronage of Sir Arthur Wellesley, later Duke of Wellington, a close associate of Peel the elder. Wellesley appears and reappears throughout the pages of this book, as his life and career, both remarkable for their longevity, intersect repeatedly with many of our eminent Victorians. Wellesley was Irish-born and Peel's fate would be woven with that of Ireland in the years to come and with that of Wellesley for the next quarter-century. At this time, Wellesley was in the throes of the brutal Peninsular War with France. His success in this conflict would see him ennobled as the Duke of Wellington and he would round off this military phase of a long public career with victory over Napoleon at Waterloo. It is clear, however, that Wellesley, as he then still was, retained the ability to influence the domestic scene too; the combined goodwill of both Wellesley and Liverpool himself was instrumental in carrying Peel forward at this critical point in his career.

For now, at the age of just twenty-four, he was appointed Chief Secretary to Ireland. This was no lowly government job but the second most prominent position within the hierarchy of the British administration in Dublin. Peel was nominally answerable to the Viceroy, since the Act of Union of 1800 the Sovereign's representative in Ireland, but in effect he was administering the country. Since Ireland at this time had a population of some six million and was perennially restive, there could be no doubts as to how challenging a task this was.

Not the least of the difficulties Ireland presented to a British politician was that, although the country had been brought into the Union, it had not been taken out of the previous century. The minuscule inbred Irish political class, the Ascendancy, was disinclined to forgo the pleasures of what might be termed the 'old corruption' of easy preferment without responsibility. Its members desired to enjoy the largesse of patronage without discharging the duties which might have been expected in return. Peel would have to learn and to strategise quickly, which he did. As his great biographer Norman Gash noted:

'The constant canvassing, the bluster and the deceit, the tendency of Irish suitors to claim silence as an assent and a friendly word as a promise, taught Peel habits of official caution and reserve' which never left him.

Peel in Ireland became a model of discretion but also one of administrative vigour, the depredations and demands of place-hungry members of the Ascendancy notwithstanding. He is best remembered for his creation of the country's first national police force, by means of a Peace Preservation Act of 1814. This policy was designed to remove the possibility of regional and religion-based militias forming across Ireland, with concomitant threats to social stability, and it worked. The Royal Irish Constabulary, its members nicknamed Bobbies and Peelers in acknowledgement of the politician who created the force, would be a feature of the Irish scene for the next century.

Peel showed the positive effects of good administration in other ways too. Poor potato and grain harvests in 1816, combined with the economic shock caused by the end of the Napoleonic Wars, brought a threat of famine to Ireland and a spreading plague of typhus. The country was fortunate in that the 1817 harvest was good, thus heading off the very worst effects of famine, but it is very much to Peel's credit that he was energetic in raising emergency funds to deal with what threatened to become a national crisis.

Departing Ireland in 1818, Peel chaired the Bullion Committee at Westminster. This was another significant position. The Committee was charged with restoring the national finances to a sound footing, in the wake of the titanic and costly struggles of the wars with France, which had forced Britain to depart from the gold standard. Peel's appointment to the Committee, which also included David Ricardo, probably the most important British economist after Adam Smith, led directly to the passage through Parliament of the Resumption of Cash Payments Act. This Act was not without controversy and some critics questioned the need and sense of placing the country once more on the gold standard. Peel himself began discussions as a studiously neutral Committee chairman. Ultimately, however, he was convinced that the gold standard must return as evidence, both symbolic and practical, of Britain's possession of a sound and well-founded currency.

As a result of Peel's financial changes, sterling would become entrenched as the global currency for the remainder of the nineteenth century. It is also important to note that Peel never forgot this relatively early lesson in the importance of financial planning and prudence and he took the opportunity to apply the lesson later in his career. His Bank Charter Act of 1844 was the second great pillar of the economic achievement upon which the United Kingdom rested until 1914. It set the limit on how much currency the Bank of England could issue according to its holdings of gold and began the process of centralising note issuance so that *only* the Bank could issue notes.* This measure provided stability and trust: Bank of England notes traded at face value, whereas other banks' issue was negotiable. It further underpinned Britain's reputation as the financial haven of choice in a stormy world with an impregnable central bank to boot.

---

* The last such private banknote was issued by a Somerset bank, Fox, Fowler & Company, in 1921.

This was for the future. For now, Peel was building a reputation for prudence and steadiness deployed in combination with an instinct for sweeping reform and an ability to cut through the cobwebs to get the required things done. This was an excellent combination and high office was beckoning for him. In 1822, he was appointed Home Secretary in Liverpool's administration, and soon he was seen to rank in the Commons just behind Robinson (later Viscount Goderich), Castlereagh and Canning in the minds of the ministry supporters. Peel's time at the Home Office was to see all his political virtues fully on display.

*

As Home Secretary Peel found himself with a considerably smaller official apparatus than he had enjoyed as Chief Secretary in Dublin. With a mere ministry to run instead of a country, his staff amounted to 'fourteen clerks, a précis-writer, a librarian and various porters and domestic officials', all confined inside the dankest offices Whitehall had to offer. What the Home Office lacked in space and light, however, it made up for in abundance in other matters, specifically an extraordinary superfluity of laws under its purview. Indeed, so many laws that nobody could reasonably be expected to grasp their mass of intricacies. When Peel became Home Secretary, nobody knew how many capital offences existed in English law. That there were a great many was evident but the ferocity of the law in theory was tempered by lax and inefficient application, not least because juries refused to convict when they felt an injustice would be done by means of an overly harsh sentence. This was English liberty in action, the liberty so admired on the Continent. In no other country in Europe did the subject have so much scope for private activity unchecked by the state. Now Peel was coming to put an end to this ostensibly prelapsarian age. His solution was to reform the legal system and to set in place a modernised police force.

It was difficult for some in early nineteenth-century Britain to contemplate the innovation of an efficient police service as being anything other than an instrument of tyranny on the continental model. The burgeoning crimes which went ever more unchecked could after all be regarded as being a price paid for liberty. According to this way of thinking, simply following God and the Church was the best riposte to vice. The application of fresh state laws, state intervention, state interference, meanwhile, appeared a rank oppression and a violation of cherished English and British liberty.

To all this Peel had a brisk reply, encapsulated in a promise of better administration and practice. The so-called Peel Acts saw laws codified and implemented with consistency. Gaols were regularised in their management, with a measure of education introduced for inmates. Archaic habits by the bench were reformed. Masses of obsolete laws were swept away and the worthy remainder consolidated into an up-to-date and reformed statute book. This new and reforming Home Secretary faced unprecedented challenges. His task was to introduce and explain his reforms, and, crucially, to handle discontent among the labouring classes without reacting in the manner of Peterloo, the state response to worker unrest in Manchester in 1819 which had led to fifteen deaths.

It is important to note that Britain's workers had true and pressing grievances. Working conditions were horrendous but the unions which spearheaded the drive for working reforms themselves became part of the problem. The so-called union 'closed shop', for example, was accompanied by demands as to what machinery could be used and how many apprentices could be taken on. Unions dictated caps on how many men could be employed and called for unpopular foremen to be dismissed. Militancy in general rose apace as money was gouged from workers in the form of union dues, union membership was made compulsory and the unions determined what work could be done by whom. Violence occurred as a low drumbeat throughout the 1820s and most dangerously early in the decade as timid magistrates and cowed owners declined to stand by the law.

To this difficult and dangerous labour question can be added more nakedly political combinations. These years saw the formation of mass political movements such as the Irish Catholic Association, and in England the Anti-Corn Law League and Chartists. They all had honest grievances but each one brought with them attendant threats to the constitutional order. To the politicians observing the scene at Westminster, it became evident that the public realm needed to be defended, so policing would have to be reformed. As incoming Home Secretary in 1822, Peel had four hundred London policemen for a city of a million. The police service, insofar as it could be said even to exist before Peel, was essentially a private militia, nominally the servant of the ramshackle courts but in practice the hired help for those with money. Competing boards might sponsor their own watches, a dozen or more to a given parish, with no central control nor any coordinated purpose. As Peel tellingly put it to his patron Wellington, 'Think of the state of Brentford and Deptford, with no sort of police by night!'

The chief defect of such ramshackle law and order was that it dealt only with the consequences of crimes once they had been committed. It did little to deter them from being committed in the first place. By 1828, with Wellington now the Prime Minister, and Peel's own policing work in Ireland to act as a useful template, he was ready to set about massive police reform in London and in these pre-Victorian years he laid suitably moral foundations for the Metropolitan Police, the first truly Victorian institution. He sought for his new police force men of the utmost probity and he saw to it that they would not be tempted by outside blandishments of financial gain. Unlike earlier forces, there was to be strictly no moonlighting as private security. There was also, from the onset, no division between officer and enlisted constable. Most significantly of all, the new police were by design *practical* men. Peel did not want distressed, genteel layabouts in it for the public dole. His designs were a success, as the formation of the Metropolitan Police gives Peel his most lustrous claim on public fame today. Most crucially, the triumphant legacy of his police reforms in London and Ireland was that they secured the situation without the recourse to reaction which occurred everywhere else in Europe at one time or another.

As always in the nineteenth century, however, the truest passions of Peel's age were excited not by moral squalor and what might be needed to deal with it but by more elevated disputes of doctrine. It fell to Peel's lot to be the decisive voice in ending the confessional state in Britain as it had existed from the settlement of William of Orange onwards. This was no small matter and in few other countries could such a constitutional revolution have been contemplated without civil war being encompassed. At much cost to his own reputation, Peel's political dexterity over these great issues, and Catholic Emancipation in particular, ensured that his new-fangled police service was not put to the test of a religious war.

*

The disparaging nickname of 'Orange Peel' had been deservedly earned, for in the first phase of his career Sir Robert Peel was no friend to the notion of Catholic Emancipation. Nor was he alone, for relief for Catholic civic and political disabilities, an enduring feature of English and British civic and political life since the Reformation, had been a neuralgic issue in British politics for two decades before Peel entered the ranks of the Cabinet in 1822, with both government and opposition deeply divided on the subject. William Pitt, the Prime Minister of the day, had hoped that Emancipation would come with the passing of the Act of Union with Ireland in 1800 but his hopes failed against the virulent opposition first of George III and then of George IV. These two kings helped to block any progress on the measure for the first two decades of the nineteenth century.

This state of affairs suited the young Peel, who by 1820 was solid in his defence of the ostensibly unified Protestant realm formed by British history. At this point, he had supported the exclusion of Catholics from the

Privy Council, colonial governorships, Parliament and the ancient universities. The issue for the young Peel, what he perceived to be the practical essence, was not the rigorous enforcement of an outdated constitutional settlement but the maintenance of a civilised, working historic compromise. If the status quo worked, at least in Great Britain, an effective, substantial, de facto toleration of Catholics, while at the same time the Anglican majority remained in control and unprovoked, why would one risk making things needlessly worse?

By 1820, Peel was out of step with his colleagues. There was by this point a substantial majority in the Commons in favour of Emancipation but the Lords was still adamantly opposed, and what had become an awkwardness in England was an infinitely worse matter in Catholic-majority Ireland. The following historical vignette gives some indication of the tension building in both England and Ireland in these early decades of the nineteenth century. Wellington's elder brother, the Marquess Wellesley, was appointed Viceroy of Ireland in 1821 and held the post until 1828. In 1825 he married an American Catholic, Marianne Patterson, and he arranged for a Mass to be said in the Viceregal Lodge in Dublin's Phoenix Park. On hearing the news, George IV, who had acceded to the throne in 1820, exploded. 'That house', the King raged, 'is as much my palace as the one in which I am, and in my palace Mass shall not be said.'

In 1823, the Irish politician Daniel O'Connell had marshalled a Catholic Association to agitate for Emancipation. The Association was a vast and enormously potent mass movement and an organisational achievement without parallel, especially given the intrinsic challenges it faced in raising funds from a poverty-stricken Irish Catholic peasantry. As late as 1826, Peel was deploying arguments against Emancipation in the House of Commons, while simultaneously observing O'Connell's daunting assertion of Catholic power in Ireland and taking the temperature of the climate in Britain itself. By 1828, mindful of both his existing Irish insights and his position as the most immediately responsible minister, he had recognised that his principles must change, before change was forced upon him.

In the summer of that year, the issue was encapsulated by the result of a by-election in Co. Clare in the west of Ireland. O'Connell squared up to William Vesey Fitzgerald in a confrontation between Catholic power and the Establishment. O'Connell had chosen to exploit a loophole in the law, which barred a Catholic from taking a seat in Parliament but said nothing about a Catholic standing for election itself. O'Connell and Catholic power won and Peel could see the shape of the future. The power of the Ascendancy in Ireland was crumbling, the power of Catholic Ireland, and by extension Catholic Britain, was growing. Peel's world would simply have to change to accommodate this unmistakable fact.

Various compromises were considered as a solution to the Catholic question. The long-standing Test and Corporation Acts refused public office to Catholics and other non-Anglicans. By the early nineteenth century, as Peel and everyone else knew, these laws were not always upheld but the very fact of their continuing existence was an affront to British and Irish Catholics. One compromise suggested the *enfranchisement* of Catholics, while continuing their disqualification from most public

17

offices, in order to uphold the Anglican character of the British state. The pragmatic Peel, who would once have supported such reasoning himself, saw that nothing less would do now but full-scale reform. Instead, he spoke with exasperation of the wilful ignorance displayed in some quarters about what was a complex issue. As he put it, 'House of Commons' arguments [are] arguments for people who know very little of the matter, care not much about it, half of whom have dined, or are going to dine, and are only forcibly struck by that which they instantly comprehend without trouble.'

It was true. Nothing about the process of Emancipation would be easy. Wellington, who became Prime Minister in 1828, was like his protégé prepared to be pragmatic on this increasingly tense constitutional point to the extent that he would presently threaten to resign if George IV did not give Royal assent to the bill. He wanted to draw on the continental model and have some kind of concordat that the British state would license and pay for Catholic priests in the United Kingdom. Peel doubted the efficacy of this approach. In the first place, because intermingling state and Rome would infuriate the country's Anglican Establishment to no good end and, in the second, because he did not for an instant believe that any such measure of state control over Catholicism would improve the attitude of Irish Catholicism in general to the Union.

The fraught measure finally came before Parliament in 1829. Peel pushed in the Commons and Wellington in the Lords for the fullest measure of Emancipation which could be obtained. Front and centre of Peel's mind now was the question of *expediency*. He wanted full civil equality, justifying arriving at that end not for its own sake but because resisting it any longer would risk harm to the Church of England. A spiteful joke did the rounds that Peel had now abandoned what was once his own fight, so now the Pope would have to respond by inaugurating a new festival in the calendar, the Conversion of St Peel.

Both Peel in the Commons and Wellington in the Lords gave the speeches of their lives and both were immediate, resounding, national triumphs. Yet it was inevitably the case that once the cheering had died down, lesser mortals would resume their carping from the sidelines. In Wellington's case, his support for Emancipation brought him scathing criticism from the Earl of Winchilsea. Remarkably, the Prime Minister met this criticism by challenging Winchilsea to a duel. It was a deeply reckless move and both Wellington and his opponent were criticised roundly, the Duke for fighting, Winchilsea for not declining to fight the Duke. Peel in turn was mocked for so neatly, as it seemed, sloughing off his previous career as an Anglican paladin and diehard Tory Ultras felt a deep sense of betrayal. This would be nothing to the sensations of betrayal they would experience later in Peel's career.

The leadership Peel had shown would bear bitter personal fruits. In 1817, he had become MP for his alma mater of Oxford University. Now, in the aftermath of Emancipation, he felt obliged to resign and stand again for election to this seat, such was the strength of feeling in the university about his having changed his line on the Catholic question. In the subsequent by-election, though he had, by his friends' telling of it, the 'quality' with him, which is to say the better degrees and titles, and the wealthier and more prestigious colleges, 'an immense number of parsons' did for him. Within weeks, Peel became MP for his family seat of Tamworth in Staffordshire, but there can be no disguising the sense of bitter humiliation he felt at the loss of his cherished Oxford seat. It is still possible to see 'No Peel' carved on a door at Christ Church.

Why did Peel stick so long with the anti-Catholic cause? In short, because he had no great hopes for the claims positively made for the pro-Catholic one. He stood by the Settlement handed down from 1689 precisely because it was tried and tested, because it had been shown to work. Catholics had obtained tolerance if not equality in England, and the Constitution which performed that miracle, among a multitude of other virtues, demonstrably worked rather better and rather more durably than did the constitutions of other, less fortunate states abroad. Peel further doubted that Emancipation would in fact transform the political scene in Ireland or the attitude of Irish Catholics to the Union. Here, his scepticism would be vindicated.

For Peel, Emancipation inexorably became a political necessity, not an action driven in any way by political conversion. In short, he was making the best of a bad job and impelled by a sense of pragmatism and duty. Soon he would find himself making the best of another bad job, this time on the matter of parliamentary reform. Peel no more wanted parliamentary reform for its own sake than he had wanted Catholic relief but he would again have to grin and bear it.

As it turned out, however, reform was to be the making of Robert Peel and of his brand of enduring political action.

*

The Great Reform Act of 1832 marks the climactic end of Whiggish politics. It allowed preceding history to be seen to be building up to this point and it was held thereafter to have set the country on its destiny towards full and complete democracy. Peel opposed its passage. Once it passed through Parliament, however, he made its provisions work and he was to be its first true beneficiary.

This attitude was demonstrated transparently in Peel's Tamworth Manifesto of December 1834. Such local manifestos, written documents, distributed as widely as necessary in the cause of electoral gain, were not uncommon. Peel's manifesto, however, had no *local* purpose since the seat was a family borough. Instead, he always intended to take advantage of the press to make this a programme presented to the entire country. Its context was specific: the Reform Bill had been passed by a Whig government, which had collapsed in November 1834. King William IV asked Wellington to form a government but a reluctant Wellington had demurred, suggesting that the Sovereign summon Peel instead. It can be seen, therefore, that Tamworth was the ultimate national manifesto, as it was the establishment of Peel's platform. It was a call for a new party and a new politics to operate within a newly reformed political system. As it turned out, Peel's first spell as Prime Minister was at the head of an unstable minority government and would last a mere four months but historians agree that Tamworth marks the end of the old ceaseless morphing and shifting Tory faction at Westminster and the beginning of the contemporary British Conservative Party.

In the Tamworth Manifesto Peel looked to both the past and the future. Summoning the stability and security of the past, he declared:

[I]f, by adopting the spirit of the Reform Bill, it be meant that we are to live in a perpetual vortex of agitation; that public men can only support themselves in public estimation by adopting every popular impression of the day – by promising the instant redress of anything which anybody may call an abuse – by abandoning altogether that great aid of government – more powerful than either law or reason – the respect for ancient rights, and the deference to prescriptive authority; if this be the spirit of the Reform Bill, I will not undertake to adopt it.

Elsewhere, he glanced into a future that was now, he suggested, equally firmly founded and rooted:

I will repeat now the declaration I made when I entered the House of Commons as a member of the Reformed Parliament – that I consider the Reform Bill a final and irrevocable settlement of a great constitutional question – a settlement which no friend to the peace and welfare of this country would attempt to disturb, either by direct or by insidious means.

The task now for these new Conservatives, Peel implied, was simply this: to say *thus far but no farther*. This was neither ignoble nor insensible, no matter how unfashionable it has seemed since. Above all else, it was necessary for stability, a quality considered all the more necessary by Conservatives as they gazed out at a country in flux, one in which such campaigners as the Chartists called for further and greater reforms, for universal suffrage, the ballot and for the abolition of the property qualification which, embedded in the Reform Bill, ensured that only gentlemen[*] of property could aspire to stand for Parliament.

Movements such as the Chartists threatened, for Peel, 'an impeachment of the whole constitution of the country', risking a needless upending of the time-hallowed system of government which had delivered 'more practical happiness [and] true liberty than has been enjoyed in any other country that ever existed'. For Peel, the task in hand was to ensure that this new dispensation, this new constitutional form, worked correctly. Some years later, in the peroration of an 1846 speech in the Commons commending free trade over protection, Peel would make his wishes explicit, claiming a desire to sate the needs of those who had no vote, precisely so that they would have confidence in the system which gave them none.

The Tamworth Manifesto can therefore be seen as a very British phenomenon, being a gradualist step towards the very idea, democracy, against which it formally set itself, and it was British because it exemplified a very British lesson: the importance of taking part and playing by the rules. The very constitutionalism to which Peel submitted was precisely the constitutionalism he urged on others, because an acceptance of the importance of the rules of the game was as important as the game itself. This helps explain his and his heirs' reluctance to accept that the rules should ever be changed other than lawfully and by the means duly provided for changing them.

Peel's sense of the working and therefore improving classes was summed up by his speech welcoming the opening of Tamworth Library and Reading Room in 1841.

---

[*] Before 1832 women were not specifically excluded from the franchise.

For gathered were, as he observed, 'intelligent men of all classes and all conditions in life [brought together], harmonising the gradations of society and binding men together by a new bond'. They were a part of the wider political community and, crucially, they were destined to become ever more fully involved in it. One reason why this was the case, at this moment, with the Victorian age in full swing, was because, as the great liberal philosopher John Stuart Mill noted, every pub and club 'had its oracles and its declaimers. Almost everybody reads a newspaper, and those who do not read listen with attention to those who do.' So they too deserved representation and consideration in the tally of *public opinion*. This in turn was a concept arguably made possible only by the existence of a mass popular press.

Peel's attitude towards the newspapers was realistic, in that he accepted that public men had to resign themselves to reading the public prints. Indeed, 'after long experience [he] had got so callous that he could read them without the slightest disturbance'. There can be no doubt that he was always a professional politician. The burgeoning role of the press, and the coalescing of politicians into formal parties, went hand in hand. The General Election of 1835 in this respect marks a pivotal moment, for this was the first election when papers published lists of candidates with 'party' labels attached. Peel by now, in the momentous aftermath of the Tamworth Manifesto, clearly led the new Conservative Party he had established but he was about to lead it into its first great and nearly fatal challenge. For, after he won the 1841 election he found himself obliged to tackle the vexed matter of trade, of protectionism versus free trade, and in doing so he struck at what his party, the party of landed interest, stood for above all else. The Conservative Party was advertising itself in the mass media but what was the party for, and what did Conservatism seek to conserve?

Here, Peel's long years of being steeped in domestic politics paid dividends. His wide experience permitted him to gain insights into the state of the nation that would prove pivotal in his decision-making in the years to come. It enabled him to understand the ways in which British economics supported, or failed to support, the welfare and needs of the great mass of the people. Specifically, it emphasised to him the need to reform the defining issue of the day, the price of food.

At this point, it is worth noting the ways in which the long period of war with Napoleonic France had left its mark on Britain's agricultural economy. War had brought tariff walls, to guard against the importation of grain from Europe and to protect Britain's agricultural sector. The war made it essential that Britain be able to feed herself. The effect of the tariff walls surrounding the country was to enable farmers to name the price of the grain they grew and thus to keep prices high. In a rapidly industrialising society, the victims of these so-called 'Corn Laws' were the urban poor. Without the means to grow their own food supplies, at the mercy of price regulation over which they had little or no control and governed by a system which granted them little or no say over the laws and regulations passed in their name, the urban masses were essentially powerless in the face of outside legal and economic influences.

When the war with France ended in victory at Waterloo, it might be supposed that the tariff walls would have been lowered and that a more natural peacetime economy be instituted but this was not the case. Instead, protectionism remained the order of the day and now, gazing out upon a political world that had passed Emancipation and passed the Reform Bill but that had failed to intervene economically, Peel was keenly aware of the manifold dangers this situation posed to social order.

Thus, he changed his mind and his habits of communication but secrecy and discretion were such that this change of mind was not quite flagged in advance. This was the usual modus operandi. Trusted fellow Cabinet members might be taken into his confidence as he methodically and sincerely addressed this or that issue but ordinary supporters were never so favoured. Hence, when the many apparent inconsistencies which taxed Peel's championing of the cause of free trade were subsequently, splenetically, put to him, Peel's response was:

[T]here are two sorts of courage ... there is the courage of refusing to accede to ... demands at all; and there is another kind of courage – the courage to do that which in our conscience we may believe to be just and right, disregarding all the clamour with which these demands may be accompanied.

This showed to his critics two pronounced Peelite traits. The first was the egotism with which he was frequently taxed and the second was the fact, frequently hurled into his face by disenchanted and embittered past supporters, that Peel habitually had the courage publicly to face down past opinions. The latter, the critics usually added, was a luxury they generally lacked the time to deal with, given that Peel's about-turns happened with such speed and secrecy.

There is an irony here, for while Peel founded the Conservative Party as we know it, he himself identified more closely with state, nation and people than with party. It was in this sense that the latter part of his career ran counter to the forces that obliged politicians to be party men first and foremost, party men before any loyalty to nation or to region. He was also deeply pragmatic. He was himself a landowner and thus a farmer but he found himself obliged to take a realistic stance on the changing, urbanising world that surrounded him. 'If you had to constitute new Societies,' wrote Peel to his estranged friend J. W. Croker, 'you might on moral and social grounds prefer Corn fields to Cotton factories, an agricultural to a manufacturing population. But our lot is cast and we cannot recede.'

Every aspect of the Victorian story is contained in those rather important words from Peel: the idolisation of the past, balanced with the practical acceptance of the future and the dutiful sense of the work that must be done in the present to secure that future. Even the self-justifying letter, written by a politician son and grandson of weavers, living on the landed estate their riches had bought, to a politician-turned-journalist friend, has the quality of a parable. For what Peel and his contemporaries lived through was what is so generally wrongly claimed of other ages, a profound time of social, economic, religious, political and intellectual change. As a wise politician he saw that he must change with the times.

If a single year in this period were pivotal it was 1845, the tipping point in the whole electrifying nineteenth century. Thereafter more people lived in an urban realm than a rural one. Moreover, the United Kingdom by 1845 was such a *young* country. In England and Wales fully 45 per cent of the population were under twenty and only 7 per cent were over sixty. In 1840 no more than a quarter of the workforce was employed on the land, compared to well over half in the eighteenth century.

Peel was Prime Minister in 1845 and he was aware of the momentous changes now underway. It was through his usual close study of the matter at hand that he had come to change his stance on free trade and to see that free trade would deliver all that it promised, economic growth that would help all sectors of society and that would lead to cheaper food. Since his return to office as Prime Minister in 1841, as leader of a majority Conservative administration, he had proceeded slowly, carefully, by degrees. *Obscurely* is perhaps the best word. He had good reasons for his stealth, for his target was the repeal of the Corn Laws, but he was acutely aware that the Conservatives drew their greatest strength from the agricultural shires, from those districts of the country with most to lose should protectionist policies end. For some time, his supporters were able to convince themselves that he remained a supporter of the principle of protection, whatever tinkering he might have to do round the edges during day-to-day administration.

This was not a sustainable situation and when the day of reckoning came at last for Peel, the air crackled with the bitterness of betrayal. The 1841 parliamentary intake had included several outspoken supporters of free trade. One of them, Richard Cobden, who became a parliamentary critic of Lord Palmerston, used his new platform to drum up further support for the repeal of protectionist policies, thus ensuring the issue remained a pressing one. At first, Peel moved with ostentatious slowness, rejecting the efforts of Cobden and others to implement change, and offering small, judicious concessions.

In the outside world, meanwhile, pressure waxed and waned. A run of good harvests in the early 1840s ensured a plentiful supply of food at reasonable prices but the potato blight had been spreading across Europe in these years and in 1845 it appeared for the first time in Britain and Ireland. There was hunger in Britain and the beginning of a period of devastating famine in Ireland. Now Peel acted. He argued in Cabinet that tariffs must be withdrawn to permit a free flow of grain imports and, as the year ended, he summoned Parliament to debate the repeal of the Corn Laws. Simultaneously, Peel resigned as Prime Minister. He was all too aware that he could not carry his Cabinet and the Conservative Party with him but nobody else could form a government either so Queen Victoria requested that Peel remain at the head of an increasingly strained administration.

As 1846 dawned, Britain was in a state of ferment. Anti-repealers agitated in the countryside and local Conservative worthies joined their ranks, in the process splitting from their own party. In May, the Commons voted on Peel's proposal to repeal the Corn Laws, with new regulations to be implemented gradually over the next three years. Prominent Conservatives argued bitterly against Peel's measure, the divisions in the Commons mirroring the splits in the country as a whole. Even the Royal Family were publicly involved in this tense situation. In January, on that first day of deliberations, Prince Albert appeared in the Commons' public gallery to listen to Peel's opening speech in favour of free trade, a move taken as a sign of Royal approval, an error of judgement never to be repeated.

Peel declared to the House that 'this night you will select the motto which is to indicate the commercial policy of England. Shall it be "advance" or "recede"?' He won the vote but lost his party, with more than two-thirds of Conservative MPs voting against the bill as it was passed only with the support of opposition votes. Wellington, meanwhile, pushed the measure through the Lords. There was no happy ending for Peel. On the same night that the repeal bill passed in the Lords, his Irish Coercion Bill, designed to quell rising public disorder in a famine-struck Ireland, was rejected in the Commons and the Prime Minister resigned.

Peel's defence to a dismayed Conservative Party was that he had *conserved* all that he could, and that free trade would lay the foundation for still more conservation to come. All the great Conservative objectives, increased trade, an end to Chartism, an intact Church of England, buoyant tax revenues but no excessive taxation and a widely accepted Constitution, had been secured by his government. Free trade, he claimed, was simply a further means to these ends. The critics, not least in the press, were having none of it. According to the *Morning Post*, Peel seemed:

> really to imagine that the more widely his measures differ from the principles which he professed when he was raised to office, the more imperatively is he called on to disparage the principles in question, and to promote the success of schemes which war with all his previous convictions. Never, assuredly, was

there devised a moral code more favourable to the growth of habits of rascality in public men.

Peel's fellow Conservative Benjamin Disraeli was less kind. He led the charge against Peel's betrayal and in lacerating style. Peel, he said, 'bamboozles one party and plunders the other, til, having obtained a position to which he is not entitled, he cries out, "let us have no party questions, but fixity of tenure"'.

Disraeli would become Peel's eventual successor, though he may have done himself no immediate favours with the sceptical middle of the country by deploying such tart language. Disraeli had hit exactly upon what most antagonised Peel's estranged supporters: the immediate canonisation of Peel by his erstwhile opponents as now being worthily 'above party'. With each attack by an inarticulate Tory Ultra given voice by the silky Disraeli, the agony of Peel's spurned supporters was doubled. With each Tory complaint, their radical, Whig and Liberal foes self-righteously ratcheted up their infuriatingly magnanimous argument that, by backing them, Peel had now transcended party.

The fact is that Peel's eventual championing of repeal split the new Conservative Party for decades. No previous battle of Peel's had prepared him for the possibility that his internal party opponents would themselves organise and resist. Now, they did precisely this and in doing so they completed the evolution of this Conservative movement into a political party for the times. Politics had moved on since Peel first evolved from one cornerstone belief to another and, now, his renunciation of the Corn Laws meant his party renounced him. Meanwhile, one

hundred or so 'Peelite' Conservatives, including Lord
Aberdeen, a youthful William Gladstone and others, joined
what was rapidly evolving into the British Liberal Party.
There can be little doubt that Peel, and the effects of
repeal, solidified a British party political system that
would endure until the early decades of the twentieth
century.

What of Peel's legacy? A large part of the reason we
remember Peel and continue to extol his example today is
that one result of his response to evident, visible, actual
change was the creation of the Conservative Party itself,
even if, in the end, he and this party parted ways. It tells
its own story that the British Conservative Party is still
with us, whereas no other European country can make
the same claim of consistency and continuity. British
conservatism conserved not least itself, which separates
it as fully from the continental political experience as
anything else. That the party Peel founded as something
new was taken in his own time, as much as now, to be
something *ancient* was his genius.

In his own era, critics sent up the tactical and ana-
chronistic cry that he was 'always really a Liberal' and
had indeed 'been in the wrong party'. It has already been
shown that the reality of party politics that evolved in
mid-Victorian Britain differed radically from the loose
groupings of Tories and Whigs, factions and splinters
that prevailed in the first part of Peel's career. Yet what
was his politics? Gash, his biographer, puts it best:

[Peel's] Conservatism was not a party label, still
less a class interest, but an instinct for continuity
and the preservation of order and good government

in a society which was confronted with the choice between adaptation and upheaval.

That Peel was to follow just this 'instinct for continuity' yet split with the party he created to serve it is the great paradox of his life. Surely, however, this very paradox provides confirmation of the sturdiness of the man's spirit. After all, he did what he felt was best by his own lights, the abuse of past friends and allies notwithstanding.

There is perhaps something slightly unfortunate about the way the great Iron Duke was forgiven by his own side and forgotten by history for doing much as Peel did. History remembers Wellington as an emphatic Conservative yet in the end he connived in all the things he fulminated against still more noisily than Peel ever did. The great issues of the day passed through Wellington's hands just as they did through those of Peel. Wellington has been forgiven by all Conservatives, probably because he defeated Napoleon so everything else is secondary, while Peel has never been because he was a professional politician.

To understand Peel and the age he brought into being is to appreciate that pivotal Victorian virtue of *respectability*. Properly understood it 'was dynamic, not static; it carried with it a commitment to self-help'. There are any number of other Victorian exemplars. Such men showed just what was industriously possible. Peel the bourgeois was explicitly glad that good honest toil meant 'opportunities of elevation and distinction'. In true Victorian fashion, however, he also knew that it was proper that 'industry, sobriety, honesty, and intelligence will as assuredly elevate the low, as idleness, profligacy, and vice will depress, and justly depress, those who are in high stations'. *Victorian values* was not the slogan of a century to come but a real scheme of morals which sought to improve, sustain and care for the community as a whole, and in hard-headed fashion to boot.

*

Finally, it is time to turn to Peel the man and Peel the politician. His industry and ability far outpaced those of most of his contemporaries: he did not found a philosophy but it is possible to catch glimpses of one in development. This is true even in the field of foreign and imperial policy, which was an inescapable consideration for Peel, as a leading politician in an age of British global power. It is an area of Peel's legacy which is rarely considered but inevitably important.

Peel's last speech before his death in 1850 was in response to the Don Pacifico affair, a bitter Anglo-Greek spat involving his contemporary Lord Palmerston, the details of which are mentioned in the following chapter. This episode hinged on the issue of intervention. When was it, if ever, allowable to follow an interventionist foreign policy?

Peel was clear. He deprecated from the backbenches the idea that Britain should strain to promote interventionism as some kind of ideological imperative. As Prime Minister too, he had been contemptuous of the Afghan crisis he inherited from the Whigs, it being 'the most absurd and insane project that was ever undertaken in the wantonness of Power'. He wanted no imperial acquisitions for their own sake, still less for the glory which might attach to those who acquired them. Rather he wanted only to make the best of what we had. This was Peel the man of business who saw patriotism as based on practicality.

Then there is Peel the domestic politician. On the hustings at Tamworth in 1841 he observed that the Reform Bill a decade before had led him to see:

... the good that might result from laying the foundations of a great Conservative party in the state, attached to the fundamental institutions of the country – not opposed to any rational change in it which the lapse of years or the altered circumstances of society might require, but determined to maintain on their ancient footing and foundation our great institutions in Church and in State.

Peel's Conservative Party was to become one of those great institutions. Its vision has always been to live on in the image of its founder, albeit to be mindful of the lesson learned by his final political act. Just as the French Revolution haunted the minds of generations of Britons, so too do today's Conservatives see the wisdom in not dividing against themselves and destroying the very party that had done so much in the service of the nation.

Norman Gash remarked: 'though the myth of Conservatism has been more often Disraelian, its practice has been almost uniformly Peelite. With that Peel would have been content; he preferred facts to phrases.' His grandson, George Peel, wrote the 1895 entry for Sir Robert in that quintessentially Victorian enterprise the

Dictionary of National Biography. Here was the perspective which endures to the present day:

> In an age of revolutions, Peel may alone be said to have had the foresight and the strength to form a conservative party, resting not on force or on corruption, but on administrative capacity, and the more stable portion of the public will.

There were other ways to conserve, resting on the power of the state or the maintenance of near feudal conditions or the ascendancy of untrammelled wealth, all of which were rejected by the political party founded by Peel.

Then there is Peel the man who was sensitive in ways a political party can never be. His manner became stiffer and more defensive with age. Disraeli observed that Peel's smile 'was like the silver plate on a coffin', and Walter Bagehot said, 'no man has come so near our definition of a constitutional statesman – the powers of a first-rate man and the creed of a second-rate man'. These are merely the words of an epigram-machine spitting out words at full pelt. Say rather that Peel personified a moral tone that in itself raised the condition of Victorian Britain. Long before there was a 'family monarchy', there was a 'family politician'. In the end, it is only possible to recognise the majestic extent of Peel's achievement by realising what it avoided. For without the party and its philosophy he bequeathed to the nation, there is little reason to suppose we would have coped with change any better than other countries did. A negative achievement when seen in full, perhaps, but a vital one, and one for which we should still be thankful.

Palmerston: 'The Shibboleth of Policy'

Henry John Temple, third Viscount Palmerston (20 October 1784–18 October 1865) was one of the great statesmen of the early Victorian period. A scion of an Irish Establishment family raised to the peerage, Palmerston was born into a world of material prosperity and political power. In the course of his long career, he fulfilled a surely manifest destiny by holding three of the great offices of state: Foreign Secretary, Home Secretary and finally Prime Minister. Palmerston, however, was very far from being simply one amid a multitude of grey political figures. On the contrary, his was a life of unusual verve. He was a Tory who became a Whig and eventually a leading player in the foundation of the British Liberal Party. He enjoyed a complicated and notorious private life, a fact which led to tensions with Queen Victoria and Prince Albert; he was a gentleman whose decisions were refracted at all times through a definite and distinct prism of political morality. It is this last quality, this inner or private philosophy brought to bear on his public politics, that this chapter explores.

*

On 20 October 1784, in the family house in Park Street in the heart of London, an heir was born to Henry Temple, the second Viscount Palmerston and his wife Mary. The Palmerston title was of the Irish Peerage of relatively new creation, the first Viscount Palmerston being ennobled in 1723. The Temples, however, had long been politically connected and wealthy. The family held vast Irish estates surrounding a country seat at Mount Temple in Co. Sligo, while both the infant's great-grandfather (the first Viscount) and his father (the second) had been Westminster parliamentarians, and from 1736 the Temples also owned the spectacular Palladian mansion at Broadlands in Hampshire, with grounds landscaped by Launcelot 'Capability' Brown.

Now, an heir had been born to secure the family line. The child was named Henry, after his father, and with power, money, influence and a title lying in wait it must have seemed a safe bet that fortune would smile on this infant. Indeed, she would smile, and warmly. Henry Temple, third Viscount Palmerston, would establish a public career second to none in nineteenth-century Britain, serving at the pinnacle of government in the course of a career that spanned a remarkable six decades.

Palmerston was thirty-four when Queen Victoria was born and fifty-two when she acceded to the throne so it could be argued that he should not be classified as a fully fledged Victorian at all. The briefest of glances at his life and career, however, reveals that such an assessment would be a mistake. The years of his greatest power and influence occurred during the reign of Victoria and he left an indelible mark on the Victorian era. His private behaviour and standards of morality were not always what we call *Victorian*. They were those of the rather racier Regency period and he was regarded with considerable disdain by more morally upright Victorians, including the Queen and Prince Albert. Today, such facts merely serve to add an undeniable zest to Palmerston's history.

Rather more pertinently, he was a fascinatingly complex politician and a figure who understood the emerging forces of democracy surprisingly well. As he remarked, 'Those statesmen who know how to avail themselves of the passions, and the interests, and the opinions of mankind, are able to gain an ascendancy, and to exercise a sway over human affairs, far out of all proportion greater than belong to the power and resources of the state over which they preside.' In this sense, Palmerston can be regarded as a populist, a politician who understood the power of a truly popular following. Yet it seems as if there were always a strongly moral purpose to Palmerston's populism, in that he used his power and authority to pursue policies that he regarded as intellectually and morally sound. He was not a man who would cry 'I am your leader, I will follow you.' Rather, he was a politician who realised fully that engaging the popular will with a laudable aim made achieving the aim easier.

Perhaps Palmerston best summed up his own doctrine in a letter written in 1833 to Sir Frederick Lamb, the British Ambassador in Vienna and Palmerston's brother-in-law to be: 'The Province of a wise government is to keep pace with the improved notions of the people; not to insist upon knowing better than those they govern.' These are the words of a man who not only understood how to keep a finger on the pulse of his people but also felt he knew best what improvements could be made to the society within which he lived and wielded power.

*

Palmerston's early life was important, unusually so, in setting the course of his future career and establishing the texture of his own moral and political philosophy. One specific and startling episode stands out. In 1792, the youthful Palmerston, then aged seven, and his parents left Britain for Europe at the beginning of a long continental tour just as events in France were building to a shocking climax. Arriving into the ferment of a revolutionary Paris in early August, the family was received in audience at the Tuileries by the King and Queen, Louis XVI and Marie Antoinette, who remained on the throne if no longer in power. This visit took place mere days before the rising tide of revolution in the city caused the Royal Family to flee the palace. Palmerston and his family personally encountered something of this disorder as they left Paris on 7 August in a pair of carriages. The revolutionaries permitted the first carriage, carrying the parents and the young Palmerston, to pass unimpeded through the barricades thrown up around the city but the second, carrying the younger children and most of the luggage, was stopped and searched. There is no evidence to suppose that the family was ever in any danger – the mob was presumably more attracted by the luggage – but it is fair to assume that such an episode would not be forgotten by Palmerston in later life, indicating as it did what might happen to a society if its ruling class failed or refused to adapt to changing times. This journey into the wider world left its mark in other ways. The family spent two years in Europe, thus enabling Palmerston to learn both Italian and French to a reasonable standard, equipping him usefully for his later life as a politician and diplomat.

The next step in Palmerston's education was rather more conventional. In 1795, he entered Harrow, where he was a contemporary of George Hamilton-Gordon, who as Lord Aberdeen would later in life prove to be an enduring political rival. Palmerston was noted at school both for his physical courage in standing up to boys much older and larger than he and for his academic qualities. In this period of his life, he also visited the Palace of Westminster for the first time, where his father introduced him to William Pitt, then in his first spell as Prime Minister.

Palmerston's academic prowess stood him in good stead for the next and, as it proved, critical phase of his education. In 1800, at the age of sixteen, he entered Edinburgh University to study political economy, at a time when the Scottish capital was at the heart of a prevailing intellectual power house which was to leave a lasting trace upon the British nation now known as the Scottish Enlightenment, a movement which asserted the primacy of rationalism and empiricism across a field of disciplines from philosophy and politics to medicine and engineering. A host of great thinkers participated in the discourse of the period. Greatest of all, perhaps, were the philosophers Adam Smith, Francis Hutcheson, Adam Ferguson and David Hume but also well known in his day was the philosopher and mathematician Dugald Stewart (1753–1828). It was Stewart who would leave a formative impression on Palmerston's political philosophy.

Stewart was unquestionably a brilliant man. He had received his chair as professor of mathematics at the University of Edinburgh at the early age of twenty-two and went on to establish a reputation as a charismatic teacher, significantly as a populariser. The texts of his university lectures in politics came to be distributed widely, spreading the import of his teachings near and far. Palmerston himself was able to observe the actions of this educational populist at close quarters, for he lodged in the Stewart household for the duration of his time in Edinburgh. That he admired Stewart himself is very evident. He wrote to his father shortly after he moved to the city, noting that 'I like Mr and Mrs Stewart amazingly, it is impossible for anyone to be kinder than they both are.' The Stewart household, moreover, welcomed a wide range of visitors. This discourse added to the academic curriculum a zest of stimulating conversation. This education, both formal and informal, had a profound effect on Palmerston, whose notes nearly thirty years later were laced liberally with many of Stewart's preoccupations, from free trade and commerce to questions of liberty and the Constitution.

Stewart proved to be a powerful influence in more systematic ways too. Palmerston imbibed the older man's influential views on what became known as Scottish 'Common Sense Realism', the theory that the philosophy of one's existence was founded upon and bound up with sound and observable phenomena. That is, upon the stuff and experiences of everyday life. As we shall see, this thread in Stewart's thinking manifests in the practicality and pragmatism that governed Palmerston's later political career. Nor was Palmerston's admiration of the sagacious Stewart by any means a one-way street: 'In point of temper and conduct,' Stewart would remark of his young friend, 'he is everything his friends could wish. Indeed, I cannot say that I have ever seen a more faultless character at his time of life, or one possessed of more amiable dispositions.'

In 1803, Palmerston left Edinburgh for Cambridge, where he completed his education at St John's College. His life had, in the meantime, changed significantly. His father, the second Viscount, had died in the previous year and his son had succeeded to the title at the age of seventeen. His juvenile years were behind him and his life as a politician and a statesman was about to begin.

These youthful years and the experiences they held in England, in Scotland, in France and Italy are relevant because they were instrumental in forming the man that Palmerston would become. Thus they were instrumental in the process of forming the history of nineteenth-century Britain in which he played such a prominent role. His eyewitness experiences in revolutionary Paris made him wary of the power of the mob but they also underscored for him the sense that political change will always manifest, that it was not only possible but *inevitable*. The challenge for the politician was to harness and direct that will for change and to channel it correctly, and towards the goal of the greatest possible human and social good. His Scottish education, in other words, had provided Palmerston with a clear set of political principles, a moral yardstick by which his public career might be measured and a vision to be implemented in a changing world.

*

Once his education was completed Palmerston moved into politics and by 1808 he occupied a seat as a Tory in the House of Commons. Initially he represented a rotten borough on the Isle of Wight and later Cambridge University. By 1809 he held the post of Secretary at War, in charge of the administration and financial well-being of the Army. It was an influential position, though one below Cabinet level. It clearly suited Palmerston, who would occupy the post without a break until 1828. His political career was now underway and it provided many opportunities for the effects of Stewart's moral and political education to be put to the test.

The consequences of this education shine through in some of Palmerston's long-standing political positions. It was one of his proudest boasts, for example, that he had voted for Catholic Emancipation virtually from the beginning of his parliamentary career. As noted in the previous chapter, anti-Catholic laws had begun to be relaxed in the second half of the eighteenth century but in the early decades of the new century sufficient measures remained on the statute books to fuel rising resentment and restlessness on the part of Catholic citizens and their supporters in both Britain and, particularly, Ireland. As early as 1807, the House of Commons had been decidedly in favour of sweeping away the remnants of anti-Catholic legislation but the outright opposition of the monarch and of powerful elements in the House of Lords ensured that no further measures were taken at this time. Indeed, it is important to note that while support for Emancipation was strong, it was relatively covert. A centuries-old fear and mistrust of Catholicism made most politicians unwilling to agitate too publicly in favour of the measure.

Palmerston, however, was happy to lend consistent support, as a survey of his parliamentary speeches makes clear. The contrast with the cautious and conservative Peel could not be more obvious. During one debate in the Commons as early as 1813, Palmerston noted that the Anglican Establishment would simply not be damaged in any way by Catholic Emancipation and went on to argue that in particular the continuing exclusion of Catholics from Parliament had disagreeable practical results. 'If it had unfortunately happened that by circumstance of birth and education, a Nelson, a Wellington, a Burke, a Fox or a Pitt had belonged to this class of the community, of what honour and what glory might not the page of British history have been deprived!' Fifteen years later he declared, 'I beg most distinctly to declare, that I am a warm and zealous friend to religious liberty – that I am as strenuous a partisan of religious freedom as the noble Lord himself ... I concur with him as far as he or any man can wish, that restraints upon the consciences of men can never be advantageous.'

These were common-sense views. This was Palmerston's Edinburgh education manifesting itself briskly and sensibly and in the face of a certain degree of political danger. Certainly in 1813, some of the voters in his Cambridge University constituency would have listened sourly to their MP's pro-Emancipation words. As was the case later with Peel at Oxford, the issue was not at all popular in Cambridge where, as Palmerston noted, 'Protestantism is very rife'. As late as 1826, with the Catholic Relief Bill at last on the horizon and common-sense change on the way, the issue nearly cost Palmerston his Cambridge seat. He was saved by a whisker and by the tactical votes of Whigs.

On other matters, too, Palmerston was willing to 'see the big picture' and take a stance that, while not necessarily to his immediate political advantage, nevertheless accorded with his own personal and political philosophy. This applies to his position on slavery, an issue that had begun to be settled in British political discourse in the early decades of the nineteenth century. William Wilberforce's Slave Trade Act of 1807 had hastened the abolition of slavery in the British Empire but not in other jurisdictions. Palmerston's own position was a settled one. He opposed all forms of slavery and was happy to do so openly even when such public opposition discomfited and vexed Britain's allies. Such a situation arose in the late 1830s, just as Victoria had come to the throne.

The ally in question was Portugal, famously Britain's oldest ally and in general terms a useful counter-balance to French and Spanish power in western Europe and on the high seas. Portugal had agreed by a treaty of 1817 to limit the slave trade but by the 1830s it was clear that slavery had not been to any great extent curtailed, much less prohibited, across the global Portuguese Empire. With this in mind, in 1837 the MP, noted abolitionist and proponent of free trade Thomas Fowell Buxton brought a motion before the House of Commons condemning Portuguese behaviour and Palmerston duly supported the measure, telling members that the British government fully shared 'those sentiments of indignation ... at the extent to which the traffic in slaves still continued under the flag of Portugal'. In discussions especially with the French, Palmerston brought the powers of Europe together in an effort to stop the trade.

Palmerston was no mere Secretary at War at this time. He had become Foreign Secretary so his words as a result carried even more weight. He was not afraid to anger the Portuguese. In the following year, he declared, 'That the slave trade, as is now carried on under that [Portuguese] flag, is a disgrace to any civilised or Christian state.' He called for the ability to 'seize slavers anywhere' and to be entitled to 'seize any ship palpably equipped for the traffic'. He was as good as his word. Britain spent heavily on naval squadrons dedicated to hunting and capturing slaving vessels and succeeded in disrupting, though not ending, the Atlantic trade in slaves.

The episode is of interest in that it helps to encapsulate Palmerston's general philosophy. He was able to combine a sense of moral indignation, which was true and deeply felt, with a practical calculation of what might also be gained from the situation. Portugal's ability to trade and profit in the Atlantic might be circumscribed and Portugal itself, ally though she was, brought usefully to heel by Britain's action in defence of abolitionism. More importantly, the hobbling and dismantling of the trade in slaves encouraged and promoted the principles of free trade and fair competition on the seas, an area in which Britain was supreme. Palmerston's rhetoric and actions against the Portuguese in these years were not without risk. His position of Foreign Secretary was not unassailable and the country's allies were not to be lightly offended but they were part of a larger picture so a risk worth taking. In his attitudes to the United States, at this time still a prominent player in the Atlantic slave trade, Palmerston was equally robust. In 1838, he remarked that 'having declared the slave trade to be piracy both they [the British government] and the majority of the people of the United States would take all adequate measures to rescue their national flag from the stain of such a degradation'. Even though he believed that 'the United States is, of all countries, that with which it ought to be our object to maintain, not merely peace, but the most intimate connection' he was still keen to exercise 'what the Americans are pleased to call an officious interference; and [trusted] that no slave will enter a British port, whether in a colony or the mother country ... without being immediately set free. An American slave-owner ought to feel, that if his slave-ship enters a British port, it is to him, as far as his slave-property is concerned, as if she had foundered at sea; excepting only that he will have the consolation to think that his ship and his crew are safe, and that his slaves, instead of having perished by a miserable death, have entered, as it were, upon a new life of freedom and civilisation'. It is highly unlikely that any slave owner would have had so noble a thought.

Palmerston's words and his approach antagonised the Americans. Yet, in spite of his desire for the closest associations with the United States, he was not afraid to irritate when he considered it necessary. British naval squadrons continued to board and check slaving ships bound for the southern United States and such actions led to periods of diplomatic tension. For the British, there was little to be lost from so doing and much to be gained. The US was a rising global force but it was not yet a military or economic rival to the United Kingdom. It did no harm to remind the Americans of the fact of British control of the seas. In addition, for the United States as for Portugal, free trade was to be encouraged and the distortions introduced by the slave trade discouraged where possible. Tensions with the Americans on this issue would end only with the conclusion of the Civil War in 1865.

These debates on Catholic Emancipation and on the slave trade underscore Palmerston's strong belief in the principle of liberty, both of the person and of individual conscience, and they prefigure the character of the rest of his political career. They emphasise this politician's belief, moral and political, in the essential validity and virtues of free trade and the moral *wrongness* of protectionism. In the chapter on Peel, the impact of these issues upon British politics has been assessed. Palmerston, as a relatively junior politician in the years that these debates were taking place, did not have a decisive role in events but he again took the opportunity to make his opinions, in this case his opposition to the protectionism of the Corn Laws and their ilk, very plain indeed. In 1832 he remarked bracingly, 'I contend that these duties, which are absurdly called protecting duties, are, in fact, nothing but disturbing duties; that they divert capital from its most profitable employment; that they check the accumulation of wealth; that they narrow, circumscribe, and destroy the full employment of labour; and that it is for the benefit of the nation to cast away those fetters by which we are still encumbered.' He went on to argue all that high duties ultimately achieved was an increase in the profit for smugglers and 'a premium to the contraband trade'.

The following year in a speech in the House of Commons, Palmerston made his views even more explicit. He claimed that as a landowner and thus as an agriculturalist himself he did not believe that the protectionist system was as beneficial to 'the welfare of the landed interest as they suppose it to be'. He denied that it was dangerous to be dependent upon foreign countries for the supply of food. His powerful argument was that 'A great portion of the population of a manufacturing country must depend upon foreign countries for the means of subsistence; for if the foreign market be cut off, the manufacturers will be deprived of the commodities or money which they receive in exchange for the produce of their labour.' In the same year, he said that 'Any restriction on commerce is as injurious to the country imposing it as it is to the country against which it is imposed.' Customs duties, he added, ought only to be there to raise a modest amount of revenue.

It is critical to remember that these were tense, strained arguments and they were part of a battle for the soul of the nation. Would Britain fully embrace the principle of free trade or would the nation cleave to the notion of protectionism, raising barriers to a flow of trade within a rapidly expanding global market? Palmerston's own views were, once more, moulded in part by his three years steeped in the debates and discourse of the Scottish Enlightenment, where Adam Smith's *The Wealth of Nations* (1776) had taken aim at the so-called 'mercantilism' that had dominated patterns of trade in the eighteenth century. Smith had deplored the notion that any government should excessively govern or direct economic activity within its jurisdiction. Such efforts were wholly unnecessary, Smith argued, and he went on to make the case for a model of free trade that would permit a free flow of exports and imports at competitive prices. 'It is the maxim of every prudent master of a family,' Smith wrote, 'never to attempt to make at home what it will cost him more to make than to buy.' For Palmerston, this was mere common sense, made more valuable by its Scottish Enlightenment imprimatur. It is better to focus on the efficient use of capital and to be aware of the risk to employment spawned by protective tariffs and duties.

These views are the product of careful thought and economic analysis and they are by no means the rushed judgements of a rash or unscrupulous populist. The easy path has always been to argue for protectionism. The free trade position is less intuitive, less based on emotion but nevertheless more truly grounded in the principle of the common good. Palmerston had taken his studies seriously and although history does not remember him for his financial skills, unlike Peel and Gladstone, nonetheless they were a key part of his political make-up.

*

Palmerston clearly relished his role as Secretary at War but in retrospect this was merely a long preamble to the greatest phases of his career. In 1828, as his tenure at the War Office ended, the tectonic plates in British party politics were shifting decisively and their movements would profoundly influence the remainder of Palmerston's career. He had begun this career as a Tory but the debates concerning free trade and Catholic Emancipation were causing internal Tory tensions. Now Palmerston was able to follow his instincts, while still preserving his career. He moved towards the liberal wing of the Tories and, when these made common cause with the Whigs to form a government in 1830, Palmerston was, as we have seen, appointed Foreign Secretary. This was a critical, a decisive, moment in his political life. In the first place, he was leaving his Tory antecedents behind as he moved purposefully towards Liberal politics. In the second, he was embarking on a period at the Foreign Office that would come to define his career.

Palmerston remained in this position off and on, mainly on, for the next twenty years and it is fair to say that he stands as the most famous Foreign Secretary the United Kingdom has ever had. He was, for one thing, remarkably dominant. He served three Whig or Liberal Prime Ministers (Grey, Melbourne and Russell) and with the latter two he had considerable freedom to follow his chosen path. This did not mean that there were no disagreements, sometimes quite fierce ones, within the Cabinet but Palmerston tended to have his way.

To his critics, his name is synonymous with interventionism, with vigorous and frequently hostile adventures abroad staged in order to bolster British influence and defend British interests and backed by what is sometimes misleadingly called *gunboat diplomacy*. Palmerston *did* believe in the principle of intervention when this was judged to be in the national interest. During his first stint as Foreign Secretary (1830–34), however, he made it clear that intervention in and of itself was not his main objective. Instead, he said, the preservation of peace was to be the 'first object' of the government. He emphasised his belief in the 'general principle of non-intervention in the affairs of other countries' and naturally he expected other nations to follow the same self-denying ordinances.

As part of this general desire for the preservation of peace, Palmerston was a believer in reform, in foreign as in domestic affairs. Reform brought about managed change and change staved off revolution but, as he surveyed a Europe that appeared utterly resistant to change, this the result of the Congress of Vienna of 1815 that ended the Napoleonic Wars and implemented a new European order, he noted the existence of subterranean political tensions across the Continent. His judgement was that a modicum of careful reform could prevent greater changes, the violent and explosive changes he had witnessed as a child at Paris. He worried that the stultifying oligarchies of Europe, symbolised by Metternich, the arch-conservative Austrian foreign minister and no admirer of Palmerston, did not and would not realise this.

This said, he did not believe that the possibility of future European unrest warranted large-scale British interventions. Instead, Britain must be ready for all eventualities while continuing to exert her influence in the defence of peace. 'There is no better or more necessary security which this country can have for the continuance of peace,' he remarked, 'than to put its navy on a footing with that of any other country.' He wanted, in other words, his nation to possess military strength and to be able to project it but he did not want to put forth such strength unnecessarily.

His thinking, his sage use of British power and his reluctance in general terms to become involved overtly in foreign adventures were all tested from the very first. In the revolutionary year of 1830, British influence was instrumental in the formation of a new and predominantly Catholic Belgian state, formed of breakaway southern provinces of the Netherlands. Palmerston also sealed an uneasy alliance in this year with France, Portugal and Spain to act as a counter-balance to a northern European alliance of Austria, Russia and Prussia. In the East, he lent British support to bolster the defences of the Ottoman Empire against the predations of Russia.

Tested but not found wanting, in each of these potentially dangerous arenas Palmerston's policies were executed without the need to send British troops into unpopular conflicts in Europe. Indeed, his first spell as Foreign Secretary underscores the sense that Palmerston's approach and his power base were under-pinned by popular support in the widest possible sense of the word. Public opinion was emphatically not in favour of foreign military adventures, not at this point, with the devastation of the Napoleonic era still within the memories of many Britons. Palmerston's genius was, first, to be mindful of this crucial fact and, second, to bring together the three classes of society who cared about foreign policy. As David Brown notes in his biography of Palmerston, quoting the *Daily News*, 'There is the aris-tocracy who nervously want to keep their privileges; the commercial and industrious class who only ever care for avoiding shocks or any threat to their existing situation; and third, the people who are unselfish in their views and dislike oppression in foreign lands.' Brown argues that Palmerston's skill ensured that the views of the second and third of these groups were heard just as clearly as those of the first, in the process broadening public support for his policies to its widest possible extent.

Palmerston's strategies did not rigidly favour non-intervention, for this was simply not the way of the world.

Nor did his policies always go according to plan, a fact most clearly demonstrated in the history of Sino-British relations in the course of the 1830s and 1840s, in which his principles of non-intervention clashed with his desire to expand a network of free trade across the globe. China was at this time in a state of relative isolation. There were no Chinese diplomats in Europe and no European representation in China. Trade, however, continued. Demand for Chinese porcelain and silks was high in Europe. This was so to such an extent, indeed, that by the 1830s the Chinese enjoyed a considerable trade surplus with Britain. In addition, economic exchange with China was highly regulated. In order to keep European influence at bay, all goods flowing into China were funnelled through the southern port of Canton. This was the so-called 'Canton System'; both it and the trade imbalance with China were sources of considerable irritation to the British authorities.

For Palmerston in particular, with his dedication to the principle of free trade, this state of affairs was vexing. In 1834, he despatched his friend the Scottish peer Lord Napier to Canton to negotiate new and more advantageous trading arrangements with the Chinese. Napier's mission was a notable failure. He lacked the necessary depth of knowledge of the terrain and of Chinese attitudes ever to be in with a chance of success. Frustrated and angry at what he perceived as Chinese intransigence, Napier counselled a military offensive against the Chinese at Canton in order to force change. The result was at this time a military stalemate and Napier retreated to his base at nearby Portuguese Macao, where he died of typhus in October.

Napier was dead but the train of events he and Palmerston had set in motion could not now be halted. Britain was obliged to remedy, if she could, a very public diplomatic and military failure at Canton and now the scene was set for the First Opium War between Britain and China, which erupted in 1839. The British East India Company had taken to transporting Indian-grown opium into China, where it was resold to local users, thus creating a wave of opium addicts. When the Chinese authorities proposed a tax on the sale of opium, Palmerston saw his opportunity and ordered an intervention. The First Opium War proved an unqualified British success, Canton was captured and Chinese opposition was swept away. By the Treaty of Nanking, Chinese ports were opened to British goods and the strategically valuable territory of Hong Kong, close to Macau, was ceded to Britain. A Second Opium War (1856–60) would complete the mission to British satisfaction, though at the cost of inflicting considerable humiliation on the Chinese nation.

Palmerston did not see the war through to victory, for he was replaced as Foreign Secretary in the summer of 1841. Yet, this was undeniably his war, his vision and his success. It violated his general desire for non-intervention but the prize of vast new Asian markets and a balance of trade surplus was clearly worth it. In addition, he understood that the Chinese would regard British caution and hesitation as signs of weakness and therefore that it was in the national interest to act. The events in China did not mark a rupture in Palmerston's political philosophy but rather a continuation or evolution of it. Where a certain course of action was warranted, it was a sensible move to ensure that this course of action be pursued.

Palmerston was out of office until 1846, returning as Foreign Secretary in that year just in time to observe the wave of revolutions which broke across Europe in 1848. Now the Liberal statesman can be seen in full view, Palmerston openly siding with revolutionary activists in Hungary as they sought to break the connection with Austria. From a pragmatic point of point, his succour of Hungarian nationalism made sense. Palmerston had always disliked Austrian hegemony in central Europe and Austrian weakness would advance British power and influence. However, the sight of a British Foreign Secretary cheering on foreign revolutionaries caused consternation at home and when Palmerston proposed receiving the Hungarian nationalist leader Lajos Kossuth at Broadlands, this alarming suggestion was vetoed by the Cabinet.

Shortly afterwards, Palmerston was faced with a motion of censure in the Commons. This move was spearheaded by the Irish MP Thomas Anstey, who put down a motion in the Commons requiring the 'production of papers', a technique still used today in the House to embarrass ministers. Anstey had form. He was a consistent and virulent critic of Palmerston, both in Parliament and outside, taking every possible opportunity to criticise the minister on all aspects of his foreign policies. On this occasion, Palmerston responded with a full defence of his thinking and an explanation of his sensible and pragmatic approach and his speech is so significant that it is worth quoting at some length:

The main charges brought against me are, that I did not involve this country in perpetual quarrels from one end of the globe to the other. There is no country that has been named, from the United States to the empire of China, with respect to which part of [Anstey's] charge has not been, that we have refrained from taking steps that might have plunged, us into conflict with one or more of these Powers. On these occasions we have been supported by the opinion and approbation of Parliament and the public. We have endeavoured to extend the commercial relations of the country, or to place them where extension was not required, on a firmer basis, and upon a footing of greater security. Surely in that respect we have not judged amiss, nor deserved the censure of the country; on the contrary, I think we have done good service.

I hold with respect to alliances, that England is a Power sufficiently strong, sufficiently powerful, to steer her own course, and not to tie herself as an unnecessary appendage to the policy of any other Government. I hold that the real policy of England – apart from questions which involve her own particular interests, political or commercial – is to be the champion of justice and right; pursuing that course with moderation and prudence, not becoming the Quixote of the world, but giving the weight of her moral sanction and support wherever she thinks that justice is, and wherever she thinks that wrong has been done. Sir, in pursuing that course, and in pursuing the more limited direction of our own particular interests, my conviction is, that as long as England keeps herself in the right – as long as she wishes to permit no injustice – as long as she wishes to countenance no wrong – as long as she labours at legislative interests of her own – and as long as she sympathises with right and justice, she will never find herself altogether alone. She is sure to find some other State, of sufficient power, influence, and weight, to support and aid her in the course she may think fit to pursue.

Therefore I say that it is a narrow policy to suppose that this country or that is to be marked out as the eternal ally or the perpetual enemy of England. We have no eternal allies, and we have no perpetual enemies. Our interests are eternal and perpetual, and those interests it is our duty to follow. When we find other countries marching in the same course, and pursuing the same objects as ourselves, we consider them as our friends, and we think for the moment that we are on the most cordial footing; when we find other countries that take a different view, and thwart us in the object we pursue, it is our duty to make allowance for the different manner in which they may follow out the same objects. It is our duty not to pass too harsh a judgment upon others, because they do not exactly see things in the same light as we see; and it is our duty not lightly to engage this country in the frightful responsibilities of war, because from time to time we may find this or that Power disinclined to concur with us in matters where their opinion and ours may fairly differ. That has been, as far as my faculties have allowed me to act upon it, the guiding principle of my conduct. And if I might be allowed to express in one sentence the principle which I think ought to guide an English Minister, I would adopt the expression of Canning, and say that with every British Minister the interests of England ought to be *the shibboleth of policy* [author's italics].

In this powerful defence of his political conduct over a span of some twenty years, Palmerston made a clear and perennial case for the sage exercise of foreign policy. Suffused with examples of what he had done, it emphasises the need to maintain a high degree of popular support and underscores the importance of commerce and the requirement for the maintenance of military strength. Palmerston also made it apparent, however, that he was no mere warmonger, nor would he ever enter into a war he thought he would lose or not easily win. Supporting liberal causes was secondary to the national interest and how other countries managed their internal affairs could only ever be of peripheral concern. Palmerston's words continue to act as an excellent basis for a contemporary foreign policy, rooted as they are in a moral and realistic vision of the supremacy of the national interest. It is certainly the case that Canning's 'shibboleth of policy' resonates to this day and it is against such a policy background that Palmerston's most famous foreign foray was undertaken.

This was the so-called Don Pacifico affair, which first erupted into the public view in 1847. Its eponymous subject was a Jewish merchant and ex-Portuguese consul-general to Greece. He lived at Athens but was in fact a British subject as a result of his place of birth at Gibraltar. He was also a man of some means and a leader of the Jewish community at Athens. In April 1847, Don Pacifico's residence in the Greek capital was attacked during an upsurge in anti-Semitic unrest. In addition, police officers and the sons of Greek officials were part of the attacking mob, thus lending a political tinge to this ugly affair. The British government proceeded to lodge a claim for damages against the Greek authorities. Greece protested that the claim was wildly excessive, as indeed it was, and assumed that the British authorities were in part using the attack against Don Pacifico as a pretext to gain some revenge against Hellenic officials suspected of misappropriating funds previously sent to the country from the United Kingdom.

Eighteen months passed without an agreement and now Don Pacifico appealed to the British government to assist in settling his claim. Palmerston himself was a philhellene. Britain had played a critical role in the establishment of Greek Independence in 1828–9, Britain remained a formal guarantor of Greek sovereignty and Britain held the Ionian Islands off the west coast of Greece. A current of benign British influence, in other words, ran very deep in Greece but, notwithstanding each of these facts, Palmerston resolved that in this case intervention was a necessity. In January 1850, a British fleet of fifteen ships sailed into the Bay of Salamis. The Greek navy was impounded and a blockade imposed on Athens, at a stroke both hobbling the Greek military and stifling the small Greek economy.

Palmerston's political enemies saw an opportunity so they went on the attack, condemning what they regarded as the Foreign Secretary's heavy-handedness and over-reaction. The result was another motion of censure in Parliament. In the Lords, a chamber that then as now was not answerable to public opinion, Lord Stanley for the Conservatives deplored Palmerston's actions that were 'directed against the commerce and people of Greece and calculated to endanger the continuance of our friendly relations with other Powers'. The motion passed.

In the Commons, however, the debate proceeded rather differently. Here, the attacks on Palmerston were founded on principles of high-minded international diplomacy. The Liberal politician Richard Cobden argued that Palmerston's display of power in Greece in fact was an indication of weakness. Cobden said he preferred a system of international arbitration to the blunt instrument of gunboat diplomacy. Moreover, he did not believe that Palmerston's intervention was primarily designed to advance liberal constitutions. It was a relatively nuanced argument. It is certainly the case that Stanley's attack in the Lords had been rather more full-throated and for this reason more successful.

Palmerston's reply to the motion of censure was an extraordinary five hours in length and constitutes the second of the two great speeches that define his career. He quoted Cicero when he said, 'As the Roman, in days of old, held himself free from indignity when he could say *Civis Romanus sum*; so also a British subject, in whatever land he may be, shall feel confident that the watchful eye and the strong arm of England, will protect him against injustice and wrong.' These were stirring words and easily comprehensible to the public. The Commons motion of censure failed, Palmerston carried the day and the events in Parliament, far from harming him, had raised him to new heights of popularity.

Here again was Palmerston's distinctive ability to harness and deploy the power of populism. The British public could after all readily understand that Palmerston was protecting an essential British national interest. His actions did not stem in the main from a personal affront at the treatment meted out to Don Pacifico, although it is significant that the riots at Athens were anti-Semitic at the root and Palmerston was not an anti-Semite. Principally, however, this was a commercial matter and a commercial calculation. British trade around the world depended upon the traders themselves being protected. In many states, there were complex internal as well as external tariffs and the risk of discrimination against international businessmen was high. The United Kingdom could not succeed commercially unless it defended the interests of business and this, quite simply, was what Palmerston was doing. Sending a fleet of ships to blockade a foreign capital not only showed the Greek government that Britain meant business, it also telegraphed the same unmistakable message to other powers, to a watching world and to the public at home.

*

In 1851, Palmerston resigned as Foreign Secretary. Queen Victoria had complained that he had not, as was required of all ministers, submitted his measures for Royal approval. Palmerston accepted the Queen's criticism and apologised. Soon afterwards, a second complaint was made. Prince Albert alleged that Palmerston had been disrespectful to the Sovereign by sending out letters in the Queen's name without giving her time to read them. On this occasion, Palmerston vigorously rejected the complaint but the damage was done. Two Royal complaints could not be weathered and he resigned. This episode will be covered more fully in the chapter on Prince Albert.

Indeed, tension between the Royal Family and Palmerston was by no means a new development and here we note a degree of spice added to Palmerston's activities. In plain terms, his private life was unorthodox. He held in some circles the nickname of 'Lord Cupid' and in his own diaries he recorded liaisons with overlapping mistresses. After his marriage to Emily Lamb, a long-term mistress, his ardour did not dim. He continued to see other women and this behaviour has coloured opinions of him during his lifetime, and afterwards. Such habits also informed the dislike felt for him by Queen Victoria and her prudish husband and help to explain the complaints she directed against him.

Indeed, as early as 1838, with the young Queen barely on the throne, the two had fallen out as a result of Palmerston's nocturnal prowling. During a stay at Windsor, he had crept along a corridor in search of the bedroom of Miss Brand (later Lady Dacre), lady-in-waiting to the Queen. Woken and startled, Brand screamed and woke the household, at which point Palmerston beat a hasty retreat. According to Albert, the Queen complained that she could not agree 'to take a man as the Chief Adviser ... who as her Secretary of State ... had committed a brutal attack on one of her ladies'. Palmerston's misdemeanours and his shamelessness reminded the Queen unpleasantly of her disreputable Hanoverian forebears. It is only fair to add that Victoria disliked Palmerston's support for revolutionary regimes abroad just as much as and perhaps more than she disliked his morals.

Such habits did his career no great harm. By 1852, Palmerston was back in the Whig coalition government of his old adversary at Harrow, Lord Aberdeen, as Home Secretary. The coalition was difficult and not harmonious and there was considerable puzzlement at Palmerston's appointment to a domestic role, when his expertise was so evidently in foreign affairs. In the pithiest encapsulation of the situation, David Roberts notes acidly, 'The proud Foreign Secretary who had snubbed the crowned heads of Europe now haggled with Vestrymen about their sewers.' Acidic but far from being the case. Vestrymen were the local councillors of the day and it was indeed necessary to haggle with them in order to ensure improvement in living and social conditions.

Haggle was what Palmerston did, with a will and with a good deal of success. Public health was to form a major component of Palmerston's paternalist work at the Home Office. He was instrumental in pressing a list of reforms the consequences of which would be long-lasting indeed. A Factories Act outlawed work by juvenile labour in the hours of darkness while a Truck Act obliged employers to pay their workers in cash instead of, as had sometimes been the case, in goods the employers themselves had manufactured, thus freeing employees at a stroke from a state which resembled medieval serfdom or vassalage.

A Smoke Abatement Act addressed the pressing problem of air pollution in the cities and a Vaccination Act rolled out a programme of children's healthcare for the first time. Penal conditions were made less stringent, maximum prison sentences were reduced and the policy of transportation of criminals to Tasmania, often for petty and trivial offences, was ended. Palmerston also began the process of upgrading London's decaying sewage system, with the result that the filthy condition of the Thames began to improve. He was obliged to deal with and sometimes be defeated by vested interests. From time to time he was also stymied by an excess of liberal ideology which quarrelled with any attempt to regulate public health. In 1854, for example, a correspondent to *The Times* declared, 'We prefer to take our chance with Cholera than be bullied into health. There is nothing a man hates so much as being cleansed against his will or having his floor swept, his hall whitewashed, his dung heap cleared away and his thatch forced to give way to slate.'

Palmerston rejected such ideologically dogmatic excesses, dismissing, for example, the idea that cholera was an act of God that could be halted by penitential fasting. Instead he pressed publicly the idea that civic works in the poorest areas were the best way to stop the diseases which led to death. His work as Home Secretary, in other words, connected with his Edinburgh philosophic apprenticeship and enabled him to bring his intelligence and learning to bear for the good of the people. It is also worth noting that twenty years later, Disraeli would be working in much the same area, asserting the political morality of such public works and seeking to define such works as explicitly the terrain of the Conservative Party. It was not only in the foreign arena that Palmerston excelled, in other words. Our collective social history tells a different tale.

*

In February 1855, Palmerston at last attained the greatest office of all, with his appointment as Prime Minister. With one brief interruption he would hold the office until his death, at the age of eighty, in October 1865. His premiership is remembered for many signal achievements, from a conclusion to the Crimean War that largely favoured the British side to forging from a tentative and sometimes chaotic Whig identity a contemporary British Liberal Party. He saw his most important goal as Prime Minister as continuing to improve the lot of the people. As he remarked, nothing was 'attended with more permanent and general benefit [above] the spread of education and the diffusion of information among the lower classes'.

He believed, as he had learned from Dugald Stewart, that the spread of knowledge would safeguard society and that consequently it needed to flourish in all parts of the nation. Education, clean water, cheap food and personal liberty: taken together, these were Palmerston's recipes for the preservation and enhancement of the nation and for the prevention of revolution. Was this a populist creed? Yes indeed, this was emphatically populist, though it was mingled with good sense and a correct morality and it was a message, moreover, that the great mass of the people could follow and approve.

He valued popular support but he was not a democrat in the sense of the term as we know it. He wanted to avoid revolution and not to destabilise the Constitution. He wanted change, not as an end in itself but because change was an antidote to revolution. As early as 1828, he had made this philosophy explicit when he argued for a limited extension of the franchise. 'I am anxious,' he said, 'to express my desire that the franchise should be extended to a great town, not because I am a friend of reform in principle, but because I am its decided enemy. I think that extending the franchise to large towns, on such occasions as the one in question, is the only mode by which the House can avoid the adoption, at some time or another, of a *general* [author's italics] plan of reform. It is my opinion that the disturbances, which on many occasions, have agitated the great commercial districts, would have been prevented, if such places had possessed a legitimate organ for the expression of their opinions.' When these modest reforms were frustrated he returned to his point in 1831, remarking in the House of Commons on the eve of the Reform Bill: 'If instead of this, the government had turned reformers on ever so moderate a scale; if the government had admitted the principle of amendment, and pledged themselves to act upon it whenever opportunities might occur, the House would not now have been discussing a plan of general reform proposed by my noble friend.'

His argument was a compelling one. He, like Peel and many others of their contemporaries, accepted that reform was indeed necessary. They felt that unrepresented large towns would be quieter with some level of representation. When citizens were accorded no representation at all, they naturally tended to back ever greater changes. At the very end of his life, however, the limits of Palmerston's support for change would be laid bare when he opposed William Gladstone's call for universal suffrage. When Gladstone remarked that every man had a moral right to vote, Palmerston countered with the statement, 'The fact is that a vote is not a right but a trust. All the nation cannot by possibility be brought together to vote and therefore a selected few are appointed by Law to perform this function for the rest and the publicity attached to the performance of their trust is a security that it will be responsibly performed.'

Nor did he want to see the aristocracy taken out of political life. He was, after all, a nobleman himself. He believed that the landed interest was essential to stability but their duty was to improve and enhance both their land and the lot of their tenants. As a landlord in Ireland, he made a considerable effort to improve the land he owned. In one speech on the government of Ireland, he noted that with slightly less than half the population of Great Britain, Ireland only generated an annual income of one seventh of that of its larger neighbour, seven million pounds compared to fifty million pounds. He attributed this to a lack of capital which came about because of poor government and on his own estates he tried to do better. As early as 1808, when he was only twenty-four years old, he wrote to his sister to tell her that the land was wholly unimproved but could be drained to enhance its arable yield threefold. He also wanted to do for his tenants what he tried to achieve for the nation decades later.

He looked to improve the condition of the people, by investing in education and better roads. Again, he wanted this partly out of natural self-interest, for a more prosperous estate would benefit him and increase his income, but he also had a sense of *noblesse oblige* and of philanthropy. This did not mean that he wanted his own privileged position overthrown. On the contrary, he was determined to preserve it but saw that the best way to hold off revolution was by means of a steady improvement in living standards. In both his political and private sphere he followed a similar approach. Adam Smith famously remarked that while the baker does not bake our daily bread out of charity, nonetheless he feeds us. Palmerston clearly saw Smith's essential point.

It is worth concluding these thoughts on Palmerston by returning to the vexed issue of populism. His success at keeping the people in his column has sometimes been used against Palmerston, in order to diminish him and to imply that he was a lesser political leader than certain of his peers. Certainly he excelled at what we might today term the 'black arts' of spin and media management. He cultivated relationships with journalists, made himself open to the press in a way that was not 'done' in those days and moulded the news agenda with a skilful hand. No wonder some people disliked him.

The point is that Palmerston, like Peel, understood the function of the press in Britain and thus he sought to influence this function. In a letter of 1831, written in the aftermath of a critical piece appearing in the *Courier*, he made his attitudes plain. His initial plan had been to argue with the editor but he recognised:

... the only influence which my office possesses over the *Courier* or any other paper, is positive and not negative. I could get him to insert any article I wish today, but I have no means or power of preventing him from inserting any other of quite a different kind tomorrow. I can impel but I cannot control ... The only communication which takes place is, that every now and then when we have a particular piece of news, it is given to the editor, and he thereby gets a start on his competitors, and on the condition of receiving these occasional intimations he gives his support to the government; but no editor would bring his daily articles to a public office to be looked over before they are printed, and no public officer who had any sense in his brains would undertake the responsibility of such inspections.

Palmerston was responsive to the press and would see any editor who came to visit him. He was also willing to help journalists in difficulties abroad, on one occasion even saving two *Post* correspondents from being shot in Spain. Rather less creditably, he was able to use secret service funds to bribe people to be supportive. He went through £2,500 per month in a secret slush fund for spies and espionage. This did not mean that the press inevitably supported his policies, which he recognised, and his attitudes began to alter and evolve. The longer he remained in office, the more Palmerston began to realise there was an opportunity for pushing his opinions via newspapers. The 1857 General Election was won, according to some, because of Palmerston mania which swept the country and this in turn was based upon his careful development of relations with newspapers including *The Times*.

Palmerston was so successful at these various strategies that some press allies were perceived to be his *personal* rather than his party's supporters. He used money and skill to place articles that put him in a good light and advanced his policies. This did not axiomatically make them bad policies, as he pointed out in a speech to the House of Commons, in answer to a charge that the people would be quiet if not egged on by reformers. 'That when the government, and the press and the public are all of the same opinion,' he said, 'it may be possible that the opinion is not a fallacy.' Later, he stated more plainly that 'the besetting sin of the late administration was a defiance of public opinion, of public opinion at home, of public opinion abroad; a belief that the firm will and steady determination of a few men in power could bear down the opinions of the many, and stifle the feelings of mankind.' He wanted, in other words, to listen to the reasonable views of the wider population. Naturally he wanted to lead, and he deployed the tools that allowed him to do it, but it was always with a clear sense of moral purpose.

'The interest of England is the polar star, the guiding principle of the conduct of the government.' Palmerston said this as Foreign Secretary in 1839 and it is a comment that was true of his whole career and the people believed him. They saw that Palmerston was on their side and shared their desire for a great and prosperous nation. He exercised his power in the national interest and served faithfully for decades. His life of duty, patriotism and political skill makes him one of the greatest Victorians.

Napier: The Great Radical

Many of the truly eminent Victorians whose lives are traced in this book are well and honourably memorialised, in busts and plaques and more the length and breadth of Britain. Few are so honourably remembered as General Sir Charles Napier (10 August 1782–29 August 1853), a bronze of whom stands grandly on its plinth in the south-western corner of Trafalgar Square in central London. Ironically, far from everyone remembers Napier's life and achievements. Indeed, some go out of their way to ignore him.

Take the scene in 2000, when the then Mayor of London, Ken Livingstone, was proud to speak boastfully of his ignorance. Who was this Napier, asked Livingstone, and why was he so visibly commemorated in the heart of London? What was Napier's relevance to the lives of ordinary Londoners? Leaving aside the obvious reply that there are no ordinary Londoners but only extraordinary ones, Mr Livingstone, who ought to know his London better, should perhaps have taken himself off to St Paul's. Here, another memorial, this one in marble, stands in the cathedral crypt and its inscription tells us very pithily who Napier was and what legacy he has left:

> A prescient general
> A beneficent governor
> A just man

As for relevance: his importance to his own peers is revealed by the note on his statue, which shows that it was erected by public subscription, with the largest number being private soldiers.

However, it may be that Mr Livingstone's disdain could have stemmed from some other source than ignorance. He might have seen something in Napier that he did not quite like: a prototype Tony Blair. For both Blair and Napier were in their way sincere patriots, whose actions were questioned in their own time on grounds of prudence and coherence. Each lustily made a case for themselves and for their virtue. Neither was at moral fault for the failures of their ambitions, though it is clear now that each might usefully ask themselves whether these ambitions, though honestly formed, were in fact sensibly held.

*

General Sir Charles Napier, GCB, late Commander-in-Chief India, and 'Conqueror of Sindh', was a grand radical. Although his ancestry and cousinhood were as elevated as they could be, these associations certainly did not stop him from holding all sorts of opinions from well beyond the confines of the pale.

This chapter will in part focus not merely on the achievements of this grand radical but on the *limits* of those achievements and this is partly to illustrate a sense of why Victorian conquest and Victorian rule were not one and the same thing, even if, as in Napier's case, they were accomplished by the same man.

Napier was not universally popular in his own era. He was accused of allowing the rape of the womenfolk of tribal Islamic rulers he had displaced and of being an enthusiastic flogger of men. The Victorian condemnation of Napier was such as to make him seem almost a Victorian caricature of a Victorian. He was smeared for his aggression, temper, bloodlust and even his supposed imperialism. To accept these slurs unquestioningly, however, would be unfair and it is worth remembering that the Victorian literary industry was almost as enthusiastic as our own in the matter of the pulverisation of reputations.

For it is certainly the case that Napier could surprise. He was a general, colonial governor and aristocrat by pedigree, who could ask of the early Victorian world through which he moved: 'Are we not the most *scientific*, and most wealthy nation in the world?', in order that he might then demand, 'Are we not so miserable, so starving, that no one can say that the poor will not rise up upon, and destroy the rich?' He did not even ask such questions in an off-the-cuff manner but deliberately, thoughtfully, coolly, in the pages of *Colonization, Particularly in Southern Australia, with Some Remarks on Small Farms and Overpopulation* (1835), a work devoted to kicking away the struts of every contemporary rationale offered up for the enterprise.

Napier despaired of the rulers, idolised the ruled and would have solved their problems with radical answers had the temper of his own age allowed it. In short, though misdrawn by contemporaries, this was no Victorian as the current caricatures would have him. Rather, he was a colour-blind colonial governor who rejected the preoccupations of race and wished to see mankind merged in one common humanity. This is not the Napier so thoroughly disliked by the critics of the contemporary world. There are two episodes in the life of Napier that help to illuminate this theme of surprise, of counter-intuition, and that stretch our conception of the man and his role. The first was his Army command in the North of England during the time of Chartist unrest, when he strained above all else to avoid another Peterloo-like riot. The second, in India, shows what a man like Napier, with his views on good government, thought governing was *for* and shows too the gulfs that then can sometimes exist between good intentions and good results.

Whether in Britain or her empire overseas, what Napier saw was that:

Justice and religion are mockeries in the eyes of 'a great manufacturing country', for the true god of such a nation is mammon. I may be singular, but, in truth, I prefer the despotic Napoléon to the despots of the East India Company. The man ambitious of universal power generally rules to do good to subdued nations. But the men ambitious of universal peculation rule only to make themselves rich, to the destruction of happiness among a hundred millions of people.

Few Victorians saw Napoleon as possessing many of the qualities they yearned to see manifest in their own lands but Napier did and this influence derived directly from his family.

*

Charles Napier's childhood was steeped in the cultures of Scotland and Ireland and was perfumed with a delicious touch of scandal. His father, George Napier, was the impoverished scion of Scottish aristocracy, while his mother was the famous Lady Sarah Lennox, who was raised in Ireland before returning to become a favourite of George III. She married Charles Bunbury, gave birth to an illegitimate child, ran away with her lover before being abandoned by him and was divorced by Bunbury all before the age of thirty-one. She and George Napier married in 1781 and Charles was the eldest of their eight children. He was born in Whitehall, in the heart of London, but the family moved to Ireland when he was three and settled west of Dublin, in Co. Kildare. George Napier took up a post as Comptroller of Army Accounts and the family was still in Ireland to witness first-hand the United Irishmen uprising of 1798, which was accompanied by an abortive French invasion of Ireland. George Napier reinforced the family home and armed the household for the duration of the uprising.

Napier's family tree was complicated but it has its hereditary radical roots that went deep and stretched wide. The Lennox kin, for example, included Charles, brother of Sarah. He was the third Duke of Richmond and was known as the 'radical Duke', on account of his keen support of all *au courant* causes, from parliamentary reform to the American colonists in their struggle against the Crown. Sarah's sister Emily married the future Duke of Leinster, who was a 'Patriot', which is to say a *popular* politician in pre-Union Ireland. Their seat was at Castletown, probably Ireland's grandest country house, and their offspring included Lord Edward Fitzgerald, who played a prominent and rebellious part in the events of 1798 and who died from the wounds received while resisting arrest on a charge of treason. Another sister, Caroline, married the prominent Whig politician Henry Holland, thus making her the mother of the dangerously radical Whig stateman Charles James Fox.

In other words, there was no shortage of radical example in Napier's family, though it is worth noting that the British have sustained and tolerated this tradition of 'hereditary radicals' only because this cosseted caste failed, at home and abroad, time after time, to achieve the goals it set out for itself. As much as anything else, it was the lesson which first the French Revolution and then the Napoleonic dictatorship taught, that inoculated the British against excess and kept these radicals from doing much harm.

George Napier, however, was remarkable not for some putative radical streak but rather because he was an honest Comptroller of the Army in eighteenth-century Ireland. His example caused his son to have no guilty, familial hesitations in his lifetime's detestation of the 'old corruption'. It is also worth noting that, although he was as much a foe of the British *ancien régime* as all in his milieu, George Napier tended to temper his radicalism. 'Our King sends millions to slaughter,' he remarked, 'and yet we cannot, in common sense, wish his crown to fall and to belong to a republic of tyrants, as all republics are.' This was the creed of a man who saw practical boundaries to even the greatest causes and he bestowed this legacy of pragmatism on his son.

There were other influences and imprints upon the life of the young Charles Napier. In Ireland, his family were essentially *dependants* of their kin of Castletown and Charles went to the village day school. He was therefore always aware of the financial and material travails of everyday life and this in turn meant that his critique of the status quo was grounded in his own observation and ran deeper than most. His financially insecure Irish youth, moreover, left him far apart from the rest of his class, both in Ireland and later in England. Not for him the rural patriotism of the Tory squirearchy, who managed to modernise their own land while retaining their traditional views. Instead there was the furious radicalism required of someone who had seen the failures of farming in Ireland and understood that the problem lay squarely with that country's absentee landlords.

Throughout his later life as a ruler of men, this problem, how the poor might provide for themselves and how the just might rearrange the structure of society and the economy to allow this to happen, was one to which Napier repeatedly returned. In Ireland, England and later in the course of postings in the British protectorate of the Ionian Islands and the Indian province of Sindh, the problem was always essentially the same, though the answer worked out unevenly, if at all. Napier's misfortune was that his response to that which he abhorred, in short, capitalist modernity, was pre-modern and uneconomic.

Like so many radicals, his urges were profoundly reactionary in origin.

*

Enlisting in the Army was the inescapable fate for a well-born but relatively poor young man. The Napier boys were nonetheless good at it and produced three generals out of five sons, which even by Victorian standards was above average. Of all his many relations, his brother William was the closest and the pair remained in constant touch, writing continually to one another. William, as a roughhousing historian, was to be of questionable use to Charles in the political battles which lay ahead. One of Napier's numerous cousins, meanwhile, was another Charles James Napier. Known in the family as 'Black Charlie', he became a renowned admiral. His sixty years of service saw him in action as a young man in the wars against Napoleon and as a veteran in the war in Crimea, and all this before he was elected to the Commons in 1855.

Napier thus had large shoes to fill when he enlisted in the Army in 1799, at the age of seventeen. He first saw action in the Peninsular War. The conflict erupted in 1807 and by 1809 Napier had retired from the field, following his experiences at the Battle of Coruña in January of that year. The battle was, on paper at least, a victory for the British. The army was in disorderly retreat at this time across the harsh winter landscape of north-west Spain and hoping to embark for home on transport ships lying in port at La Coruña. When they arrived at the coast, however, the ships were not there. They did finally arrive and the British repulsed a last-minute French attack, boarded and sailed but the price was high. The retreat was felt as a bitter humiliation, with *The Times* noting, 'The fact must not be disguised ... that we have suffered a shameful disaster.' Worse still, the British commander, Sir John Moore, was killed in the battle and worst of all, at least from his family's point of view, was that Napier himself was grievously injured in the retreat and taken captive by the French as a prisoner of war.

Years later, 'Black Charlie', now an MP, described to the Commons his cousin's experience in battle:

Something occurred to impede them – [Charles] was surrounded by French troops – received a cut on the head with a sabre – was stabbed in the back with a bayonet – a bullet went through his leg, and two of his ribs were broken by a cannon-ball. 'I think (said the gallant officer) that was a dose enough to settle any man.'

French arms caused the injuries but French medical treatment saved Napier's life. He had been left for dead by the British and indeed had not the French picked him up and behaved impeccably towards him, he could not have lasted the day. In England, his will was read and it revealed provisions he had made for a Mrs Kelly, the wife of the Hythe Barracks master whose husband was still very much alive. Within a few months, Napier was back in England. A British ship was sent to enquire after the injured and dead and, upon discovering that he was among the living, an agreement was struck with France to permit Napier to return home.

Napier was no coward but he never exulted in war. To his mother he wrote, 'Military life is like dancing up a long room with a mirror at the end, against which we cut our faces, and so the deception ends. It is thus gaily men follow their *trade of blood*, thinking it glitters, but to me it appears without brightness or reflection, a dirty red!' Throughout his life as a fighting general or as an administrator of law and order, Napier would strive to avoid blood being spilt. He detested too the practice of flogging that was so common in the Army, even going so far as to write a book denouncing it.

Napier returned to service in Iberia, seeing service at Badajoz and a range of other battles. His next Army service took him to North America, where he saw action in the War of 1812 as part of the 102nd Regiment. This regiment had a reputation as the 'worst in the Army' and Napier's task was to fashion this body of men into an efficient fighting force. He loathed the conduct of the war in the United States. He hated to hear the American enemy speak his own tongue and was disgusted with the atrocious behaviour of British units formed out of French deserters. Yet he was still Charles James Napier, full of vision and schemes for change that would never be fulfilled. This time, in the American theatre, he argued that slaves should be armed, and that he should be at their head. No reply came from high command and years later Napier was still improving on his plan, settling in his mind that, had he been permitted to give the slaves their liberty, he would have resettled them in Canada. At a stroke providing them with a livelihood and at the same time populating Canada itself against possible aggression from the United States.

As the war with the United States ended, Napier was awarded the sinecure of Governor of the Virgin Islands, a role which did not require him to visit the archipelago. Soon he was back home, returning to Europe in 1815 and missing Waterloo by one day. His time abroad had done nothing to trim his radical instincts. Napoleon had been swept from the field but Napier admitted to a thinly disguised admiration for the Corsican's vision and achievements. Looking back at the personal trauma of the Peninsular War, his regret was that he had suffered essentially in vain, for, having freed Portugal from Napoleonic rule, the British had simply returned the country to its previous despotic government. The rigours and bloodshed of war had been for nothing:

> We have flattered their vanity and deprived them of no public custom or ornament: we meddled not with their religion, we paid their soldiers when their own prince did not; and we might have done more on a sound system, but we always act on the confined basis of – present expediency. We might have regulated their whole civil government and founded a free nation, entirely and truly regenerating them as a people.

On the brink now of preferment to his first important job, as administrator in the Ionian Islands, Napier had learned certain lessons and noted certain errors. Portugal was a mistake Napier intended *not* to repeat, now that he had the responsibility for 60,000 souls on the island of Cephalonia.

*

In 1815, the strategically significant Ionian archipelago, that chain of islands off the west and south-west coast of Greece, was emerging from a stormy spell of government. It would remain a British possession until 1864. Indeed, an Anglophile thread in the culture of the islands can still be detected today.

When Napier arrived on Cephalonia in 1815, his observations rapidly confirmed all his theories about what proper government could do for the people or at least what it could if it was in his hands. His superior was Sir Thomas Maitland, Governor of Malta and Lord High Commissioner of the Ionian Islands, who maintained a seat of administration on Corfu. Maitland was also something of an aristocratic military radical, imperious but sufficiently progressive as to disapprove of building barracks, for fear they would lead to military despotism, and to permit Napier himself a large measure of autonomy on Cephalonia itself.

Venetian rule over Cephalonia had been swept away but an Italian-speaking, Catholic Venetian elite continued to hold sway over an impoverished Greek Orthodox peasantry. Napier was determined to implement change and bring something of justice and fair play to the island. He positively relished tilting the scales against the powerful in favour of the weak, especially in the course of the legal proceedings over which he presided. His vision was perfectly clear. His role was to rule in the interests of the poor and against those of corrupt local elites. If that required being unfettered by the letter of overly fussy laws, so be it.

Napier and his trusty Irish deputy John Pitt Kennedy introduced one improvement after another. Roads, canals, quays and a lighthouse were constructed and they all rapidly proved their economic worth. In the marketplace,

British officials displaced crooked middlemen taking advantage of illiterate peasants. Reliable British scales saw peasants get a true and fair price for their crops. Napier, in his road-building schemes, laid down a manual of extraordinarily progressive health and safety regulations for the labourers and, rather more to the point, their responsible overseers. What Napier did in the course of his absolute rule of Cephalonia was to master the administration of the island, through rational rule, detail, questionnaires, regulations being promulgated, officials being disinterested and authority being *just*.

Napier was well aware of the arbitrary nature of his rule but he regarded it as a moral solution to a pressing problem. After all, why should the people of Cephalonia *not* get the benefits of the good government he could and should give them? Were not Greeks people? What reason was there to suppose they were in any way unfitted for the gifts and advantages he could bestow upon them? It was an inescapable truth that the programme he offered was rule by technical experts *for* the common people and not rule *by* the (sadly as yet) inexpert people themselves. His biographer Edward Beasley, however, contends that Napier anticipated John Stuart Mill in embracing a progressivist solution. That is, evidently thinking that the only way to habituate people to the exercise of rights is to grant them first, albeit in a controlled environment.

Napier believed in his rule, in the rule of the state, embodied in this case by him, as a force for good. He saw this centralised notion of good as being a great deal more practical and moral than anything that private charity could offer. What was the point of the state if it could not function well and smoothly and with agility and if it could not head off problems before they materialised? Prompt action by Sir Robert Peel did precisely this in Ireland at this time. He managed to fend off famine by swiftly distributing relief where it was most needed and it was to Napier's satisfaction that he in the same way pre-empted and defeated the prospect of famine in Cephalonia by swift, determined government action.

He was aware of the utility of visual cues too, in keeping the people onside. Until told by his superiors to trim it, Napier sported a beard reaching down to his chest in emulation of the Greek revolutionaries now planning a war of independence on the Turkish-ruled mainland. He went 'native', as it were, in more personal ways: his commitment to the island only deepened when his Greek nationalist mistress gave birth to his two daughters. (He, with their mother's disinterested consent, took both girls with him when he eventually left Cephalonia and both in due course acquired a future general as a husband.)

Napier's life intersected with another and rather better known champion of Greek independence at this time. The great Romantic poet George Gordon, Lord Byron moored his boat *Hercules* in Argostoli harbour on the west coast of Cephalonia in August 1823. Napier was absent so Pitt Kennedy welcomed the poet to the island. Napier returned to Cephalonia a few days later. After a few weeks he persuaded Byron to leave the *Hercules* and enjoy his hospitality on dry land instead. He and Byron kindled a friendship, although Napier could not agree with Byron's views on the wickedness of religion and took to addressing him as 'Your Atheistship'.

There were many points of similarity between these two men and not least was this. Unlike many other British philhellenes they shared a belief not simply in the *principle* of Greek independence but also in the idea that freedom would not come by means of fine words. Greece would have to arm herself to be free, she would have to invest not only in cultural regeneration but in military hardware. This said, however, Napier was forced to decline the London Greek Committee's offer to command the forces they were prepared to fund. He had a job to do on Cephalonia and he was the servant of the British government. This sense of duty was not quite enough to stop him travelling to London to raise funds for the cause of Greek independence and this in turn convinced his military superiors that he was wildly and dangerously anti-Turkish in his political views.

Napier had found something like a personal paradise in Cephalonia, which made his exile all the harder. Byron died of a fever at Missolonghi in April 1824 and Napier himself was removed from his post in 1826. He had returned to England on leave with Elizabeth, his wife (the aforementioned Mrs Kelly, who had married him a decorous year into her widowhood) and the blow of removal was the more bitter because they had returned home for the sake of Elizabeth's health. She died in England. The context of this sad business, meanwhile, demonstrates how poorly Napier played the game of strategy. His brother William conducted a furious press campaign to have Napier returned to his post on Cephalonia but his efforts were counterproductive. The Army dug its heels in and Napier was never to return to his beloved Greece. He is remembered on Cephalonia today in the form of the Napier Gardens at Argostoli.

The course of Napier's life had, though, been set. He was to rule men and for their own good. The question was, where next? The answer seemed to be the Antipodes, for he was offered and accepted the governorship of the fledging free, that is, non-penal, colony of South Australia. However, he then declined the post when it became clear that the London-based administrators of the scheme would not give him the resources he had expertly determined were necessary to make a success of the new colony. His decision to renounce the role led directly to the publication of *Colonization*.

In the pages of *Colonization*, Napier, such a central figure in the story of the Victorian colonial project, attacked at every turn each intellectual premise on which the enterprise of colonisation rested. Were planted colonies an outlet for 'surplus population', for example? No, for what was 'surplus population'? Nothing but a shockingly under-protected home population. *Colonization* vigorously pitted itself against the teachings of such fashionable theorists as Robert Malthus and James Martineau. The work of Malthus was much debated against the background of the Corn Laws but he also busied himself in the field of demographic theory, arguing that the 'poor' constituted a problem for society that could be addressed by checking their tendency to reproduce, a theory that disgusted Napier. Martineau, meanwhile, was criticised by Napier for merely directing fine moralising words towards the poor without doing anything concrete to alleviate their distress. All the other current cases made for Empire, a market for 'over-produce' or as an outlet for British capital, were likewise dismissed by Napier as misconceptions, which supplied retrospective justifications for things which had already been settled upon.

Beasley notes that a key influence on Napier was the Swiss historian and political economist Jean Charles Léonard de Sismondi. Sismondi argued that the key task of the state was to maximise happiness not private profit and this in turn could best be achieved by ensuring that poor farmers had secure possession of their land. Revolution and rule by the mob was pointless, continued Sismondi. Rather, what was needed was rule by a competent, activist state. Every advanced idea was present, correct and approved of by Napier: a limit on the hours worked in the week, old-age pensions, an end to child labour, health insurance, profit-sharing and even 'reform' of landownership and inheritance rules.

What did this mean in practice? For Napier it meant a step towards a socially just utopia. His goal was the creation of a mass of peasant-proprietors. He wanted an end to the detested class of prosperous, middling farmers, the innate conservatism of which spoiled the view of his vision. Napier contemplated no great harm to his own class. Instead, the 'bottom' rung on the social ladder would be rigorously protected and its role in the economy enhanced. Curiously, the 'top' would be protected likewise and the whole middle of the yeomanry swept away.

Nonetheless, there was no element of self-serving pretence in Napier's philosophy. 'I would rather see Civil War, than see the people of England treated as they now are,' he said and he meant it. His philosophy hung on the notion that people behaved badly only because they were governed badly. Hence those who must truly be held responsible were those bad rulers, whether those bad rulers were absentee landlords in Ireland, decayed Venetian aristocrats on Cephalonia or native rulers further afield.

Napier was not alone in his views. He had a good deal of contemporary radical company, for others, not least in Britain itself, were also in favour of annual parliaments, universal suffrage and the ballot. He was not alone either in calling for flogging to be abolished by the Army. Other officers agreed with him here, too. While Napier pressed for other rights to be granted to the private soldier – pensions, a savings bank for pay so that soldiers would not literally have to carry their money with them – there was always sound military reasoning at work. His views in many cases are not especially radical at all but are simply common sense. No, where Napier astounds is on his views on the Empire's gravest failing, race.

In the free colony of South Australia as Napier would have governed it, he would have made the murder of an Aboriginal Australian a capital crime, to be punished as such. In India, suttee, the burning of a widow on her husband's funeral pyre, would be the crime it would have been in England. Why not, argued Napier, when there was no human difference between the people of Sindh and the people of Britain, save for the fact that one had enjoyed British law for longer than the other.

His philosophy firmly rejected any distinctions on the basis of ethnicity. In India, his aim for the native popu-lation was to 'give them justice, give them riches, give them honours, give them a share of all things till we blend with them and are one nation'. Unlike liberals today, Napier thought that there were no innate divi-sions between peoples. Rather, only their separate pasts made their presents different. Treat them the same and they would be the same. In his journal he was explicit: 'Let children of many races be brought up in a country foreign to all and they will all be as the men of that country are.' This was a noble vision.

These assumptions, of equality in the eyes of the law, combined with deference to the one true law, are now very unpopular among people with 'correct' opinions. The laws Napier upheld were *his* laws, British ones. By whose authority did he impose them on others, other than conquest? What right had he to do so? Napier's test would have been *moral utility*, the very rightness, self-evidently so, of the laws he was bringing to people who had been unfortunate enough to go without them. The sincerity of his feelings can be seen when we consider what he thought of the woefully inferior British laws and customs he so heartily detested. Napier did not assert that what was *British* was right. Rather, he said that what was *right* was right and that people like him were gifted in detecting it. In the Britain in which he remained, instead of sailing forth to govern South Australia, he found error and villainy enough to be going on with, in the North of England.

*

In early 1839, Charles Napier was given command of the Army in England's Northern District. It is unknown whether his much-broadcast political views played a part in his being chosen. This was a man who had publicly written of his loathing for 'the child-torturing murderers in the manufactories', in which the North of England abounded. Yet he was the man entrusted by the Whig Home Secretary, Lord John Russell, with the task of maintaining peace in the industrial north during the Chartist unrest, which constituted the greatest period of domestic alarm since the end of the war with Napoleon.

Napier had no doubts about how any fighting would go. The Army would win, for how could they not? They were trained and equipped and well led; the would-be rioters were none of those things. This certainty only reinforced Napier's desire that nothing their cruel and incompetent government might do should provoke the Chartists into any disorder, given that it could only end in such unfair bloodshed. On meeting the Home Secretary and his officials for the first time, the now Major General Napier was astonished to discover that they shared his aims, that they too were anxious to avoid violence, never mind provoke or pursue violence. Delighted but astonished as well, for this was not what his diagnosis of government had led him to expect. He was unabashed at this failing of theory, however, and set about his usual meticulous, professional work.

Napier was a great systematiser and now he wanted as much information collated as soon as possible about his new command. His languid predecessor cheerfully announced that he could tell him all he knew about the state of affairs in the north inside half an hour, which was not quite what Napier had in mind. He began touring his district to the great discomfort of Whitehall, where Thomas Babington Macaulay was the unfortunate civil servant who relentlessly pursued Napier to account for his travel and lodging expenses.

It is important to note that no consensus existed inside the government at this time. *Did* the Chartist activity constitute the worst crisis since the war? If it did, what should be the response? Napier immediately identified one mistake London was making. The government was empowering and arming militias, to supplement such police and army as existed in the region. This could not possibly be conducive to good public order. He was correct but the real reason for his opposition to the existence of such militias was his dislike of giving private armies to the local well-off, that is to the very same people he fully expected to provoke the poor into riot and disorder in the first place. He further disliked many of the magistrates with whom he had to deal, believing them prone to panic and exaggeration. Much of his early work was spent trying to coordinate them and to ensure a uniform official response to Chartist meetings.

The Chartist gatherings in the North of England had been imagined apprehensively as 'monster' meetings but they turned out to be smaller than had been anticipated. Napier took all of them, however, in his stride. Sympathetic as he was to the workers' predicament and in agreement with their basic claims, he remained resolutely unalarmed. As he said to one of his junior officers, 'we want more oil with our vinegar'. Yet there were real dangers. At Hull, for example, miners dug a shaft under the barracks in the town, the better to cause the structures to subside. Napier might have been phlegmatic but such actions can hardly have encouraged a veteran of Wellington's armies.

The propertied classes noted that Napier was not precisely on their side and they protested that he would do well to listen to what the Chartists were actually declaring aloud. At Rochdale, for example, a Chartist leader told a cheering rally: 'Arm yourselves well with pikes and firearms and get plenty of powder, for the time is near at hand when we must either put down the Government or the Government put down us.' Moreover, for all Napier's confidence in the prowess, should matters come to a head, of the Army, northern factory owners and landowners were practical men of business too. They knew the potential for lethal trouble. They knew that if anyone could produce the weapons of war it was the industrial men of the north. Lord John Russell, however, was on Napier's side. He was not ill disposed to the rallying of Chartism in the north, for it bore out much of what he believed about what could flow from the absence of proper local aristocratic influence in the industrial towns and the want of true religion in such communities. A correction might come as a result of this imbalance and, if it did come, that was all to the good. The Home Secretary left Napier to take the decisions and assess whether his ameliorative methods could prevent something close to revolution.

Then in Newport, South Wales, in November 1839, a Chartist march led to disaster. Troops opened fire on the crowd of 10,000 demonstrators. Twenty-two men were killed and now the country was riven with rumours of more coordinated revolts being imminent. Newport was outside Napier's own district and the deaths had not been his responsibility. He was aware of the nature of the calamity but he refused to be alarmed. He still discounted the military potential of the Chartists, their vastly superior numbers notwithstanding. The most they could do, he remarked, was murder him, which would be good news for the 'one hundred and sixty-four other major-generals, all anxious to be employed'. Even if they were all accounted for, one after another, 'it would only be a godsend for the colonels'.

It was noticeable that, although very often highly strung, voluble and excitable in print and private correspondence, Napier was a much calmer individual now that he had a real job of work again. For the first time since his important labours on Cephalonia, he had something substantial to do. The corollary of this, however, was that he was dismissive of the reactions of what he saw as the 'panicking rich'. Every concern or fear raised by the mercantile classes with Napier was either downplayed or, worse still, rejected flatly as being provocatively counter-productive. For Napier, the *vigorous* measures' demanded against Chartists were 'idiot measures' sought by 'Member John Donkey'. Indeed, throughout his command of the Northern District, Napier was pointedly clear that in his view the Chartists needed protection from the threat of violence at least as much as the 'entitled rich' did.

Against such a context, cynics might well snort that if there was nothing ever really to fear, what real *difference* did Napier's hard work make in the end? The answer is that there was nothing to fear precisely because of his active advocacy in the shadows. He was up at 5 a.m., and seldom in bed before 1 or 2 a.m. He spoke to as many Chartists as men of property and willingly walked among them. Napier always felt that the danger to avoid was that of another Peterloo, which is to say a gross overreaction by the authorities, so he fought untiringly to ensure that another Peterloo did not occur. He stoutly maintained, moreover, that his role was not to intervene in private industrial disputes, for almost certainly to do so would be to take the side of the haves against the have-nots.

On relinquishing his command in 1840, Napier dreaded what would happen next. He was convinced that the state would provoke violence after he was gone. Yet in his absence, his nightmares failed to come true. There was no bloody uprising nor heavy-handed repression, and he had demonstrated that it was perfectly possible to rule the United Kingdom without recourse to violence. Napier's next call to service came from the Indian border with Afghanistan, a corner of the Empire where order and security were proving to be an intractable problem.

*

Appointed in 1842 to a command in the Bombay Presidency, Napier found that the British in India had become embroiled in a disastrous invasion of Afghanistan, a 'stupid' war, as Wellington called it in the House of Lords, reminding his fellow peers that Afghanistan was a fearsome place of 'rocks, sands, deserts, ice and snow' and a land over which the British could not possibly hope to sustain any form of control. Wellington, indeed, fore-told the entire course of the First Anglo-Afghan War with uncanny accuracy. The British might succeed in invading Afghanistan and capturing its cities but their supply and communication lines would from that moment be under sustained attack and any invading army would either starve to death or be lucky to escape with its collective life.

Hence, it came to pass. In the spring of 1839, the British invasion began and by the onset of winter much of the country was in British hands but as time passed it became clear that a vast standing army would be needed simply to maintain control. The country rose against the occupiers and in the depths of a bitter Afghan winter the order came to evacuate Kabul. Some 16,000 people, soldiers, with their families, servants and camp followers, left Kabul in mid-January 1842 and just one recorded survivor reached British-controlled Jalalabad, at the foot of the Khyber Pass. The dreadful aftermath of this calamity, one of the worst reverses in British military history, was later captured by Elizabeth Thompson, Lady Butler in her famous painting *The Remnants of an Army*. It depicts William Brydon, a surgeon who also survived the Siege of Lucknow.

The Earl of Ellenborough, Edward Law, was the new (and aggressive) Governor-General of India and he gave the newly arrived Napier the unenviable task of concluding the withdrawal of British forces from Afghanistan. This should ideally take place under cover of some kind of showy, punitive 'victory' but regardless of whether he achieved that or not, the most important thing was to ensure that the withdrawal happened, and fast. Yet all these designs became redundant when Army officers George Pollock and William Nott secured victories at the Khyber Pass and Kabul sufficient to enable the British to leave the region with some tattered semblance of dignity intact.

The result was that Charles Napier was instead given the task of resolving a situation that had developed in what is now the region of Sindh in Pakistan, which was of considerable interest to the British. Much of this stemmed directly from its location. It was on the way to the wealthy and strategically vital region of the Punjab and if Sindh could be more securely managed, so too would be the

Punjab. Thus was the logic. In British India, wider still and wider the boundaries ever ran. Sindh was at this time theoretically autonomous and was, with depressing predictability, ruled extremely badly by a confederation of forty amirs or local rulers, a confederation much propagandised against in the British press.

One of the aspects of Sindh especially to excite the British press, both at home and in India, was the existence of lush, green hunting preserves, the property of the amirs, ranged along the banks of the Indus. These vast landscapes stood in sharp contrast to the barren, uncultivated countryside beyond them. They were highly covetable. Indeed, the entire British sense of very public affront against the amirs of Sindh may be seen through a covetous lens. Nearly everything the amirs did was seen as thoroughly provocative. In particular their habit of parlaying with one another by way of ceremonies conducted by sailing their hundred-foot pleasure barges along the Indus from hunting preserve to hunting preserve was seen as dreadful because of the land it took from the indigenous poor. It was more in the style of King John than Queen Victoria.

The British, as part of this campaign to delegitimise the political status quo in the region, also grumbled continually that the amirs had only been in control of Sindh for a paltry sixty years – the subtext being that they did not, therefore, really deserve to control the region at all. There were no strong moral or legal grounds for the British to object to the presence of anyone else on the lengthening frontiers of their possessions in the subcontinent and there was little need for grumbling in any case. By 1839 amir control of

Sindh was highly circumscribed. The region was falling inexorably into the British sphere of influence, it had become subject to the usual treaties, whereby it was placed formally under British protection, with tribute to be paid, the Indus made navigable for British trade and no negotiations to be entered into by the Sindhi authorities with foreign powers without first obtaining the approval of the East India Company. Yet, suddenly, this was not quite enough. Sindh would have to be absorbed into British India and quickly, for a situation was developing in the region in the aftermath of the Afghan disaster. The amirs, sensing momentary British weakness, were restive and a rebellion against the British not to be ruled out.

Napier's task was to calm Sindh, although he clearly thought about the region as he had about Cephalonia. That is, in terms of the civil engineering opportunities it presented, once a peace had been restored and what he could in general do for the region's wretched inhabitants. He saw a golden opportunity, another one, to effect some good in the world. Ellenborough, who was an extremely able politician, if never a successful one, had been President of the Board of Control, effectively the minister at Westminster responsible for the East India Company. This meant that he knew, even if Napier did not, that securing Sindh would accomplish another objective, one that had nothing at all to do with civil engineering. It would ensure that the opium trade, the movements of which had tended to flow around British borders, would have no choice but to fall under the control of the British authorities. This was no small objective, for more than half of British revenue in India in this period was accounted for by duties levied on the trade in opium. In the end, British interest in Sindh had everything to do with realpolitik.

For Napier, there were rather larger fish to fry. The moral case behind his presence in India had to be made and thankfully it was simple. It had nothing to do with opium. It was this. Intervention was a *moral choice*, because wanton amirs did not deserve their grossly exploited realm, where the 'wretched people [are] frequently seen to pick the grain from the dung of the officers' horses to eat!' In consequence, '*Mene! mene! tekel, upharsin!* How is all this to end? We have no right to seize Scinde [Sindh], yet we shall do so, and a very advantageous, useful, humane piece of rascality it will be.' Rascally or not, a case can be made that Napier was trying to achieve in India what he had achieved in the North of England, albeit by different means. In his dealings with the amirs, he was outrageously high-handed, deploying language tinted by arrogance of the first order, but arguably this was a *deliberate* policy. This was a move to avoid bloodshed and by his reckoning this could best be done by overawing the amirs, who would be more likely to settle if confronted by imperious behaviour and words. This was, in theory, a sound psychological approach, though Ellenborough, with memories of the appalling recent happenings in Afghanistan still fresh, doubted, as it turned out, correctly, that the ruling caste in Sindh would submit without resistance.

The official who dealt *directly* with the amirs was the highly experienced political agent Sir James Outram, who, because he felt it would be highly provocative, had withheld Ellenborough's ultimatum from the amirs: that they must stop interfering with British policy and conspiring with foreign powers or face being deposed. Ellenborough had given Outram permission to withhold this threat *if* he concluded the amirs were not in fact plotting against the British and Outram duly held his tongue, even though he knew for sure that the amirs *were* plotting. At the edge of the Empire, the man on the spot was often taking decisions like this but in Sindh in 1842 much was at stake. A country and a war turned on the outcome of this case.

In such a serpentine business, the grounds for division were endless but what emerged in the strategic discussion between Napier on one side and Outram on the other was essentially this. How was the Empire to be managed? Napier set himself against the governing philosophy of Outram, with what might be termed his 'Old India' logic. He thought that local habits and customs must be acknowledged where possible, even if one privately thought them barbarous. Local rulers must be respected, even if one knew them to be rogues and knaves. To Outram, conversely, this Napier, a general new to India and full of current and untested theories, was both 'profoundly ignorant' and more seriously, 'a theorist who invented systems, and acted on them as if they were realities'.

This criticism of Napier hinges on the claim that he did *not* do in India as he had done in the North of England. That, although in both cases he sincerely loathed war and wanted to avoid it, he did *not* engage with the Sindhi as he had with the Chartists and that he had no firm grasp as to what the Sindhi rulers really wanted. One possible reply to this is that Napier knew, as a certainty, that war with the amirs was inescapable and also that this war might yet prove to be providential. After all, it would allow him to bring history forward by a few years. For was not Sindh starving? Were not her rulers corrupt and irresponsible? Did not her people deserve better, and should they not get this 'better' as rapidly as possible?

Convinced that they were sincerely willing to accede to British terms, Outram requested a gathering of the amirs at Hyderabad in February 1843. Napier disagreed with this meeting. He thought that the amirs were temporising in order to build up their combined armies prior to attacking the British. Outram urged Napier to come along, alone on a steamer along the Indus, to remove the doubts the amirs entertained (it must be said, with good reason) about him. Napier was proved correct. 'Unquestionably,' he observed later, with admirable dryness, 'it would have removed all doubts and my head from my shoulders.' In February, a Sindhi force maybe 8,000-strong attacked Outram's hundred-strong garrison in the Hyderabad residency, with the agent only just escaping down the Indus by the very steamer on which he had wanted Napier to arrive.

Miani, the battle which followed the attack on the residency, was Napier's first and greatest victory as a fighting general. Heroic on the close-fought battlefield, he may have been assisted in his daring frontal attack by the fact that the fire of the enemy artillery was being laid down by a coerced, captive British officer, who diligently set it off target. It was a famous victory. The British were outnumbered perhaps ten to one by the 30,000-strong force of Sindhi troops. Napier lost most of his junior officers in the ferocious hand-to-hand fighting. There is a tendency now to suppose that when West met East in those days, to wage war was to win it, but nobody in India at that moment supposed anything of the sort, not with the retreat from Kabul still fresh in their minds. Thus we must not diminish Napier's victory or his strategic skill. The victory at Miani was an extraordinary feat of arms and with good cause Napier became 'the first commander in British history to name the common soldiers in his dispatches and not merely the officers. And he named Indian soldiers as well as British troops.'

In the aftermath of the British victory, Hyderabad opened its gates and Napier gallantly returned to the amirs the jewelled swords they had ceremonially surrendered to him in token of defeat, no small consideration in an age when bounties still existed. He further ensured that the Sindhi women were guarded and went unmolested. And indeed, when the editor of the *Bombay Times* claimed that they were systematically violated by the army, all 104 of Napier's officers who had survived the battle immediately signed a letter refuting this. For Napier believed in the moral force of intervention and of intervention with honour.

Dubba was the next battle, on 24 March, just as the hot weather was settling on India in advance of the monsoon. This engagement was fought against the 'Lion' Shere Mohammed, whose men had not come to Hyderabad and who outnumbered the British force merely by a factor of 5:1. Again, and still bearing an open wound from an accidentally exploded rocket earlier in the year, Napier was valiant in battle. The general was on his horse for four full hours of running cavalry battles, barely able to sit, sixty years old, in 110-degree heat with almost no junior officers left. Sindh was now British territory. It was annexed by Napier in the aftermath of the battle but it is well to remember that, in so doing, he had in fact exceeded his orders. He had been ordered to put down any rebellion but not formally to annexe the region.

At home, *Punch* had a field day with this 'mission creep'. A famous pun of Catherine Winkworth's described a victorious Napier astride the battlefield, despatching a message to his irked superiors in London. *Peccavi*, it read, a pun on the Latin 'I have sinned'. Napier had been correct not to trust the amirs. Their attack on the Hyderabad residency proved this beyond doubt and to allow them to have concentrated their forces would have been to run the risk of the Afghan horrors being dismally repeated in Sindh. Yet as much as Napier thought he was simply anticipating the inevitable so, by exactly the same logic, could the same be said of the amirs themselves.

The criticism at home did not come only from *Punch*. Outram's predecessor, the illustrious Sir Henry Pottinger, thought Napier simply rash and guilty of ignorance. The *Edinburgh Review* was scathing:

> [Needless to say] we attach no value to the random statements of men like Sir Charles Napier, who, having made up their minds to have the country [are] seized with a strong feeling of sympathy for the subjects of those termed by them oppressors, whose place they are anxious to take.

In Parliament, Lord Ashley MP (the future Lord Shaftesbury) led the charge against both Ellenborough's forward policy and against Napier, its celebrated instrument. A vote of censure was called and now Radical MP

John Roebuck, a friend of Napier, experienced in Indian politics and ally of the Chartists, rallied the defence, defeating Ashley's motion 202 votes to 68 in the Commons.

There were other critics too. Although Sir Robert Peel publicly defended the action in Sindh, he was privately scathing of British treatment of the amirs. 'We have taken their territories and despoiled them of their private property,' the Prime Minister noted, 'surely we need not inflict further punishment and privations ... It makes one ashamed of Indian policy.' Retired Old India hand and Scottish statesman Mountstuart Elphinstone added, 'Sindh was a sad case of insolence and oppression. Coming after Afghanistan, it put one in mind of a bully who had been kicked in the streets, and went home to beat his wife in revenge.'

Napier was outraged by accusations levelled that he had started the war out of a bloodlust. Such sensations were antithetical to his entire military career. He denied too that he had acted out of self-serving glory or even just for prize money. To his journal he cried out:

It is hard ... for an honest man serving his country in the midst of dangers and trials, physical and moral, and acting from the honourable feeling of doing his duty ... to be exposed to the insolence, the falsehoods of men like Lord Howick [a parliamentary critic] ... To give him personal chastisement would give me pleasure, such as one feels at cutting a village cur dog with a whip, but I forgive all of them. After anger, contempt succeeds. I never feel angry in my heart against anyone – beyond wishing to break their bones with a broomstick!

The best way, he felt, of disproving his critics was to show just how he would rule Sindh, now that he had it.

For, criticism and objections notwithstanding, Napier was made both governor and military commander of the newly annexed Sindh. Now he had a chance to demonstrate the moral case for intervention. 'My object now,' its new master proclaimed, 'is to ... make roads, buildings, open streets, to secure justice. O! how I long to begin thus to live, and to rest after the horrid carnage of these battles!' Soon it became clear that Sindh was no Cephalonia. Shortly after peace was restored and in punishing 132-degree heat, thirty-two Europeans, including Napier himself, were struck down by sunstroke within minutes. Three hours later, all bar him were dead. Sindh was not to be an easy country to rule.

Napier might have been excused for wishing to return to Britain. His health was battered yet he remained, reckoning that his status as 'conqueror' would save native face and allow them to accept reforms from him they would bridle at from his civil successors. Ellenborough, however, was recalled, an act without precedent in British Indian policy and illustrative of how divisive Indian policy had become. He was replaced by his brother-in-law Henry Hardinge, who was sufficiently enamoured of Napier to name his favourite horse Miani. Even Hardinge, though he arrived a partisan of Napier and remained an admirer, began to question the general's temperament. He wondered if Napier's now marked eccentricity aided good government, and he began to despair of the poisonous coverage of affairs on the subcontinent, both in the Indian press and at home.

Still, Napier persevered. He retained what worked in Sindhi law and custom but ardently reformed that which he found wanting. He sought to enforce murder as a capital crime, in other words as something which could not be 'bought out of', as was customary in Indian justice. The 'honour killing' of women too was to be recognised as murder and the statutes against it reinforced. Troops were forbidden from plundering; abusive landlords were, without too much hidebound procedural squeamishness, dealt with severely; infanticide was outlawed; and slaves were emancipated, with their owners uncompensated, unlike in the rest of the Empire. Suttee was prohibited and in a final picturesque flourish, Indian peacocks were solemnly protected by law, just as English swans were at home. Napier remarked:

> This burning of widows is your custom, prepare the funeral pyre. But my nation also has a custom. When men burn women alive we hang them, and confiscate all their property. My carpenters shall therefore erect gibbets on which to hang all concerned when the widow is consumed. Let us all act according to our national customs!

This was Napier's imperialism, moral, liberal, just and implacable. This was the good that not merely could be done with power but the good which *must* be done, in order to justify possessing that power.

Napier's quest was to pull Sindh out of the feudalism he saw as being responsible for the starvation and squalor which was visible to every British official. Specifically, his plan was to encourage local notables to reject their previous role as armed chieftains and embrace a new role as improving resident landlords. Here Napier's relative lack of local expertise told, with negative consequences for his policy of moral intervention. He confirmed the rights and privileges of the *jagirdars*, that class immediately below the more princely amirs. His decision, however, was based on a degree of ignorance, for these *jagirdars* were not as he supposed them to be. They were not as greater gentry on the European model but were military holders of feudal land rights whose privileges flowed from a medieval past. Moreover, their bailiwicks were *temporary* appointments. They were not districts they were born into, or knew and loved, and this in turn meant they were not necessarily predisposed to invest in them for the long term. Worst of all, when bearing in mind Napier's views of the absentee landlord class in Ireland, the *jagirdars* habitually were not even resident in the vast estates the British in effect had given to them. Perhaps the closest parallel is the Russian oligarchs who happened to be well-placed bureaucrats at the time of the dissolution of the Soviet Union, and who in consequence reaped vast private rewards from public property.

For this was the key thing to understand about the land bestowed by Napier. It was effectively freehold public property given away to a landlord class he had himself created. Worst of all, in building this new social order, the problems of which bedevil Pakistan to this day, Napier inadvertently also created a disaster. He caused the formation of a landless peasantry on the Irish pattern where previously there had been a caste of peasant-proprietors who may not have been wealthy and who sometimes were desperately poor but who were at least secure in their land tenure. This situation underscores the brutal and inescapable fact that in Sindh Napier was out of his depth.

In addition, Napier's rule also suffered owing to the fact that, palpably over-worked though he was, he also chronically under-delegated. The precepts of rational administration had not caught up with his private office. One of his earliest and most distinguished successors in Sindh, Sir Henry Bartle Frere, took a dim view of the quality of Napier's civil administration. In Frere's expert judgement, Napier's governance had lacked uniformity and coordination. Yet honest government did have its own rewards. Starvation retreated in Sindh, the province recording its first grain surplus, and exports to Britain duly got underway. As the new administration bedded down, there was a general atmosphere of peace, for Napier was as keen as ever to avoid civilian casualties.

In 1848, Napier resigned his post on grounds of ill health and retired, or so he thought, to England. Travelling home in the leisurely fashion befitting an honoured British official, Napier saw first-hand in Europe some of the events of the revolutionary year of 1848. It was almost as if the activities in this Year of Revolutions had been got up specifically to please him, so suitable were they for this viewing. 'Great events,' as he remarked approvingly, 'have been succeeding each other like flashes of lightning. Tyranny has got such a shake as has taught our Rulers in this world that the people they have misgoverned will bear these things no longer. I am delighted at this tolerably broad hint.'

But India had not yet finished with Charles Napier. He had barely returned to England when events on the subcontinent demanded his immediate return. The Second Anglo-Sikh War was looming, with at stake the very thing that Sindh had been occupied to secure, not the opium trade but the route to the strategically vital Punjab region. With the Indian military establishment reckoned entirely inadequate to the task, *The Times* began a vigorous public campaign to have Napier returned to India to sort everything out. A public clamour grew and now the politicians joined in. Supposedly when asked for three names for the job, the aged Wellington replied: 'Sir Charles Napier. Sir Charles Napier. Sir Charles Napier.' Old, aged and in constant pain, Napier resisted the clamour, until eventually Wellington told him that if he didn't go, he, the seventy-nine-year-old Iron Duke, would have to go instead.

Napier had Wellington's not insubstantial support but there was much institutional resistance by Old India hands to the notion of Napier returning to the subcontinent. In London, for example, the Court of Directors (of the East India Company) manoeuvred to keep the new Commander-in-Chief off the Supreme Council of India but fate intervened to calm Napier's role in India, for even before his return the war against the Sikhs had been won. Turning up at Calcutta in 1849 in time for the victory service, Napier was on hand to see the Punjab annexed, and the Koh-i-Noor diamond given to Queen Victoria in recognition of a great victory, ready for its display at the Great Exhibition two years later.

Napier would happily have returned immediately to England but as the Marquess of Dalhousie, newly appointed as Governor-General, was keen to have him stay on to cast a reforming eye on British India, Napier set about instituting reforms in the Army. Officers were obliged to learn native languages and pass tests to show that they had done so but Napier was undone by politicking above his head. He discovered that, with Dalhousie's consent and encouragement, the rule of the Punjab was rapidly becoming despotic. Isolated rebellions were dealt with harshly, with homes burned and crops destroyed. Public opinion was turning against the British occupation.

The relationship between Dalhousie and Napier soured and eventually, as would happen so often between Viceroy and Commander-in-Chief in India, the two men became irretrievably estranged. They cut one another socially, briefed against one another in the avid British and Indian press and constantly sought to undermine the other in their respective spheres of authority. Reluctantly Wellington took the side of Dalhousie and Napier resigned. Napier would, perhaps, have the last laugh in this specific context but a bitter laugh. Dalhousie's mismanagement of Indian affairs is widely seen as having led to the calamity of the Mutiny against the rule of the East India Company in 1857.

Thus Charles Napier left the India he had wished to serve in the interests of the poor and against those of the strong. Almost a decade previously, he had been unambiguous about precisely who these 'strong' were, and they were us:

[A] more base and cruel tyranny never wielded the power of a great nation. Our object in conquering India, the object of all our cruelties, was *money – lucre* ... Every shilling [has] been picked out of blood, wiped, and put into the murderers' pockets; but, wipe and wash the money as you will, the 'damned spot' will not 'out'.

These were not the sentiments of the generality of men who became Commander-in-Chief, India, during the time of British rule.

*

There is something emblematic about the fact of Napier's birth in Whitehall, the standard term today for the heart of government in Britain. It seems that he stands as the heroic model for what good, benevolent government ought to try to do, which is simply to be honest, systematic and well intentioned. His work on Cephalonia stands as a noble testament to this attitude, in that he saw weaknesses and he intervened decisively to replace them with strengths. The result is that his legacy on the island endures to this day both in built form and in a collective Anglophile memory in this place far from Britain. Napier's policies on this island, indeed, can be taken as an example of what today is called 'soft power' at its most precise and effective.

In Sindh, however, the limits of this form of power can be seen, for it paid little heed to the intricacies and differences of Indian culture, thus disproving the theory that one size can fit all. It is, after all, the greatest irony of Napier's professional life that while he saw the evils of inadequate land laws in Ireland, he actually created an inadequate land legislation in India, with enduring consequences. Napier's intentions were always good, he was brave and fair. He opposed evil practices such as suttee. He deserves his place in the pantheon of heroes but that does not mean everything he tried succeeded. If that were the standard there would be no heroes.

Sleeman: Moral Purpose

Thuggee did not exist. It never existed.

No: it was merely the product of lurid Victorian sensationalism. It was a classic product of what we must call an 'Orientalist' mindset, by which is meant a wilfully disdainful and ignorant Western attitude towards all things Eastern. These Orientalists were capable of all kinds of wickedness in the form of tales, stories and accounts. Their intent being to criticise and patronise Eastern civilisations, to diminish them in the eyes of Western readers and consumers and in so doing to justify Western predation, exploitation, settlement and theft of land and assets. Hence, Thuggee was a concept that had to be dreamed up because Indian civilisation had to be labelled as violent, murderous and beyond the pale. If any country urgently required civilising, that country was India.

Enter the Thugs, the stranglers of India.

Thus runs the prevailing academic approach to the phenomenon of Thuggee and its untold thousands of victims. This contemporary approach, indeed, bears remarkable comparison to the attitude of complacency and collusion towards Thuggee, towards the act of Thuggery, which predominated among the civil servants who ran British-administered India in the first half of the nineteenth century. Why lift a finger, or a pen, to combat the actions of murderers and villains, when one could instead avert one's eye, and rationalise them out of existence? It was so much easier to pretend that the phenomenon did not really exist or, if it did exist, that it was someone else's problem.

In the end, as we shall see, these stranglers were defeated both by pen and by difficult and laborious work in the field. The individual who took up this great burden, who worked both pen and muscle, was the British soldier and administrator William Sleeman (8 August 1788–10 February 1856). His long residency in India afforded him the deep insights necessary to understand the complexities of culture and society on the subcontinent. It also enabled him to look clearly and frankly at the weaknesses of his adopted home. This chapter aims to tell a story of graft, endurance and honesty, to show how the moral integrity and everyday administrative zeal of one Victorian helped to lift a curse from Indian society.

This is a story of redemption.

*

William Sleeman was almost a prototype Victorian in that the greater part of his mission was accomplished before Victoria came to the throne but his success exemplified that great, if unsung, Victorian virtue of sound, strong administration. Indeed, he was a classic administrator. Such a phrase does not make the blood course with excitement in the veins and this is not the story of a colourful *Flashman* character, his life filled to the brim with wine, women and song. It is not even the story of the sort of passionate evangelism which was such a strong current in the Victorian era. Rather, Sleeman simply did his job, which was, as he understood it, to see justice being done in the interest of those who had been placed in his care. If this attitude had not necessarily prevailed prior to his arrival on the scene, so be it. He would set certain policies and structures and frameworks in place. Moreover, they would remain in place long after he had departed the scene. The tasks he accomplished would stay accomplished. This is the very idea of being a good Victorian.

If one aspect of Sleeman's philosophy can be regarded as placing him apart from so many of his peers, it was that he, in common with his Indian contemporary Charles Napier, did not regard life in India as being cheap. He valued all life equally. This clear, uncomplicated attitude provided him with necessary ballast when a challenge otherwise beyond comprehension came hurtling in his direction. It meant that he was simply not willing to accept the status quo, if that status quo cried out to be altered. Life could not be permitted to trundle along in the same manner if it might be changed. In this, Sleeman was something of an example of a key Victorian characteristic. He did not understand and would not tolerate fatalism.

How fortunate, how providential, that such a man was on hand in the subcontinent to take a look at India in the round and to identify precisely those aspects of its life and character that must change, that must be swept away. For who would tolerate the phenomenon of Thuggee, when it might be exterminated? What man of morality *could* put up with such a cult, when the means existed to remove it from the face of India for ever?

*

The Sleemans were an old Cornish family whose gentility varied according to the teller of the tale. William was the fifth of eight children, seven boys and a girl, of Philip and Mary Sleeman of Stratton, a village on the north Cornish coast. Philip Sleeman was an excise inspector. His forebears had been deeply involved in the smuggling trade that had always prospered along this rocky and isolated stretch of coastline and his generation of aspiring Sleemans was, as can be well imagined, in continual reaction to their rather less respectable ancestors.

Sorrow and financial want soon descended upon the family. In 1799, when William was eleven, his brother Lewis was lost at sea. Three years later, Philip Sleeman died, thus depriving the family of an income that had been steady albeit slender. William now had to grow up fast and to assume that sense of responsibility and duty, so Victorian, that would mark his character for the rest of his life. He had in particular to renounce the dream he had nursed since childhood, of becoming an officer in the regular Army. In those days before profession-alisation, officers purchased a commission. It would be decades before Gladstone's first administration reformed this particular aspect of military life. Clearly, after Philip Sleeman's death, the funds to effect such a purchase were entirely beyond the means of the family.

The other option, for the Sleemans as for so many British families in this era, was for William to look to India for his livelihood and specifically to throw his lot in with the East India Company. The appeal of such a move was obvious. The Company ran British India on behalf of the British government, a position it would maintain until its power was removed in the aftermath of the 1857 Mutiny, when the government imposed a form of direct rule on the subcontinent. Ruler and governor of this vast territory, the Company required a standing army, in fact three standing armies, and appointment to one of these armies meant a salary, in a part of the world where there were potentially fortunes to be made. Sleeman's specific interest was in one of the several hundred Army cadetships on offer each year. Open entry and exams for these were still another half-century away and the Sleemans, though they were far from being a powerful family, did retain enough influence to have William gazetted an ensign in the army of the Bengal Presidency. In March 1809, William Sleeman sailed for India, arriving six months later. He never saw England again.

Sleeman ought to have sailed at an even earlier age but, in an early sign of his always slightly awkward relationship with the rest of British India, and of his independence of mind, he had declined to join the Company college for cadets at Basaret. The college suffered from its closeness to Calcutta. Its cadets were at the time reckoned to be 'in a continual uproar, blowing coach-horns and bugles, baiting jackals with pariah-dogs, fighting cocks, and shooting kites and crows'. Sleeman instead had opted for a course of private tutoring at home in England and this meant that, aged twenty, he was

117

reckoned rather old to take up a cadetship. However, he arrived well equipped, in particular his private tutoring had revealed a gift that would stand him in the very best of steads for his career in India. He was a marvellous linguist. From the start, he showed his extraordinary facility with a range of indigenous languages. Indeed, his independent efforts at preparation proved rather more useful than did the official Company handbook, which he had taken care to study thoroughly in the course of his long journey from England. This document lacked any form of military instruction and was instead filled with hints on the number of servants one might bring with one to India and on the necessity for gentlemanly behaviour.

The India in which Sleeman arrived was undergoing two great changes, one obvious, the other less so. The obvious one was political in nature. Britain, in the form of the East India Company, was consolidating her position following a long period of relative unrest and strife. The Company had been founded explicitly as a trading enterprise, having received its Royal Charter from Elizabeth I, with a focus on the spice and textile trade. The eighteenth century on the subcontinent had seen the decline of the Mughal Empire. Simultaneously, the British gained the upper hand over French traders in the region, and a series of significant military victories saw the Company evolve slowly from a trading enterprise into a governor of much territory in Bengal and elsewhere. When Sleeman arrived in the autumn of 1809, the Company was at the height of its power. Its *formal* rule over territory was accompanied by *informal* control over a string of nominally independent princely states. The result was that British suzerainty over India was to all intents and purposes complete, which everyone knew.

The second change was rather more subtle, though arguably just as visible to those in India. It had to do with a culture change, with the moral attitudes and behaviour of the British population in India and how these would alter as the culture at home went from tyranny to Victorian. The challenge in particular was to find a role and a code of behaviour in conservative Indian society for British women, who were arriving in greater numbers as British influence across the subcontinent was consolidated. It is important to remember that in the more precarious but also more relaxed world of the previous century, there had simply been no capacity for the British to consider imposing too many of their morals on India. They had neither the inclination nor the practical strength to attempt to do so. As the nineteenth century began, however, this started to change and as the Victorian age approached and a reaction grew against what was perceived to be Regency licentiousness, so the climate of India changed too under pressure both from moralists in London and memsahibs in India. Where it had once been considered good form for the British in India to sport local apparel and relish authentic local curries, now these agreeable customs began to fall away in favour of what would be a much more starched state of affairs.

This was the slowly changing backdrop against which Sleeman set out on his Indian adventures and against which, as would soon become clear, he set his face. It is important to note that he never moved from his principle, which was that British culture was superior to all others, including the manifold civilisations of the subcontinent. Accompanying this, somewhat counter-intuitively, was his very strong sense that India was a place of the greatest value that was worth getting to know fully and intimately. His linguistic skills would provide the key to this knowledge but his cast of mind was critical too. He was open to India, to its beauty and vibrancy, but to all other aspects of life there too, including its shadows and its darkness, and this cast of mind would be critical to what he achieved there.

William Sleeman's first great encounter with the complexity of Indian life and culture was rather conventional. It came in the form of the so-called Anglo-Nepalese Wars. Border tensions between the Nepalese authorities and an East India Company intent on inexorably widening its sphere of influence and trading network led to a two-year conflict beginning in 1814. This conflict is better known as the Gurkha Wars, which concluded with Nepal forced to cede its western provinces, enabling the Company to control the lucrative trade in Himalayan wool. As a mere foot soldier, Sleeman played no great or glorious role in the conflict but his time stationed in the lofty foothills of the Himalayas provided him with the sort of valuable insight into local life and custom that would prove valuable in his later career. His experience proved useful in the short term too not least to Sleeman's own happiness and contentment. His superiors observed that he was better suited to a quiet life in the hill country than to the social whirl of Calcutta, so when the wars ended he was permitted to remain in the highlands, learning his administrative trade and watching the local scene.

He proved superlatively good at this, his textured and revealing reports proving of the greatest use to the Company, so it was no surprise that in 1820 he was transferred formally from the Company's Bengal army to its political department. In other words, to be the eyes, ears and brains of the Company in India. His command of Indian languages widened and deepened further and wherever he travelled he continued to take a marked interest in all classes of Indian life. He talked to Indians, about Indians and, crucially, *for* Indians, advocating for their interests both against their own landlords, when faced with occasions of injustice, and against the Company itself on those occasions, which were hardly infrequent, when its behaviour seemed unjust. His life now was very far from being quiet. The professional duties of a 'Political' could hardly be anything other than exciting, not to mention exhausting. In times of crisis, such help as existed might be several days' ride away. All the time the man on the spot was responsible for the welfare of maybe 100,000 souls.

In 1828, on a break from his posting to recover from malaria, Sleeman travelled to Mauritius, and there he met the beautiful, intrepid and intelligent Amélie de Fontenne, the daughter of a sugar plantation-owning noble exiled from France by the Revolution. They married and theirs was a love match, so much so that Amélie joined her husband at his various postings and later on some of his most gruesome journeys of investigation. Their life together was accompanied by the all too common Victorian heartache: several of their seven children died and those who lived were sent, each in turn, to an England none of them had ever known. As each one left, moreover, it was to be the last they saw of their father or he of them. Five-year-old Henry was packed off from Calcutta with a small sword in case of shipwreck and this serves as a chilling reminder of the dangers faced on journeys to and from Europe in those days. At least it can be said that the family shared a good life in India, when, that is, there were all under the one roof.

The newly married Sleeman was transferred to Jubbulpore in central India, now the city of Jabalpur, in those days a place so remote the route there was not marked on such maps as the Company possessed. In addition to a stable family life, his fame and reputation were about to flourish, and his attention to and study of India would pay great dividends. As noted above, fatalism was not a characteristic one associates with the Victorians. Certainly, William Sleeman was not, when a challenge presented itself, prepared to accept that things should just continue in their usual course even if the challenge in question was almost beyond comprehension. This was why, when the existence of a horrifying cult in Indian life made itself known to him, Sleeman set to work. It was another case to be dealt with, another memo to be addressed, another file to be studied and resolved. Such was the attitude of this excellent administrator. The case in question was the opposite of a common or garden case study but there is much to be said for taking facts on the chin and being practical, regardless of the context. At any rate, such an approach worked for William Sleeman, for whom duty and morality, energy and sincerity were all part of a professional whole.

Naturally, he was not above taking righteous pride in his achievements. When his friend Charles Fraser became the foremost magistrate involved in the unrelenting campaign about to be set in motion, Sleeman wrote to him as follows:

Do not I pray you get tired of the duties – neither you nor any other man can ever be employed in any more interesting or important to humanity. I shall look back with pride to the share I have had in them as long as I live ... Believe me, Fraser, I would not exchange the share I have had in this work for the most splendid military service that man ever performed in India. I glory in it and ever shall do.

This 'splendid military service' was accomplished against the presence of Thuggee in Indian life and the great achievement of Sleeman's career was to grapple with this phenomenon and sweep it away. Let us turn to examine Thuggee, in all its complex horror.

*

Even at this remove in time, the phenomenon of Thuggee remains unfathomable. There had been many glimpses of it long before William Sleeman's era but never any serious, coordinated effort by the Company authorities to tackle it, much less eradicate it. This was not least because the British did not truly know what it was. It is only fair to add that any attempt to describe what Thugs did is to appreciate the difficulties anyone then or since has encountered in believing that such practices ever existed.

Simply put, Thugs travelled the highways of India as groups or gangs. They behaved and spoke as conventional travellers and they befriended others travelling like-wise. Then, at some prearranged point, they strangled and robbed their victims. It is all too evident that this confederacy was in its essence and nature evil but it is important to add that, as the phenomenon is studied further and each deeper stage perceived, Thuggee becomes not merely evil but also utterly incomprehensible. Incomprehensible, both that it *could* happen at all and that it *did* happen and happened for so long before the arrival on the scene of William Sleeman. His part in encountering and then exterminating Thuggee came about by chance. He happened to be on the spot when several incidents occurred. On the other hand, perhaps fate or destiny had ordained precisely *that* Sleeman be on the spot, for it needed such a man as he to deal with a situation that so many before him had failed to resolve.

It is necessary to emphasise that the Thugs were not what is named in Hindi *dacoits*, the fiendish bandits who had plagued a war-afflicted subcontinent for decades. *These* gangs were most certainly highly disagreeable, they assembled in large numbers, were open in their movements, moved swiftly and sped away after they had attacked, dissolving in formation only to reassemble elsewhere at some later point. The dacoits were perfectly representative of a thread of criminality present in many disordered states. Such gangs had existed for centuries and they would exist for another century to come, as the experience of Republican China was to show. Every society has had to deal with antisocial elements and every society finds ways of doing so but at least such gangs tend to be visible and comprehensible. It is possible to take steps to avoid them and a functioning justice system will deal with them. Moreover, travel in India for the unguarded had in any case rarely been safe. The country had few roads to begin with. In addition, it was home to an infernal Noah's Ark of tigers, snakes, wolves, jackals and bears, the presence of which made transport a trying affair, even before men, especially Thugs, entered the picture. India had her thieves: common or garden thieves, light-fingered thieves, violent thieves, murderous thieves, thieves in every imaginable form. Yet the Thugs were something quite different with no known parallel anywhere, ever.

For one thing, they got themselves up with special care. They were noted at the time as being 'closely shaved and oiled all over, so that if caught they could slip out of your grasp like eels'. They also exploited what many observers recognised as a weakness implicit in Indian society as a result of the governance of the East India Company. Because the subcontinent was split between regions ruled directly by the Company and native states under varying degrees of British sway and regulation, such law and order as there was tended to be fragmented. Justice did not work very well in any case but it habitually failed the victims of Thuggee. The British attitude to the syndrome can be partly explained by a degree of ignorance as to how India worked while many local chiefs actually connived in Thuggee by means of taxes greedily levelled on men whose income came from this crime. There was, in other words, a dysfunction implicit in Indian life and governance. This in part stemmed from ignorance of the language and local culture and custom but it allowed Thuggee to slip through the holes in the net, leaving its victims with no recourse to justice.

Thuggee, a term which itself emerges from the Sanskrit word for *cover* or *conceal*, tended to be hereditary in nature. Thugs hailed from long lines of Thugs before them. Father to son, the habit would be handed down and, when flushed into the open by Sleeman, it emerged that long oral genealogies were claimed. There was, in other words, a complex subculture to the phenomenon. Some of the venerable family trees held by practitioners of this dubious art, stretching back to the days of Alexander the Great's rampage through Asia and into India itself, were deemed highly implausible but it does seem apparent that Thuggee had probably been practised, in one form or another, for several centuries but certainly for more than a century. Moreover and heredity notwithstanding, the gangs habitually included many outsiders. One of the most striking things about the Thugs is just how heterogeneous the gatherings were by the standards of their times. Muslim and Hindu, high and low caste, newcomers and old-established members, all were to be discovered as having Thugged together, in murderously multicultural abandon. Gangs might be in the order of twenty men, although their numbers could fall lower, depending on the charisma of their leader, or swell, although probably never to more than fifty individuals. While gangs could have core members, individuals were as likely to go 'Thugging' with one gang as another. As for the season, attacks were more likely to take place during the brief Indian winter, simply because it was the period during which travel was more tolerable.

Thugs retained something of an honour code. They were, according to their own lore and traditions, not permitted to murder women, together with a whole range of sub-categories of men. These included fakirs, dancers, musicians, bards, lepers, elephant drivers, oil vendors, washermen, sweepers, Sikhs (in some though not all provinces), the halt and otherwise physically afflicted, and anyone who was accompanied by a cow. This is by no means a comprehensive list nor was it always observed. In general terms, however, a failure to follow these rules was taken seriously, as a result of the evil that might flow from a violation of a taboo. In *general* terms, sometimes, a certain blasé spirit of 'necessity' governed the actions of Thugs in their choice of victim.

This, the actual process of choosing, was to European minds one of the most infernal aspects of the whole business. Wealth *per se* was not, as far as could be made out, the sole settling factor. Cult rites could see almost anyone being murdered. The poor were generally regarded as being unfortunate choices for a first victim on a Thugging expedition. There were byzantine mysteries to the whole process and the sheer absence of reason, by British lights, thereafter added its own peculiarly hellish flavour to how Thuggee was reported.

As for *how* it was done, Thuggee was managed by stealth, deceit and well-honed technique. At least one of their number would seek to insinuate his way into the affections of a traveller, who might be journeying alone or, more likely, as part of a group. The aim was to befriend them and travel together, for greater security. Thugs might travel with their would-be victims for days or even weeks. Then, at some appointed hour, a secret signal would go up among the Thugs. Perhaps a victim would be urged by his new friend to look at the stars. Often these final journeys together were started before dawn, at Thug prompting, so that they might be surer still of avoiding prying eyes, while another in the party of strangers would be behind him. This was the strangler and to be an accomplished one (a *bhurtote*) was to have risen high in Thug esteem. The cry would go up and he would slip the *roomal* (a simple piece of knotted cloth) round his victim's neck, while the hand-holder did just that and the deed was done in seconds, as many times as they were victims in the group and Thugs to slaughter them.

Strangulation is a most appallingly intimate form of murder and this fact adds to the horror. That bands of men actually existed who committed this crime time and again makes the Thuggee still more nauseating to imagine. Further detail deepens the fear. Dusk was another favoured time for striking. A seated victim, tired and resting from the labours of the road, was easy prey to a man standing behind and, for this reason, sleeping men were generally stirred into rising by a false alarm about a snake or scorpion, as recumbent forms were apparently surprisingly hard to despatch. Then, further repellent details: Thugs on dry land, for example, might stab bodies in the eyes to make sure they were dead, victims travelling on the Ganges would have their backs snapped after strangulation, to assist the work of the following crocodiles. In both cases, victims were disposed of speedily. Experience gained over years of Thugging meant that gangs tended to have favoured spots (*matarbur beles*) for committing their murders. Likewise, they had long lists of charnel houses for disposing of the bodies, from wells to groves. India turned out to be defiled by them. When Thuggee was finally challenged by Sleeman and its secrets revealed, legions of bodies emerged from the deep, an aspect which particularly disgusted Indian sensibilities. It showed that both Hindu prescriptions (cremation) and Muslim ones (burial facing Mecca) had been ignored and the bodies of the dead desecrated.

Yet, if scandalously disrespectful of the rites of others, Thugs were deeply attached to their own. Where shallow graves were to be dug, a pickaxe sacred to Kali, the Hindu goddess of destruction, albeit idiosyncratically employed by the Thugs, would be used. No Thugging expedition could begin without all the correct obsequies having been performed towards this ritual object, which in turn was carried in several pieces, to disguise its purpose if the gang were ever searched for any reason. To add to all of these gruesome details, bodies might be dismembered and deliberately disfigured, further to obscure their identity while enabling India's plentiful fauna to take care of the evidence. Which inevitably leads to the same problem as confronted by Sleeman himself. Not only was Thugging inexplicable, it was then as now impossible fully to ascertain the range and scale of its activities.

Thuggee *may* have originally been an outgrowth of a perverted understanding of Mughal-era law. The Hanafi school of Islamic jurisprudence held that murder entailed capital punishment only if a weapon was involved which *spilt* blood. Hence, the theory went, the Thugs strangled precisely because, even if they were discovered, they would not meet the same end as their victims or, more likely, any of the varied range of local punishments, which included being trodden upon by an elephant or, as the British were to do themselves after the Mutiny, being strapped to the mouth of a cannon which was then fired. British observers speculated that the appeal of strangulation lay in leaving so little physical evidence. Yet, this did not make sense either, given the fact that the Thugs were as likely to dismember their victims as not.

Problem piled upon problem for the unsuspecting authorities. By the very act of murder being done on travellers far from home, the victims were removed in time as much as distance from their families and friends. For when should the alarm be raised, as when was it apparent that they had gone terminally missing? In the absence of a body at the scene of the crime, when could the alarm be raised there? Even when remains were discovered, the impossibility of identification, almost regardless of what was physically left, of someone so far from home was obvious. In the nature of Thugging, whole parties entirely annihilated out of sight with no witnesses left behind, was its dreadful success. These problems were virtually insurmountable.

To add to their ghastly cleverness, Thugs tended to array themselves in imitation of the Company's native military ranks. An individual gang was led by a *jemadar*, while a leader of leaders styled himself a *subadar*. The *jemadar* brought his group together, he was the individual on which group cohesion depended. Individual Thugs might drift between different gangs, they might take a break from Thugging in any given season but the *jemadar* was required to be consistent and visible. Accordingly, when the spoils of a Thugging expedition were divvied up at its close, the *jemadar* took the largest, fixed share. He was followed by the *bhurtote*, with an equal division thereafter for the rest of the gang.

Many specialised roles existed. Scouts identified travelling groups of victims and warned of the approach
of forces belonging to the Company or local rulers.
The *sotha* was especially expert at inveigling, as the
art of insinuating oneself into the confidence of strangers became increasingly difficult to master. As often as
not, the *jemadar* himself did the inveigling. He had the
clothes and patter to be able to convince wealthy strangers in particular that their group and his should come
together for mutual protection. Children could be found
on Thugging expeditions. This was in part so that they
might be initiated into its mysteries but their presence
also entitled their families to a share of the proceeds.
Most heinously, sometimes the children with the Thugs
were those whose parents had been murdered by them.
It was a staple of the Victorian accounts of Thuggee to
reflect on the children thus taken, who themselves grew
up to be Thugs, as part of their new families.

*

That we know so much about the intricacies of this
murderous Indian subculture owes everything to the
labours of William Sleeman, and the reason that Sleeman
made these discoveries was that chance set one fact after
another under his eyes. Until he took an interest, the
authorities were aware that *something* was happening
on India's roads and waterways, something criminal and
murderous, but had no conception that a plethora of
individual incidents were part of a greater malignant
whole. As a result, owing to the sense of fragmentation
across the Indian network, no systematic efforts were

made to understand these transport-related crimes, much less to eliminate them. In some quarters the dawning notion that something diabolical was taking place was dismissed as an implausible fantasy. Those of Sleeman's predecessors who had the courage to ask questions were often censured by their superiors, their local police were dismissed and even in some cases imprisoned for having pressed charges against suspected perpetrators. This was the context within which Sleeman was working.

In 1835, however, an Indian named Feringhea was arrested and this arrest supplied Sleeman with the key to the rest of his work. Feringhea was a fifth- or sixth-generation Thug and a *jemadar*. He was tall, plausible, rich and, as a Brahmin, high-born. He was by no means driven to Thuggee by reason of poverty or hunger. Of his own initiation into Thuggee, made by consuming the sacred *goor* (sugar), Feringhea recalled:

I never wanted food; my mother's family was opulent, her relations high in office. I have been in office myself, and became so great a favourite wherever I went that I was sure of promotion; yet I was always miserable when absent from my gang, and obliged to return to Thuggee. My father made me taste the fatal *goor* when I was yet a mere boy; and if I were to live a thousand years I should never be able to follow any other trade.

In Feringhea's mind, the code of dubious honour that characterised Thuggee was paramount and he was clear in his own mind that his own downfall and that of Thuggee as a whole was because he had dishonoured the cult's own rites. In his own case, he had been responsible for the murder of a *Mughalanee* (a high-born young Muslim woman), a transgression he became ever more convinced had accounted for his capture, although the crime in question was never discovered until he confessed to it.

When Feringhea was revealed to Sleeman as being a leading Thug, Sleeman had his family placed in custody. He knew that Feringhea was devoted to them and would not be able to resist staying close so that he might hear of them. The 500-rupee reward placed on Feringhea's head also spurred endeavour and eventually two boys in the service of the Company tricked Feringhea into revealing himself. He fell into Sleeman's hands as the best-connected *jemadar* yet. He took Sleeman and his courageous wife to a mass grave to verify the extraordinary claims he made in the course of his confession and he named his accomplices. The campaign had begun.

Feringhea's arrest was the pivotal moment, and it remained the most famous incident of Thuggee in the collective consciousness. Indeed, the tale of Feringhea spawned a novel, *Confessions of a Thug*, published in London in 1839. It sold wonderfully well, proving that a silver lining can sometimes be taken from the most unprepossessing of situations. Before this crucial moment, Sleeman had been convinced of a pattern of murderous behaviour in the Indian countryside and had set himself to solve the puzzle. He had noted the crimes of various lesser Thugs and had slowly become convinced that these crimes were part of that puzzle, that the practice of Thuggee, not that he knew it yet by this name, was a real one and that the East India Company was failing

133

grievously in not paying attention to deaths taking place, by the hundreds, in territory under its administration. Now he had something material on which to build a case.

Sleeman showed his ability to think through a problem. Aware of the unwillingness in many quarters to open up the vistas of this appalling case, Sleeman wrote an anonymous article and sent it to the *Calcutta Literary Gazette*. The article detailed the material on Thuggee which had so far been accumulated and even in its slenderness it was ghastly enough. The piece was quickly picked up by the mainstream newspapers. The story of Thuggee landed on the breakfast table of the Governor-General, Lord William Bentinck, and suddenly there was no avoiding doing something about these crimes. Indeed, it is worth pointing out the significant thread which runs not only through this story of Sleeman but through so many of these Victorian stories. Many of their great works were underpinned by having a strong and energetic press willing them on in their endeavours and able to support their works.

Following the arrest of Feringhea, Sleeman had another stroke of luck. Sepoys, armed Indian infantrymen, had long been a favoured target of Thugs. Their return home on leave meant they had their pay with them and their disappearance was something which would only eventually be noticed when they failed to return to the ranks from leave. Sleeman's second piece of luck was that for once a victim, in this case a sepoy, *did* escape the clutches of his would-be killers. He was able to raise the alarm and the gang members were then captured. On top of this train of good fortune, moreover, came a third piece of luck. This incident happened in Sleeman's own district, ensuring that he saw at once the opportunity, the chain of evidence, that fate had handed to him. The pieces of the puzzle were forming now before his very eyes.

What made Sleeman *unique*, however, was that he was the first British official to extrapolate outwards from the evidence afforded him by the capture and trial of the Thugs. After all, he was not the first magistrate or political officer to stumble upon Thuggery but he was the first to set a system in place. He gathered his knowledge piece by piece and applied it methodically in a fashion which European police work would take another fifty years to match. Most significantly, he challenged the laws which had enabled Thuggery in the first place. Archaic Mughal provisions meant that prisoners' words could not be used against other prisoners. This was swept away, because central to Sleeman's scheme were so-called *approvers*, Thugs who turned informer. These individuals had to satisfy him that they had given a full confession. Then they would go out in the field, offering him full cooperation in catching Thugs still at large. If they failed to do so, their conditional pardons would be void, and they would be hanged. If they were seen to cooperate, on the other hand, their fate was life imprisonment, with pensions arranged for the families they could no longer support with murder.

There was seldom glamour in Sleeman's approach but there was heft, power, quiet authority, an iron will to succeed. The scale, ambition and energy of Victorian industry is something to be wondered at but this sense of limitless ambition, this Victorian trademark, was at the heart of what he did. He had maps made where none had previously existed and he compiled Thuggee genealogies, essentially as another form of mapping. An exhaustively detailed collation and indexing of the evidence enabled him to set about a process that had seemed impossible. He established the identity of the Thugs and their victims. The evidence Thugs gave was checked, as much as was possible, against testimony from such relatives as could be found and against the physical remains exhumed once approvers had led Sleeman and his officials to the makeshift graves. These were all aspects of 'Sleeman's machine' and, as revealed in one of the thousands of detailed interrogations still available, Sleeman himself took the form of an avenging angel:

Q: Have you ever heard of Capt Sleeman?
A: Yes, for years we heard he was hanging and banishing Thugs, and that he has made a machine, for torturing Thugs! For breaking our bones ... some said that the Thugs were ground to death in this machine!

Rather than literal torture, these were the mills of justice at work, something which rightly terrified those who had been beyond the reach of justice for at least a century.

To consider only the victims of Feringhea is to recognise the scale of Sleeman's achievement and to recognise, incidentally, the form of the happy hunting Thugs had enjoyed as a result of the peace the Company's eighteenth-century victories had restored to India. On the course of just one Thugging expedition, Sleeman wrote, as well as 'the usual mass of undifferentiated "travellers", "Marathas", "Rajpoots" and "Brahmins" ... the Thugs had murdered two dozen sepoys, eight bearers, six merchants, three *pundits* [learned teachers of religion and the law], a messenger, a fakir, two shopkeepers, an elephant driver and a bird-catcher. Their victims also included four women.'

Although Indian legal officers had bridled at such innovations as general warrants, which allowed Sleeman to get hold of suspected Thugs for interrogation, central government, once aroused by the publicity Thuggee quickly attracted, acted decisively to back the political officer. Calcutta, as an extraordinary provision required to tackle the unique menace of Thuggery, set aside its usual squeamishness about intruding upon the prerogatives of local rulers and now Thugs would be chased wherever they hid. These developments inevitably gave rise to resentment. Sleeman, by now Superintendent of the splendidly named Thuggery Department, had to put up with sour looks directed by his peers. British Residents in the Princely States bridled at these legal intrusions into their bailiwicks and protested loudly to the Governor-General that the 'delicate balance' upon which British rule of India rested was being heedlessly upset by Sleeman and his agents.

Yet higher authority, to its enormous credit, stood firm. George Swinton, Secretary to the Government of India, commended Sleeman's crusading:

[the Governor-General] relies on the approved zeal and activity already displayed [by] Captain Sleeman, in bringing to condign punishment some of the most notorious of these inhuman wretches, and [if] the

abominable [Thugs] should be ultimately exterminated, your services in the cause of humanity would
entitle you to the highest meed of applause.

When all was done in the anti-Thuggee campaign,
perhaps one in seven Thugs were hanged. It is important
to note that this was no orgy of extrajudicial slaughter
in response to the evil which was discovered. Rather,
justice prevailed in its extirpation. It was justice rough
at the edges, without doubt, but always proceeding by
design, as per the law it sought to uphold. Evidence
was sought and crimes treated proportionately. To be
a scout, for example, was not to be a strangler and
was not to be punished as such. It is important to note
too that, whatever jealousy Sleeman provoked, most of
his peers admired him, and his superiors backed and
promoted him.

Occasional reverses were inevitable. Even when he
began to assemble hard-won facts and to compile a dossier
of irrefutable evidence, Sleeman was then forced to battle
the 'blind prejudice' of some senior judges. Their refusal
to accept that any sort of plausible evidence had been
presented for Thugging meant that Sleeman was more
than ever reliant on the approval of public opinion and
on the support of his political superiors. In his lengthy
reports to the latter, he admitted, 'These proceedings are
voluminous, but [Thug] depredations ... which under the
sanction of religious rites ... make almost every road in
India between the Jumna and the Indus from the beginning of November to the end of May a dreadful scene of
hourly murder, are becoming a subject of awful interest,
and these proceedings have swelled from my anxiety to

collect all the material that would be found to bear upon this particular case.' In the face of such external pressure, the courts were obliged to back down, and mete out justice where it was due.

As for the trials themselves, these were duly sensational, especially given that the Thugs were revealed as ordinary, regular Indians. As Sleeman himself was to put it, 'These common enemies of mankind [who] strangle other people of whatever age or sex without the slightest feeling of compunction, feel towards their relations as strongly as other men.' It was exactly these discordant virtues which served to deepen the fascinated British horror at what Sleeman's work revealed. Thugs at home could be and almost always were upright and entirely correct. Of one who was a cloth dealer, for example, Sleeman noted that he 'was so correct in his deportment and all his dealings, that he had won himself the esteem of all of the gentlemen of his station'. The Thugs also rejected absolutely any idea that they were merely common thieves. Indeed, upstanding men that they were, they deprecated 'low and dirty' robbers. To provoke a Thug, all one had to do was to accuse him of mere criminality:

A Thug rides his horse! Wears his dagger! And shows a front. Thieving? Never! Never! If a banker's treasure were before me and entrusted to my care, though in hunger and dying, I would scorn to steal. But let a banker go on a journey, and I would certainly murder him. Dacoits and robbers are contemptible, I despise a dacoit. Let him come before me!

Remarkably the evidence from their trials shows that many Thugs really did believe they were discharging something that resembled military service and that, in doing so, they were honourably providing for their families. The consequence of this, as one displayed in one confession, was that legitimate loyalties could easily switch in the mind of a Thug. 'I am a Thug,' one such captured said, 'my father and grandfather were Thugs, and I have Thugged with many. Let the government employ me and I will do its work.'

*

Sleeman had uncovered what the Thugs thought, what their victims' families thought and eventually what the Indian courts thought. As for what the British themselves thought of the fantastical specimens upon whom they inflicted justice, that was always bound to be a much more exotic undertaking. Certainly, Thugs were part of a delicious mystery to the Victorians. There was nothing the Victorians relished more than a delicious mystery, all the tastier for being revealed a safe distance away. Add to the list of ingredients a dash of the cult of Kali, of which there was no need for the spectating Victorians to worry too much about the metaphysical complexities, and the mystery improved still further. Here was a crime, stupendous in scale, incomprehensible in its motivations and form and, best of all, irresistibly easy to tell as a story. What could be more unsettling in an age, where any mind could easily comprehend the banditry of dacoits, than to be told that the innocent were also stalked by killers who turned out to be among the most unassuming and well-spoken men in all the land, to be the Indian equivalent of a British gentleman?

The role of Thuggee in the Victorian imagination is a central part of this story not least because the stranglers' actions played to both of those central and cherished British Victorian virtues, fair play and honour. On the one hand, the Thugs, by 'ganging up' on their victims, were unfair. There was nothing manly in this aspect of life's struggle. Had the British themselves been studied and typified as they did others, their 'cult of fair play' would doubtless have been identified as having been gravely transgressed by Thugging. On the other hand, the Thugs were seen as having, however appalling, an honour code of their own. They were, in their own minds, no mere 'ordinary' criminals or bandits. As one East India Company magistrate put it, 'The histories of these men are as romantic as the most ardent lover of Oriental adventures could desire.'

It would be wrong to say the Thugs filled a want the Victorians barely knew existed. Equally, it would be ahistorical to imagine that the Victorians simply enjoyed tales of Thuggee as we might enjoy a horror film. British Victorians were obviously as aware as British citizens today that casually strangling passers-by was neither honourable nor fair. However, there can be no denying that Thuggee became an irresistible legend of the Empire. It was simply too good a story not to tell. If Thugs were felt to have their own perverted honour which separated them from the lawlessness of dacoits and other bandits, then so much the greater was the achievement in finally putting an end to them. This was where the industry of a Sleeman came in and in large part why his story was instructively told for so long.

It is significant that one aspect of the Thuggee trials provided a particular point for Victorian Britain. This was the bloodless way the Thugs themselves recounted their crimes. There was no melodrama here, only a litany of unexceptional deeds recounted at steady length. That eminently quotable Victorian Fanny Parkes recorded that it was said of the condemned Thugs, 'It would be impossible to find in any country a set of men who meet death with more indifference than these wretches; and, had it been in a better cause, they would have excited universal sympathy.' In comparison to the absence of Victorian fatalism, the very evident fatalism of the *East*, as manifested in these trials, caused especial shock and moral outrage. Victorian observers watched as the Thugs gave a collective metaphorical shrug. They had no sense of reproach for having Thugged, for was it not provided for? Kali had demanded it. Indeed, it was their failing to observe her precepts by murdering women, for one thing, which occasioned their downfall. Such was their reckoning, as the Victorians looked on agog.

Sleeman himself cast a cold eye on this cult of Kali, concluding that the murders were not *for* Kali. The more mundane truth was that Kali was an indispensable tool to the Thugs. She assisted the stranglers as much as did an individual gang member. In this way, Sleeman stepped away from any process of 'othering' the Thugs. Their psychology was no different from that of an English murderer. The blame could not be pinned on Kali and on an Oriental mindset, not when the truth was infinitely more recognisable and more horribly mundane.

The success of *Confessions of a Thug* was followed by a wave of other creative endeavours. Marie-Joseph 'Eugène' Sue's *The Wandering Jew* was one of the most popular novels of the nineteenth century. In it the Thugs, the 'Etrangleurs', became the first characters from the East to be taken out of their own context and placed into a Western novel where they promptly teamed up with the more familiar figures of unscrupulous Jesuits. Later, Wilkie Collins placed a murderous Indian cult in the pages of *The Moonstone* and a half-century later Mark Twain recalled the story of a movement called the Thuggee, now swept away but capable in their own time of inspiring the greatest fear:

We understand what Thuggee was, what a bloody terror it was, what a desolating scourge it was. In 1830 the English found this cancerous organisation embedded in the vitals of the empire, doing its devastating work in secrecy, and assisted, protected, sheltered, and hidden by innumerable confederates – big and little native chiefs, customs officers, village officials, and native police, all ready to lie for it, and the mass of the people, through fear, persistently pretending to know nothing about its doings; and this condition of things had existed for generations, and was formidable with the sanctions of age and old custom. If ever there was an unpromising task, if ever there was a hopeless task in the world, surely it was offered here – the task of conquering Thuggee. But that little handful of English officials in India set their sturdy and confident grip upon it, and ripped it out, root and branch!

143

Even in our own time, the trace of Thuggee occasionally registers, as in the murderous Indian cults pursuing Harrison Ford through subterranean tunnels in *Indiana Jones and the Temple of Doom*. Let it never be said that Victorian stories have no staying power.

*

In the Waterloo Chamber at Windsor Castle there lies to this day a two-ton piece of carpet, a distinctive memorial to the life and works of William Sleeman. It arrived at Windsor via the Crystal Palace, where it was a prized piece at the Great Exhibition, but it originated at Jubbulpore, where it had been woven at the School of Industry. The school had been established by Sleeman himself, who had set it up to house and confine reformed Thugs. This is an instructive reminder of Sleeman's method. For those Thugs who were not executed could never again be set free but they must be given something to do for the years of their confinement. Let us not imagine Sleeman, in other words, as anything else but a classic Victorian.

Sleeman died off the coast of Ceylon, en route to England. He was buried at sea. His life was a vindication of the Empire he served and was spent in service to the peoples who lived in it. Contemporary fashion might sneer at the happy morality tale Victorians fashioned of his life but this sneer stems from a contemporary retreat from sincerity. It speaks volumes about today's culture, while saying little of note about Sleeman himself. In his vigorous and virtuous Victorian way, he saw the chance to do good by his charges and he seized the chance. He is an example to us and he was certainly an example beloved of the Victorians, precisely because he personified what they wanted to believe was the best of their culture. He encapsulated the highest hope of their moral purpose and through administrative efficacy did good and beneficial work.

Pugin: The Hand of God

The life of the Anglo-French Catholic convert, architect and designer Augustus Welby Northmore Pugin (1 March 1812–14 September 1852) was relatively short but it was full of lasting cultural achievements. The scintillating Gothic interiors of the rebuilt Palace of Westminster are Pugin's crowning glory and in them along with a range of ecclesiastical and other buildings scattered across the Empire we see a substantial legacy. The greatest of these achievements, however, is that we take Pugin's legacy so much for granted. The Victorian character of the nation's landscapes, its built-up spaces, its mindset. This is so ubiquitous that people have almost ceased to be aware of it. Instead, it forms the backdrop, familiar and omnipresent and comforting, to daily life. Yet such a context could not be achieved without much struggle, and no party to that struggle spoke in quite the same idiom as Pugin.

Pugin was also fated to be what could be called the first 'eclipsed' Victorian. Even in his own lifetime, despite this very great architectural and cultural legacy, his people virtually lost sight of his achievement. He was the first victim of the backlash, which began long before *the Victorian age itself came to an end, against what Lytton Strachey's Bloomsbury contemporary Virginia Woolf called the 'crystal palaces, bassinettes, military helmets, memorial wreaths, trousers, whiskers, wedding cakes' of the age. This chapter attempts to reassess the legacy left by 'God's architect' and to give him his due.*

*

By the age of twenty-one, Augustus Pugin had already lived a lifetime. He had signed up the monarch as a client and been imprisoned, shipwrecked, widowed and become a father. Less than twenty years later he was dead, having by then experienced madness, fame and a reordering of his personal belief system. His *Contrasts* publication of 1836, written when he was twenty-four, was regarded as the first true manifesto of architecture. It proclaimed that the discipline was a moral force, to be deployed for the greatest possible good. He died in the knowledge that he had packed four-score years and ten into forty and in the knowledge too that the bulk of his achievement had been squeezed into a mere half-dozen of those years. He was steam-powered, as much of an engine as the age in which he lived.

The French Revolution was responsible for the presence of Augustus Pugin in the British firmament. His father and namesake, a draughtsman and writer on matters architectural, was born in Paris but around 1798 he departed the revolutionary cauldron of France, bound for London. Here he studied at the Royal Academy Schools and later obtained a position with John Nash, best known for the neoclassical design of Buckingham

Palace, Regent Street and the stuccoed terraces surrounding Regent's Park. This was a design, a philosophy and a way of encapsulating the world that the younger Pugin would utterly reject. In London, too, the senior Pugin met and married Catherine Welby, the Presbyterian daughter of a wealthy Lincolnshire family. Her money enabled the young couple to set up home in Bloomsbury and it was here that their only son was born.

Catherine was responsible for the young Pugin's first encounter with Christianity, although it bore little resemblance to the High Catholicism which influenced his work as an architect. He attended Presbyterian services with his mother but he experienced these as cold ceremonies held in austere surroundings. The plainness and, as he felt it, sense of labour which accompanied these services became sources of alienation rather than devotion for the impressionable Pugin. His mother, however, remained the dominant intellectual influence on her beloved son. Sharp, a snob, keen to joke at the expense of others, though less keen to be the butt of jokes herself, Catherine was enamoured of certain causes such as female emancipation and animal welfare, long before they were fashionable. As a result, she cut a distinctive figure in the London of the day.

The young Pugin was precocious and cossetted. His parents cut into the attic of the house in Bloomsbury, transforming the top floor into a model theatre for him, complete with working scenery. Here, Pugin's imagination ran riot and no doubt was where his sense of how to handle volume, space and decoration first came to life. He grew up with the notions a child in his circumstances might almost have been expected to have. Like his near contemporary (and fellow Bloomsbury resident) Benjamin Disraeli, he set about fashioning a grand and noble lineage for himself and like Disraeli he had foreign and exotic backdrops on which to draw. In this case, he was able easily enough to imagine the history of a family obliged to flee the persecutions in France.

When the Napoleonic Wars ended and British visitors were again safely able to go to the Continent, the Pugins visited the basilica at Saint-Denis in the northern part of Paris. Since the tenth century, the church had been the resting place of French kings but on their arrival the family discovered that the royal tombs had been destroyed by the Jacobins, the patrimony of almost a millennium lost in one violent day. For Augustus Pugin, such a sight and such an experience did little to inspire confidence in revolution, 'reason' and secularism.

He attended Christ's Hospital school in the City of London, though his education was not all it might have been. It seems clear that he was more influenced by his father's publications and drawings than he was by any tutelage he received. He was, moreover, surrounded by a fragmentary past in a form that might have been designed expressly to set aflame the imagination of an impressionable boy. He could, at that time, with a child's modest pocket money buy for loose change precious medieval treasures of the type which now form the basis of collections across our foremost museums. For this was an age in which the current attitude to the fragmentary past had not yet evolved. These fragments, disregarded and discarded by Regency Britain in the name of a thrusting modernity, were to be had in abundance from any antiquarian shop. The result was to furnish

Pugin with a practical attitude to the relics of history. They could all be seen as eminently serviceable and as an adult he would regard the masses of triple-decker pulpits, sounding boards and other paraphernalia scorned by modernisers as artefacts to be pressed into the service of architect and God.

The young Pugin was not alone in communing with an imagined past. The first decades of his life, in the age of modernity though they were, also witnessed a rising interest in interpreting and from time to time actually enacting history. This was the age of Romanticism, which reacted sharply to the mechanisation and industrialisation at work on all sides. As the century progressed, so this reaction took a variety of forms. Take the Eglinton Tournament of 1839, in which 100,000 spectators gathered in the pouring rain in Ayrshire to watch enactments of medieval jousts. The knights, by rank, were as real as the horses and the armour, and the underlying idea, a community of bonds and reciprocation, obligations and duties, was real too.

This pageant was in itself a response to Walter Scott's *Ivanhoe, a Romance* (1819), which depicted a fanciful, medieval world and became a bestseller. It was also the era of 'Young England', a group of youthful Tories at Eton and Cambridge invested in the ideal of a medieval feudal golden age. Disraeli was associated with the group and his novels *Sybil* and *Coningsby* set out on the page some of the swirling ideas of these years. Pugin was not to be immune to the power of such ideas and he would do more than anyone else to sculpt such ideas into a form of material reality. As Rosemary Hill notes, he would absorb such ideas of mutuality and reciprocation and turn them into an imagined model society, a 'coherent Christian civic order in which the poor would be fed, the old cared for, the children taught. As the Victorian age began, it was a compelling thought.' Such a vision would become central to his life.

Pugin was absorbing, sponge-like, the swirling currents of his cultural context but he was also learning his trade. Upon leaving school, he began working for his father and he made several more visits to France where he also began to collect commissions. These were for jewellery and furniture which included vast and immovable sideboards for Windsor Castle, which after a long period of neglect and stagnation was being stirred into renewed life by George IV. He went to design sets for the Theatre Royal, later the Royal Opera House, at Covent Garden. Here, he would go on to work high up among the rigging sometimes working late into the evening. He would even spend the night sleeping in an opera box.

This polymath developed an interest in sailing too. For a brief period, he commandeered a schooner trading between Kent and Flanders. This allowed him to develop an eye for the design prevalent in the Low Countries and to import occasional pieces for his own use. Not that these voyages always went according to plan. In 1830 he was shipwrecked on the Scottish coast near Edinburgh and with this brush with death came a decision to leave the seas and devote himself as much as possible to land-based design. He established a furniture business but this failed too and he spent some time in prison on account of unpaid debts.

In 1831, at the age of nineteen, he met and married Anne Garnet. Soon his wife was expecting their first child. Alas, in short and tragic order, she was to die in childbirth, although the baby girl survived. Pugin lost both his wife and his parents before he was twenty-one. His second marriage came in 1833, when he married Louisa Button. Their child was Edward Welby Pugin, who also became a noted architect, and moved with them to Salisbury. It was here that Pugin put down significant roots.

*

By now, the neoclassical world epitomised by Nash and his peers was in retreat. The monumental front of Buckingham Palace was impressive, but the palace redesign had been scandalously expensive and the building itself was cordially disliked by its Royal inhabitants. George IV had breathed new life into Windsor Castle but nobody had managed to discover how much the works had cost. Such ruinous expense was, it seemed, of a piece with the period itself, and the Regency, necessitated by a mad king, was raucous and rakish, overrun by licentiousness, in which scant attention was paid to order, morality or higher thinking. As the cities expanded, infernally, many thought, without much in the way of planning, and still less of poetry or beauty on display, so the public's attitude to its environment began to change too. When the crowds gathered to watch the Eglinton pageantry or read *Ivanhoe* or *Sybil* and dreamed of a coherent world, so they began to hunger after a glimpse of this world, of a poem, rendered in bricks and mortar. Pugin would be the man to deliver this world to them.

The Gothic Revival was a response, in architectural form, to these changing times. Several generations before Pugin, the style had been on the rise in England and later throughout western Europe. It was of a piece with a version of Romanticism which took stock of the world as it was and found it wanting. It manifested in a range of ways. Tentative forms of ornamentation sought to echo the Gothic lines and play of the Middle Ages. Later, a more confident mood began to expand into novel forms of old design. Vernacular Gothic emerged in more humble settings, expansive and expensive forms manifested in such wealthier places as Cambridge, Oxford and European university towns.

The movement's philosophical and ecclesiastical context is of importance. As well as being a response to the social and industrial changes, the movement also had deep roots in a *religious* and liturgical context. Specifically, it mirrored the slowly renewing confidence of Catholicism and of High Anglicanism in eighteenth-century Britain, following the rigours of the Reformation and the wars of the seventeenth century. It would be decades before this confidence was echoed in legislation but times had begun to change. The lush and elaborate symbolism of Catholicism and Anglo-Catholicism underpins much of the Gothic Revival and it must also inform any discussion of Pugin's own vision.

At Salisbury, Pugin set about creating his own expression of the Gothic vision in brick and stone. A few miles from the city, in Alderbury, he designed his first house, naming it St Marie's Grange. 'To the astonishment and often undisguised mirth of passers-by,' remarks Rosemary Hill, 'a turreted, fortified, red-brick house, apparently blown out of the pages of a book of hours, began to rise rapidly next to the main Southampton road.' The Grange was and remains, though it is today much altered, a singular house, with its moat and drawbridge, its tower, its windows arranged the better to view the building's private chapel than for any more practical reasons and its ranges of impractically interconnecting rooms. It was a strange and unusual house but is possessed of its own beauty and it was Pugin's first essay in a craft that he would presently perfect.

In 1834, he made another decisive change. He had long since sloughed off the Presbyterianism of his youth but now he converted to Catholicism and was received formally into the Church the following year. In his own words:

> After a most close & impartial investigation I feel perfectly convinced the roman Catholick church is the only true one – and the only one in which the grand & sublime style of church architecture can ever be restored.

It is important to emphasise that Pugin's journey towards Catholicism was in all likelihood not a long one. Although he had been steeped in his mother's Presbyterian austerity, his father was probably, it is impossible to know for certain, originally a Catholic, albeit one who pragmatically converted to Anglicanism as a means of rising within British society. Pugin's conversion involved rather less in the way of courage than would have been the case in previous years, for Catholic Emancipation was now a fact. It was nonetheless a move not without professional risk.

Pugin might have hoped that his conversion would also open different and unexpected doors to him and this proved to be the case. He was now firmly in contact with the world of English Catholicism. He had lately met John Talbot, sixteenth Earl of Shrewsbury. He was one of England's leading Catholic aristocrats, a de facto role with some significance as a result of English Catholicism's centuries without Hierarchy or any form of formal leadership. Talbot himself was something of an outsider. He was not born to be Earl, having inherited the title from his childless uncle. He was the first Catholic to sit as such in the Lords since the Reformation and he had received only an uneven education. In short, he had been held to little account before he succeeded to the earldom, whereupon this kind, shy, gentle man inherited a fortune and, to everyone's surprise, turned out to possess an ambitious vision.

This vision was one shared with Pugin: the return of a Catholic England after centuries of suppression. Shrewsbury 'combined, in a chivalrous manner, the public flamboyance suitable to his rank with a modest private austerity' and now he enlisted Pugin to develop his estate at Alton Towers in Staffordshire and to rebuild and extend his residence in the Gothic style. This was a turning point for Pugin, his first great commission and the beginning of a sequence of such commissions, including his first full essays in ecclesiastical architecture.

In 1836, Pugin followed his conversion with a publication that must be viewed as his own personal manifesto and as in itself something of a personal spiritual document, as well as a blueprint for a new world and a new and better society. *Contrasts; or, A Parallel between the Noble Edifices of the*

Fourteenth and Fifteenth Centuries, and Similar Buildings of the Present Day; Shewing the Present Decay of Taste did what its title implies it would do. It made the argument that an architecture derived from the pre-Reformation medieval world was infinitely superior to the horrors of the Renaissance or neoclassical world. It was the only *fit* form for a society that aspired to Godliness and the ideal of human perfection. *Contrasts* was above all a denunciation of urban life of the day. It attacked 'the world of the Regency, that Vanity Fair of stucco-fronted manners, high taste and low principles'. It confronted the Britain that had by means of its industrial revolution created the modern world and squalor and misery in monstrous proportions such as the world had never previously seen. As ever for Pugin the question, and thus the answer, was moral. This was a matter of creating the right city and rejecting the wrong city. It was a study of morality, more than planning or aesthetics. It claimed to be a work of rigorous impartiality, while simultaneously asserting that no fair mind could find in favour of the work of the present century over that of the Middle Ages. Pugin's conclusion was that true buildings were the ones which 'emanated from men who were thoroughly embued [*sic*] with devotion for, and faith in, the religion for whose worship they were erected'. *Contrasts* never stopped being comic and readable, as well as honest, melancholic and sincere.

Contrasts was handsomely and richly illustrated but it was a classic polemic. It focused on a series of contemporary buildings, set them against a medieval equivalent and supplied illustrations designed to magnify the beauty and harmony of the one and to diminish the beauty of the other.

Rosemary Hill singles out Pugin's comparison of the new King's College London with a view of Christ Church, Oxford. The one hunches gracelessly between two larger buildings, while the other, its more contemporary Tom Tower edited out, is shown as a picture of grace. Another view showed a fine medieval monastery, complete with gardens and charity for the needy and compared it with a monstrous panopticon, where the needy were not saved but allowed to die and were despatched after death to be dissected in an anatomical laboratory. At Alton Towers, Shrewsbury had commissioned Pugin to build exactly such a medieval hospital, one which would help the needy, not merely the sick. The ideal shared by both gentlemen was that to cure the body was a good thing but to match the soul with life was the best thing.

Pugin was being not quite fair then yet *Contrasts* accomplished what it set out to achieve, encapsulating in visual terms the fundamental and moral point that its author was seeking to make. Further texts would follow in the remainder of his career: in *The True Principles of Pointed or Christian Architecture* (1841) Pugin invented his work anew and showed how it could be applied to everything, from a church to a chair. This was indeed the 'functional' nature of his Gothic. In Pugin's view what others called 'symbolism' was also functional, much as a wafer does, as understood by the Catholic doctrine of transubstantiation, become the Body of Christ. His churches were functional by virtue of their pointed roofs shedding rain *and* heralding the Resurrection. Pugin extolled the virtues of careful and skilled craft over mechanisation. This became part of his influence on the future and such words seem to anticipate the later works of William

Morris. Nonetheless, it is important to note that Pugin's essential purpose differed greatly from that of such individuals as Morris because his vision was anchored in religion itself.

As commission followed commission and as his writings were disseminated, so his fame began to spread. He was a careful curator of his own image, for in dress and speech he appeared shabby and eccentric. He designed his own clothes, wore billowing multi-pocketed cloaks and appeared often as the fantasy of the sailor he had in his varied youth actually been. He spoke to bishops and builders as one.

While he criss-crossed the country sketching medieval churches, his sense of theatricality served him well. His early work hanging high above theatre stages, for example, had rendered him fearless of heights. He was comfortable perched on an eyrie below the vaulted roof of Lincoln Cathedral, drawing, observing and noting and he became part of the local colour, with tour guides pointing him out, as much a cathedral point of interest as its wonderful gargoyles or the worn stone where pious pilgrims still kneel to ask for St Hugh's intercession.

Not that it could possibly all be plain sailing. It was all fine to champion the virtues of the medieval world, as Pugin and Shrewsbury liked to do, and to relate it to a contemporary Catholic world but the challenge came in explaining both the utility of this world and the ostensible perfection of the Catholic vision, to a country steeped for centuries in Protestant liturgy and Protestant culture. A nation which industrialisation and mechanisation were making wealthy and powerful, the first superpower. How to explain the wonders of the Gothic in such a context?

How to explain his own form of Catholicism, which was woven with an idea of England in the Middle Ages that was idealised and that never in fact had existed at all? Especially when this Catholicism bore little relation to the reality of the present Church. As Pugin's work and career were to develop, this was to set the stage for innumerable and bitter disputes with those whom he might reasonably have hoped to be closest to him.

There was a tremendous harmony and simplicity to Pugin's moral vision. Gothic churches had, for him, grown out of a truly Christian world. Therefore, they 'were not simply buildings *in* which, but rather *with* which one might worship God'. All of the church contributed to the whole. The cruciform shape was the Cross, verticality in form was the Resurrection, the spire marked out Heaven while the altar was Calvary again on Earth. The Gothic was, in its totality, not merely a style with which to decorate a church, still less a meeting house for a congregation. It was a sacred *organising principle* which enabled the building to be used in the way for which it was intended: the worship of God. This is religion before architecture, and it is architecture deployed to serve the needs of religion. This was the encapsulation of the man himself and the purpose, as he saw it, of his art and his gifts.

At the heart of Pugin's vision, however, there was an essential contradiction which could not for ever be ignored or set aside. At first, as we have seen, Romantic Catholics stood undivided with other British Romantics. When the Anglo-Irish writer and Catholic convert Kenelm Digby wrote about what might have happened had the Reformation never occurred and England remained a

159

Catholic country, he was fully in the mainstream of a critique of a century. 'It is possible', Digby suggested, 'that Birmingham and Manchester might not have attained their present character, for merciless inhuman industry would not have been tolerated.' It is important to emphasise that this is not a discussion about the merit of some counterfactual speculation, nor the rights and wrongs of 'Manchesterism'. Rather it is the common criticism and concern for the physically and spiritually poor, which stretched from liberated Catholics to so many other quarters in Victorian Britain.

British Catholics such as Pugin, however, diverged from these mainstream preoccupations in certain critical ways. Their glorification of the medieval caused them to see the sermons and boards listing the Ten Commandments of the Established Church as being inescapably and inextricably linked with the wider socio-spiritual malaise. Pugin and his patron Shrewsbury were tormented by the knowledge that their suggested antidote to this problem was a Gothic vision which relied upon an antediluvian world. It was one in which a powerful laity played a critical role in the Church and by means of the Church, in the wider world. The problem with this vision was, in short, that this Church and this world no longer existed. Pugin wished to build churches that Catholics themselves no longer used as once they did.

This painful truth was manifest in Rome itself, where the Renaissance and the return to the earliest classical forms stood as the city's visible heritage. The very Senate House of ancient Rome, the Curia Julia, had survived the ravages of time essentially intact but for more than 1,200 years it was not a place of pagan government at all but the Christian church of Sant'Adriano al Foro. Catholicism itself, in its mainstream and necessarily practically minded form, had altered. The great mass of Catholics appreciated that the Tridentine rite, which had reordered continental churches to accommodate *it*, was by now centuries old and was serving the flock well. In other words, certain recusant English Catholics and certain converts such as Pugin were firmly in the minority and were regarded as dwelling in the past. They were emerging into the post-Emancipation world only to find that this world had changed and that Catholicism had too.

For Cardinal Wiseman, the Irish cleric who would become the first Archbishop of Westminster upon the re-establishment of the Catholic Church in England and Wales in 1850, the Pugins of the world were intent not on glorifying the Church in England but on establishing an English Catholic Church, a crucial and potentially dangerous difference:

[They] thought that no more authority should be allowed [the Pope] than what was barely necessary for keeping up communion ... Such opinions if acted upon would lead directly to schism ... I would rather see all the splendid cathedrals on earth levelled to the ground, than a jot or tittle of Catholic truth allowed to pass away & I would rather hear the pure doctrines of the Church preached in barns than dangerous theories or principles that would weaken unity preached under richly fretted and gilded vaults.

No wonder, perhaps, that *Contrasts* entirely justified the little ditties which were sung about its author:

161

But now it's clear to one and all,
Since he published his lecture,
No church is Catholic at all,
Without Gothic architecture.

This dilemma, this spiritual and liturgical conundrum, was far more tragedy than comedy and one that would unfold through the bitter legacy of his work, as he attempted to put English Gothic to the service of a restored Church which no longer, by its own universal lights, had any call for it. Indeed, the keenest usage of Pugin's Gothic eventually ended up being certain Anglo-Catholic parishes of the Established Church. A Church whose existence he bewailed but the form of which to this day Pugin has done as much as anyone to settle. How did Pugin set his course through these disturbed and difficult waters?

*

The great period of Pugin's professional life began now, in the aftermath of *Contrasts*, of his conversion and of the onset of his friendship with Shrewsbury. He was commissioned by the Earl to design a series of key ecclesiastical buildings in England and Wales, including St Giles at Cheadle, and aspects of St Peter and St Paul at Newport. He also designed a series of new Catholic cathedrals across Ireland, including St Mary's at Killarney and St Aidan's at Enniscorthy. This was his vision behind a range of new buildings at St Patrick's seminary at Maynooth, near Dublin. In a demonstration of his range and reach, he despatched a set of designs to Australia.

Pugin churches survive today in Queensland and New South Wales and the distinctive Pugin vision of Gothic ecclesiastical architecture has planted deep roots into the national psyche.

Pugin called St Giles 'my consolation in all afflictions' and it remains a splendid building. Shrewsbury's deep pockets ensured that Pugin had all the resources needed to turn a vision into material reality. This in the end was a rather larger one than the first sketch plans might have suggested, though Shrewsbury was as pleased about this as Pugin. He visited the ancient churches that stud the landscape of Norfolk, as well as those of northern France, in search of inspiration, and Shrewsbury opened a new sandstone quarry on his land to supply the stone deemed necessary. Red sandstone, white sandstone, gypsum, elm and oak were lavished on St Giles, bespoke tiling and enamelwork were commissioned for its interior and the cost of the purpose-carved rood-screen at length caused even Shrewsbury to blench. The building was consecrated on St Giles' Day, 1 September 1846.

Other English commissions included St Chad's Cathedral at Birmingham, consecrated in 1841 and the first large-scale church building Pugin had had the opportunity to design. For St Chad's, he looked to the Gothic architecture of northern and central Europe. The cathedral, with its brick fabric and its sheer height, is deliberately reminiscent of Munich's glorious Frauenkirche and its wooden ceiling, ornamented and richly carved and decorated, glances at the lavish equivalents at Ely and Peterborough cathedrals. Much of the building's furniture and fittings were also personally designed by Pugin, the bishop's chair, all oak and velvet, for example, or collected from Europe and brought to England by Shrewsbury. Pugin was careful to use the finest contemporary craft, in accordance with his artistic vision. Windows, metalwork and vestments were designed by him and manufactured with loving care in Birmingham itself. St Chad's stands as an example of *why* certain forms of work should be done and *how* they should be done and with what exalted purpose.

Spiritually serious as these schemes were and all-consuming as Pugin invariably found them, a certain degree of pathos can from time to time be discerned. In 1839, at the consecration of St Mary's Catholic church at Derby neither Shrewsbury, the building's patron, nor Pugin stayed for the ceremony. It was one of Pugin's earliest completed schemes so of considerable importance as one of the first new English Catholic places of worship in the post-Emancipation world. Regrettably the officiating priest declined to don the specially designed medieval vestments supplied for the occasion. Nor would he permit the singing of *authentic* plainchant to accompany the service. Instead, the London Philharmonic Society orchestra and choir performed a Beethoven Mass for the good Catholic people of Derby. Pugin and Shrewsbury did not stick around to be affronted, they simply went home. Wiseman called St Mary's 'without exception the most magnificent thing that Catholics have done in modern times in this country' but sadly Pugin's purity caused him not delight in his accomplishment, only pain and anger.

Similarly, at his son's christening in the non-Pugin-designed church at Margate, God's Architect confined himself to the stairs. He would not enter the main body of the church, the better to avoid what he deemed the worst sights of the building. When asked for costs for the new St George's Cathedral in Southwark, consecrated in 1848, the exasperated architect replied, 'Who ever heard of a complete cathedral being built in the life of one man?' He may have designed St Chad's and seen it through to consecration yet in Pugin's sure view, far better an unfinished good and true church than a completed bad one. Such purity tended to get him into trouble and such vignettes serve to underscore the ways in which his overarching vision clashed with the facts of the real world and of the real Catholic Church.

There was more to Pugin's life and profession in these productive years than churches and church furniture. Although self-criticism and self-revision had been a constant throughout his life, he was boosted by occasional sense of what might be possible. In his *Apology for the Revival of Christian Architecture in England* (1843), his last, highly successful written work, Victorian architecture was there with 'nature as a model, the return to the vernacular, the escape from mere copyism' and a Gothic which could turn itself to anything and anything to Gothic. It is impossible to say where he might have leapt next but in his final years he had come to terms with many of his earlier self-imposed frustrations. As ever, the cause was theology and 'development' theory was the key. The *Apology* set out how he now believed that things could be designed in accordance with the *principles* of the past, rather than just in *imitation* of them. 'Development' held that while divine revelation was final and absolute, human understanding of it was not. This suited Pugin's forgivable habit of letting his theories lag behind his practical discoveries. In consequence, he now felt he could build things that were new yet still true.

One opportunity came courtesy of Balliol College, Oxford. By the early 1840s, the college authorities were sufficiently concerned about the state of the ancient Balliol buildings to propose a wholesale renewal of much of the college's fabric in the Gothic model. George Basevi, architect of the illustrious neoclassical Fitzwilliam Museum at Cambridge, was commissioned to draw up Gothic plans for the college but these were rejected when Pugin, asked for his opinion, damned them as 'not bad enough to be rediculous [sic], nor good enough to be commendable'. The issue factionalised the college, so Pugin was approached by one faction to undertake the work himself.

This was the beginning of what became known as the 'Civil War of 1843' at Balliol. The choice of Pugin was in itself brave, if not foolhardy. The college's Broad Street frontage, which it was proposed Pugin tear down and rebuild, occupies one of the most prominent positions in Oxford. Moreover, it faced the new Martyrs' Memorial, the form of which Pugin had loudly opposed in print, this despite the fact that the designer was George Gilbert Scott, a Pugin disciple. Balliol's governing body divided viciously among itself and against its Master. Its members began to leak copious details of the squabble to the press, which was itself hungry for news of the savage ecclesiastical battles being waged in the highly heated Oxford of the day. Such was the temperature of the quarrel that all records of it have been removed, literally torn, from the Balliol records. In the end, nothing was done. The scheme was abandoned but nobody told Pugin, leading to humiliation and trauma for the architect.

His domestic and private life was similarly chequered. He had sold his curious house outside Salisbury and left the district in 1841, removing temporarily to London. Louisa died in 1844 and was buried at St Chad's. By 1848, his life and circumstances had changed again. He married his third wife, Jane Knill, at St George's, Southwark (their child would be the architect Peter Paul Pugin), and by now he was focused on creating the building that today stands as his personal testament, The Grange, which perches on chalk soil at West Cliff, above the sea at Ramsgate. The Grange captures the domestic transformations that Pugin pioneered in the course of his career, the ideas for which he is remembered today with respect and admiration. In particular, he is loved because he emphasised the notions of truthful and honest living, with buildings to match, ideas as far removed as is possible to imagine from the mad Modernist dream of houses as machines for living.

Pugin transformed the ideal of domesticity by moving away from the symmetry and gravity of the Georgian home, instead having the external form of the house reflect its inward purpose. Rather than living being determined by what the Georgian façade outside required, what was done was what you saw. Perhaps this concept came from the difficulties and traumas of his own home life, his loss of two wives, his eight children and his peripatetic searches for a home finally to call his own. St Marie's Grange at Alderbury proved to be a mere essay in the craft and it was not until he settled at Ramsgate that the essay became material and set reality. The Grange adhered to the template of which Pugin and Shrewsbury were so fond. It was an organic jumble of buildings, including a chapel, all constructed on an elevated site overlooking the sea, the Goodwin Sands and distant France, with the luminous Kent sky arching overhead.

In its essence, this house was *simple*, plain on the outside, with a central hall functioning as a room in its own right and with other living rooms branching off it and into each other. Here as at Salisbury family life and work were blended. Unlike in most Victorian homes, neither children nor servants were banished to the back stairs or out of sight. The briefest glimpse of The Grange reveals the truth of the matter, the interior of the building being designed first, with the exterior added later. It could almost be called a machine for living, before this ugly phrase was thought of, but a machine shaped into the warmest and most democratic form imaginable. Add the adjoining St Augustine's, the private church designed by him and completed by his sons, and Pugin's dream is revealed incarnate and fit for any British Victorian life.

The Grange also exemplified the life of the private Pugin. To his children he was a loving and present father when, that is, he was in their presence. Home life would start before dawn with eldest son Ned wandering the house with a hand-bell waking everyone and throughout the day bells for offices would ring, with religion woven into the lives of the family. Delightful glimpses of this life may be caught in action. Once, when his son was fourteen and should have been asleep, Pugin was overjoyed to find him still awake in bed finishing off a drawing of the Crucifixion.

Such a home, a relatively modest, detached dwelling fit for the new middle classes, was an aspect, a by-product, of the world as it had become and it is in such insights that the irony in Pugin's life and work can be seen. In particular, lives such as the one lived by the Pugin family overlooking the Channel at Ramsgate were made possible by technology and by one form of technology above all. This was the railway. The monstrous machine of steam and heat that brought Pugin's seaside life within range of London and professional engagements, that opened up such prospects to Britain's rising bourgeoisie and that brought cheery, sunny Ramsgate and other such locales within the reach of an even greater swathe of the population. Pugin's life of transformation was, in other words, made possible by the modern transformations of the Victorians.

Pugin's contemporary William Powell Frith demonstrated this transformation with his painting *Life at the Seaside (Ramsgate Sands)*, which was exhibited at the Royal Academy in 1854. The painting shows a cheery and almost shockingly mixed group of Britons intent on enjoying a day at the seaside. The scene is crowded with a Victorian paraphernalia of bathing machines, a Punch and Judy show, a boy with his mouth organ, performing animals and, there in the background, Pugin's house on West Cliff. Here was an expanding democracy and an expanding world captured on canvas. Pugin was both an intrinsic aspect of Frith's dizzying painting and of the world it portrayed. He made this modernity work for him. Whether it was in pressing Birmingham foundries and workshops into his service or installing plate-glass windows instead of leaded panes or enjoying the comfort of water closets or 'any modern invention which conduces to comfort, cleanliness or durability', Pugin was pleased to apply the contemporary world to his cherished Gothic. Nor would he be the last architect to eschew ideological purity in favour of every mod con to be had and surely because of this he is the more popular. Turning from the domestic to the public it is time to look at the schemes which placed Augustus Pugin at the centre of national life.

*

On 16 October 1834, a fire began in the basements of the Palace of Westminster, the ancient home of Parliament. The fire spread rapidly through what was a decrepit medieval building, parts of which dated back to the eleventh century, and before long the greater part of the Palace was ablaze, in what proved to be the greatest conflagration London had witnessed since the Great Fire of 1666. Elements of the sprawling complex survived, most notably Westminster Hall and the Chapel of St Mary Undercroft, but the remainder of the building was burned to the ground, together with centuries of historic treasures in the form of tapestries, furniture and paintings. The sheer scale of the fire was captured by Turner in his two paintings entitled *The Burning of the Houses of Lords and Commons*. He, together with others, including Constable and Pugin, had walked to the south bank of the Thames and watched as the conflagration grew and spread.

It was a calamity but also an opportunity and almost at once recognised as such. In some quarters there were calls for Parliament to rebuild elsewhere – William IV offered Buckingham Palace, hoping in the process to dispose of a cordially disliked London residence – but in the end a decision was made to rebuild on the existing and historic riverside site. As to how to rebuild, it is significant that when proposals were floated to embrace the neoclassical it was decided that such notions were alarming. After all, Washington DC had been built along such lines and any idea that the British Parliament might cleave to republican ideals must be rejected.

Instead, it was decided from the outset that the new building must hark back to an earlier English age. It must be Elizabethan or Gothic in its form and it must incorporate those original buildings that had survived the fire. When the Royal Commission chosen for the task reported back in 1836, it chose a design submitted by the English architect Charles Barry.* The new building would be explicitly Gothic, although its design was underpinned by neoclassical conceptions of symmetry, with a great tower at its centre, another tower, a clock tower, at its eastern end and a dazzling river frontage created partly on land reclaimed from the Thames. Barry had chosen his prospective design well and, significantly, he had chosen his collaborator well too. He had asked Augustus Pugin, at this point still resident at Salisbury but at the age of twenty-three already gaining a reputation for the clarity of his vision, to contribute ideas for the internal design and form of the new building. Pugin did not let him down, adding his own distinctive touches in the form of a cornucopia of vanes, spires and other Gothic motifs. Construction began in 1839.

Pugin had been instrumental in the choice of building but until 1846 he played no further part in its construction. It was not until the scheme threatened to spin

* Barry, passing in his coach, had seen the fire too, and had rubbed his hands as he proclaimed, 'What a chance for an architect.'

entirely out of Barry's control that Pugin was summonsed back to work. At every stage, the vast project had attracted controversy and even malice. Barry was taxed almost to defeat by his struggle over the vast contrivance responsible for blowing hot air through the Palace and which threatened the new building once more with incineration. The Commons and Lords clashed on the matter. In the midst of this crisis and faced with understandable press ridicule, Barry lost his prime government supporter when Peel was felled in the aftermath of the repeal of the Corn Laws. At this nadir in his fortunes, Barry implored the return of Pugin. Formally he became 'Superintendent of Wood Carving' but this title, for which he was paid a pittance, utterly fails to capture the centrality of his role.

When his association with the developing building was at length renewed, Pugin set to work to fill the vast building with his own vision of carvings and gilt, panelling and a range of furniture. His attention to detail knew no bounds. Even the door knobs were bespoke by Pugin and those with an eye for such things understood that the real architect in this gargantuan project was not Barry, but Pugin himself. Charles Voysey remarked it was considered 'an acknowledged fact that Mr Pugin was the real Architect of the Houses of Parliament'. Pugin himself felt obliged to issue a refutal:

A misconception prevails as to the nature of my employment in the works of the new palace of Westminster ... In fulfilling the duties of my office, I do not do anything whatever on my own responsibility; all models and working drawings being prepared from Mr Barry's designs and submitted to him for his approval or alterations prior to their being carried into effect. In fine, my occupation is simply to assist in carrying out practically Mr Barry's own designs and views in all respects.

Pugin was clearly constrained by the needs of diplomacy, because it is very evident that he was no mere dogsbody in the process. The respective roles of Pugin and Barry would later become an unseemly feud. A generation later, a new wave of Pugins and Barrys would publicly squabble over what recognition was deserved by whom for the Palace.

In any case, in 1847 Pugin received no invitation to the inauguration of the House of Lords, the first phase of the building to be completed. Not that Pugin sought much in the way of adulation from the project. He went to Italy at the time so he deliberately avoided the event. It is impossible to know for certain the facts in this case. What is clear, however, is the lack of attention his work received at the time. This almost certainly had something to do with his very visible Catholicism. The renewal of the Catholic Hierarchy in England and Wales had, after all, occasioned the last strong outburst of anti-Catholic prejudice in the country. Thus it makes sad sense that Britain's most famous Catholic should be barred from receiving plaudits that were his due for designing the nation's Parliament. In any case, Pugin certainly has had the last laugh. For while the exterior of Parliament, Barry's testament, may not quite deserve Pugin's famous quip of 'All Grecian, sir; Tudor details on a classic body', anyone who steps inside the building can see the wonders that have been achieved.

Indeed, Barry freely admitted, not least by beseeching his draughtsman from the distant days of competition success to return to the fray, that 'only Pugin could have done what Pugin did'. Pugin's work received a Royal imprimatur too. Prince Albert himself chaired the Royal Commission on Fine Art which oversaw the interior decoration of Parliament. Shrewsbury was another member and neither the Prince nor the Earl had any doubt that only one man in the country could manage the vast work in wood, glass, metal, furniture, upholstery, lighting, wallpaper, tiling and decorative schemes which the new Palace needed before it could be finished. That man was Pugin.

Latent anti-Catholic feeling continued to linger in the country and it appeared once more in Augustine Pugin's career, this time amid the glittering surroundings of the Crystal Palace. Prince Albert's awareness of Pugin meant that his presence at the Great Exhibition of 1851[*] could be no real surprise.

Yet in Protestant England suspicion of Rome could erupt, geyser-like, at any hour and in any place, even within the Crystal Palace. One such eruption occurred over Pugin's conception of a 'Medieval Court', planned as a star exhibit at the Great Exhibition and consisting of a deeply atmospheric display of ecclesiastical furnishings, Marian statues, metalwork, textiles and sculpture. In truth, he was not enthusiastic about the Crystal Palace, which he dismissed as a 'glass bubble'. He dismissively told its designer Joseph Paxton, 'You had better keep to building greenhouses and I will keep to my churches and

---

[*] See chapter on Prince Albert.

cathedrals.' It was not only the glassy surroundings that ought, by rights, to have repelled Pugin and prevented him from going near Hyde Park that summer. The Great Exhibition was in its essence a thrusting display of technological wonders and the power of modernity, neither of them ideas which pleased such a man as Pugin.

Most of all, the *scheme of organisation* for exhibits at the Crystal Palace was the antithesis of everything Pugin believed. That in itself should have prevented him from taking part. It was all divided into categories and in the applied arts all was subdivided by material. Instead of Pugin's transcendent idea of the unified, Christian whole, there was a form of ghastly material division, the opposite of everything he stood for when it was housed in a building of which he despaired. Where for others the Crystal Palace represented a staggering achievement of British ingenuity and engineering, to Pugin this glazed cathedral of man erected in months had all the demerits of something which had manifestly *not* taken centuries to build and did *not* serve God.

Perhaps the lure was simply too much. To assemble a showcase of medievalism, its beauty and sacred meaning set off by the false and profane sparkle of its surroundings, was too glorious a chance to pass up. Thus, in that inevitable, truly Victorian way, Pugin broke the rules. He pitched his idea, he was accepted and he triumphed. No artist at the Great Exhibition was supposed by rights to be individually named and certainly none was supposed to do what his Medieval Court did. Certainly none was supposed to insert Catholicism, of all faiths, into this pagan milieu. No wonder some critics and viewers were scandalised, some claiming that this shameless Catholic architect was brazenly attempting to insert a Papist chapel into the heart of the Crystal Palace, complete with a statue of the Virgin and Child. How much more outraged they would be when Pugin's exhibit was among the greatest successes of the hugely successful Exhibition. The claims of craftsmanship, care, devotion, all triumphed in the age of the machine and it was for this that Pugin received full laud and honour. It was his crowning glory.

Unfortunately the story of Pugin does not end with his note of glory, for the details of how his life ended are miserable. In February 1852, while on a train bound for London, Pugin suffered a catastrophic mental breakdown. He arrived in the capital unable to speak and seemingly unable to recognise his friends and family. By June he had entered Bedlam, the Royal Bethlem lunatic asylum adjacent to his own Catholic cathedral of St George's, Southwark. By September he seemed to have recovered sufficiently to be removed to The Grange at Ramsgate but recovery was impossible. He died at Ramsgate on 14 September and is buried at St Augustine's.

*

Fortunately, Pugin's legacy ripples across the years and the continents. The great Victorian architect George Gilbert Scott was, as we have noted, deeply influenced by Pugin's ideology. His Gothic buildings include such fine and dispersed examples as the Midland Grand Hotel at St Pancras in London, the eponymous Anglican cathedral at Christchurch in New Zealand, which is due to be recreated after its destruction by earthquake, and Holy Trinity at Shanghai in China. All of these can trace in their lines and ornamentation a direct link back to Pugin. In Pugin's own Ramsgate, Gilbert Scott designed Christ Church. It is profoundly Puginesque, though erected by public subscription as a furious Anglican riposte to Pugin's feared Romanising tendencies. Scott later insisted that the dead architect must be commemorated on the relief at the base of the Albert Memorial in London. Pugin's son Edward, meanwhile, created the soaring Gothic cathedral overlooking the harbour at Cobh (then Queenstown) in Ireland and scores of other buildings which owe their provenance to his father.

In *The Stones of Venice*, published in 1851, a year before Pugin's death, John Ruskin damned him as 'not a great architect but one of the smallest possible or conceivable architects'. Although his words were condemned, they cast a shadow over Pugin's legacy that could not readily be dispelled. A century and more later, the august historian and broadcaster Kenneth Clark mourned Ruskin's malign influence on the future, noting acidly, 'If Ruskin had never lived, Pugin would never have been forgotten.' Indeed, it is only in these latter years that Pugin's lasting influence had been acknowledged and honoured. The shape he gave to his buildings transferred to the shape that Britain herself assumed in the national psyche, lending his work a potency that none of his contemporaries can possibly match.

As for Pugin himself, perhaps he outstrips Ruskin in negativity, for he was his own worst critic. He felt his work to be uneven and erratic and he came to despise many of his early and best commissions. In 1850 he lamented, 'I can truly say that I have been compelled to commit absolute suicide with every building in which I have been engaged, and I have good proof that they are little better than ghosts of what they were designed [sic].' Time shows what his inordinately busy and productive life rendered obscure to his own eyes. He created a body of work never seen in the Middle Ages themselves but which was as honest and coherent as anything done in that deep past. Pugin took the language of the past and placed it in the service of the present and in doing so he created marvels which affect our lives profoundly if Churchill's famous quip 'we shape our buildings; thereafter they shape us' is to be believed.

The purpose of his writing, his drawing, his rhetoric was clear, honest, open, evident. It was to serve a higher purpose and never simply the purposes of a profane human life. A sight of his life and work shows a man who could only ever have been what he was because he had a cause greater than himself. His achievement is all around, rising effortlessly above the sniping of the critics then and since. His punishing life reveals much about the self-sacrifice being a Victorian so often involved and the price he paid was made manifest in the words spoken at the funeral celebrated in the Ramsgate church he himself had built:

zelus domus tuae comedit me.
Zeal for thy house has consumed me.

Albert: Behind the Throne

Prince Albert of Saxe-Coburg and Gotha, Prince Consort
of the United Kingdom (26 August 1819–14 December
1861) is a central figure in the story of Victorian Britain.
He stands at the side of Queen Victoria in any number
of paintings from the age the loyal and devoted husband,
the father of the Royal couple's nine children, the grandfather of kings and queens and dukes and empresses the
length and breadth of Europe. The patron of a host of
worthy causes, the power and energy behind the Great
Exhibition of 1851, the campaigner against slavery,
the diplomat, the crusader, the architect, the tentative
liberal. The lonely and distressed child of a shattered
marriage in a minor German duchy, who became almost
the de facto king of another realm. The man who held
no official power at any point in his life, who upon
marriage was denied even the governance of his own
household, who was scorned as a foreign carpetbagger
but who went on to wield extraordinary influence as
the partner and equal in what had to be a profoundly
unequal union. All this, plus any number of assassination attempts with which to contend. Albert emerges

from history as a Renaissance man and as a thoroughly dutiful individual.

*

Sometimes and in some circumstances it is best to be an outsider. To be the stranger, new to a nation, a family, or a firm. The newcomer must work hard to learn and adapt. He or she might be put in a gruelling situation or expected to take on unfamiliar tasks immediately. In every case, the process of adapting to a new set of circumstances, to a new culture, will take time. The trick is, sometimes, not to let the strain show, to present a certain comfortable face to the world and not to show weakness.

It is necessary to make the best of the situation, to take the freshness of the circumstances, to turn it to the best possible end. As well as to remember this lesson, that it can be easier for outsiders than for those born into a given context to take stock of a situation and to recognise that the status quo can and sometimes must change profoundly and swiftly.

This inevitably leads to a famous consort of the Victorian era, a representative of minor German royalty who married a youthful Queen Victoria and installed himself, or found himself installed, at the centre of the British Royal Family. The presence of such a man had the effect of introducing new energy to the House of Hanover at a moment when such an infusion was most necessary. From the Royal Family, Albert's influence spilled out into wider British society, leaving a mark on everything from culture to science to the public realm. All this was in the course of a life in Britain that lasted a scant two decades. Who was this minor princeling and what influences and philosophies drove him on?

*

Prince Francis Albert Augustus Charles Emmanuel, of the House of Saxe-Coburg and Gotha, was born on 26 August 1819 in Schloss Rosenau, near the town of Coburg in the historic Franconia district of what is now northern Bavaria. The Schloss and its estate had been in the possession of the Coburgs since the middle of the eighteenth century. Debts occasioned its sale but in 1805 the family repurchased it and commissioned a well-known Prussian architect, Karl Friedrich Schinkel, to mastermind its splendid redesign.

There was nothing remarkable in this. The Coburgs were a venerable family and one of the dynasties that held sway over the myriad minor German dukedoms before the consolidation of these patchwork territories into a German Empire later in the nineteenth century. There was little by way of actual grandeur or majesty in the family's circumstances. Albert's father, Ernest, Duke of Saxe-Coburg Gotha, ruled no empire, but rather a duchy less than half the size of Somerset, but the Duke had some right to a degree of pride. He had fought Napoleon, he was of an ancient lineage and was well connected and wealthy. He invested his riches in part in the enhancement of Coburg and of the duchy and in the interior of the Schloss itself, where his son grew up surrounded by an atmosphere of cultured beauty. As for the grounds at Rosenau, these were beautiful too, for they had been landscaped in the English picturesque style so popular in the Germany of the time.

Cultured beauty but not stability. The Duke's marriage to his kinswoman Princess Louise of Saxe-Gotha-Altenburg was not a happy one. They had two children but the Duke's infidelity put a strain on the relationship and Albert's mother followed her husband's example. The couple officially divorced in 1826. Louise had been banished from the household two years previously and after her departure, she never saw her children again. She died at Paris in August 1831.

Albert was close to his brother Ernest but his difficult, fractured childhood showed in aggression towards other children. He was not fortunate enough to enjoy a mother's love even though his father would marry again in 1832. For his formative years, Albert had no maternal presence in his life. Instead, he relied on the friendship and support of his tutor, Johann Christoph Florschütz, an intelligent, enlightened graduate of the University of Jena, whose influence was vital and long-lasting. From Florschütz, the young Albert learned the virtues of independent thinking and of hard work. He drove himself to succeed, writing in his journal at the age of eleven that he 'intended to train myself to be a good and useful man'. By the age of fourteen, he had adopted the habit of dividing his days into eight one-hour-long slots, the first beginning at 6 a.m. and the last ending at 8 p.m. He permitted himself a break between 1 and 5 p.m. which was scarcely a break at all as he used this period to study history, classical literature, French, English, mathematics and Latin composition, with vigorous games pursued outside during whatever time was left to spare. Albert was no idler but rather an exemplification of the daunting phrase *mens sana in corpore sano*, 'a healthy mind in a healthy body'. His studies were often interrupted by his father the Duke, to whom Albert was devoted, but his nature was nevertheless hard-working. The young Albert's habits of industry were to last to the end of his life.

Albert's education took him from Germany to the new kingdom of Belgium, ruled over by his uncle, and eventually back to Germany. Then, as was the custom for many German princes, he studied at the University of Bonn. This young man's ultimate destiny, if not quite established, was at least approximately delineated. As a member of a European Royal house, Albert was expected to marry a fellow Royal. The continental nobility was astonishingly self-regarding. This was his duty and there is no indication that he ever questioned the general form his future life would take.

As for the marriage that was ultimately arranged for him, the key figure in bringing Albert and Victoria together was Leopold, King of the Belgians since 1831. As early as 1821, when both Albert and Victoria were a mere two years old, the idea of a useful dynastic union was being bandied about by relations on both sides. The two young people were already related by blood. They were first cousins, as Victoria's mother, Princess Victoria of Saxe-Coburg-Saalfeld, was Duke Ernest's sister and thus Albert's aunt. The case was, nominally at least, already set fair.

Leopold, however, can be credited for driving the idea forward. As brother of Princess Victoria and Duke Ernest, he was uncle to both Victoria and Albert, in the way of Europe's intricately related Royal houses, and he had accepted the newly created throne of Belgium, having previously rejected the throne of Greece. He had further connections. His first wife was Charlotte, daughter of George IV, who before her untimely death had been heir presumptive to the British throne. It can thus be safely inferred that Leopold knew more about dynastic marriage policy than anyone else in Europe.

Moreover, he was on excellent terms with all the principles in the case. Victoria told her journal delightedly that Leopold 'is so clever ... is indeed like my real father, as I have none, and he is so kind and so good to me'. He was assiduous in keeping in touch with her, no doubt partly out of genuine avuncular affection but also because he knew that she would, in due course, become the Queen of the United Kingdom. It should be added that Leopold was a great one for interfering. Victoria would, in the future, sharply rein in this tendency, although she would continue both to admire him and to remain fond of him. She once said that hearing 'dear uncle speak on any subject is like reading a highly instructive book; his conversation is so enlightened and clear'.

Leopold was thus in a good lobbying position when the question of Victoria's marriage arose. A sort of beauty parade of eligible suitors was arranged for the gratified Victoria, with the choice coming down to, on the one hand, Prince Albert, and on the other the equally eligible Prince Alexander of the Netherlands, who was the preferred choice of her uncle, King William IV. This was in 1836, when Victoria was barely seventeen years old and Albert sixteen.

Leopold now worked assiduously to bring about the marriage, conspiring with Victoria's governess, Baroness

Louise Lehzen, to pave the way for an alliance. Victoria immediately seemed to warm to Albert, describing him as 'extremely handsome; his hair is about the same colour as mine; his eyes are large and blue, and he has a beautiful nose and a very sweet mouth with fine teeth'. She was less enamoured of Alexander, noting that the '[Netherlander] boys are very plain ... moreover they look heavy, dull, and frightened, and are not at all prepossessing'. Albert was less enraptured by the beauty pageant in which he was forced to participate. He objected in particular to having to stay up late for an assortment of entertainments. Moreover, he disliked, as some visitors do, the generally delightful nature of the British climate. These onerous duties eventually ended and Victoria and Albert did not meet again for three years.

Leopold in the meantime continued his matchmaking. On their second meeting, Victoria was as delighted as ever with her German prince. It was with some emotion, she told her journal, 'that I beheld Albert – who is beautiful'. Victoria's status had changed fundamentally in the course of the intervening years. Her uncle the King was now dead and she was the Queen of the United Kingdom, probably the most important person in the world. Victoria had a close relationship with her first Prime Minister, the Whig Lord Melbourne. He spent a great deal of time counselling the Queen in the ways of rule and government. This was constitutionally proper as well as personally agreeable and now she sought Melbourne's guidance on her marriage.

His advice to her was fair and frank. He warned the Queen that the Coburg family was unpopular in Europe, adding bluntly that her own difficult mother, with whom the young Queen had a complicated relationship, was a fair specimen of them. The Russians hated the family and, to cap it all, Melbourne added that the British public was nervous of foreigners. He also reminded her that Albert was, after all, her own first cousin. Against this list of disadvantages there were no other suitable Protestant Royal suitors and Victoria herself was reluctant to marry a subject, noting, as she put it squeamishly to Melbourne, 'marrying a subject was making yourself so much their equal, and brought you so in contact with the whole family.' When all was said and done, it was clear that Albert was the obvious choice.

Hence, Victoria proposed to Albert while they were out riding at Windsor. Albert accepted but elements within the nation were less enthusiastic, their disdain for what was taken to be Albert's ungentlemanly motives summed up in this mean little stanza: 'Here comes the bridegroom of Victoria's choice, the nominee of Lehzen's voice; he comes to take "for better or for worse" England's fat Queen and England's fatter purse.' Albert was viewed correctly as the most minor of royalty and less fairly as an impoverished grasper intent on rising in the world and with Catholic relations to boot. It was not a good beginning.

Nor, in the short term, did matters improve for the Prince. Parliament would not vote through the usual grant of £50,000 per annum out of the Civil List. Albert's allowance was cut to £30,000, though this was more to do with Parliament's hostility to Melbourne, who ran a minority Whig administration, than to any dislike of Albert. In addition, Victoria could not persuade Melbourne, or anyone else for that matter, that Albert ought to have the title of King Consort. Such a move would have required an Act of Parliament. In the sixteenth century, Philip II of Spain had required such an Act to assume the role of formal King Consort to Mary I and in the seventeenth, William of Orange had required a similar measure to assume the role of formal King Consort to Mary II. In both cases, Parliament had obliged but in this case Victoria was forced to accept that neither Parliament nor people would clasp Albert to their bosoms any time soon. 'The English,' she wrote gloomily, 'are very jealous at the idea of Albert having any political power or meddling with affairs.'

Thus foiled, Victoria tried a new strategy. Albert might not be King Consort but at least his rank and precedence would for ever be preserved and now Victoria put pressure on Parliament to pass the necessary legislation so 'that the Prince, for his life, was to take precedence in rank after Her Majesty, in Parliament and elsewhere, as Her Majesty may think fit and proper, any law to the contrary notwithstanding'. Alas for Victoria, Parliament declined this measure too and in the end the Queen determined his precedence by means of letters patent, which could not affect the statutory rules of the House of Lords or the Privy Council.*

This was a difficult beginning and such a parade of quarrels, petty, party political but unrelenting, cannot have made Albert's early introduction into British life very amusing. He was also not granted a peerage and here we catch a rare glimpse of Albert's vexation. His

---

* The present Queen did the same for the Duke of Edinburgh, who takes precedence over the Prince of Wales by letters patent.

tart response was that a British peerage would be a humiliation and 'almost a step downwards, for as a Duke of Saxony, I feel myself much higher than a Duke of York or Kent'. At length, however, the squabbling ended. Victoria and Albert were married in the Chapel Royal at St James's Palace on 10 February 1840 and Albert became a naturalised subject of his wife.

*

Initially, Victoria was not keen to allow Albert a role in her official life. Even before they were married, the Queen had made clear to Albert that her duty must come first. He proposed a long honeymoon, maintaining that the usual custom in England was 'for newly married people to stay up to four or six weeks away from town and society'. The Queen would have none of it. 'I am the Sovereign,' she told him, 'and that business can stop and wait for nothing. Parliament is sitting and something occurs almost every day, for which I may be required, and it is quite impossible for me to be absent from London; therefore 2–3 days is already a long time to be absent.' Upon their return to London, moreover, the Queen made it clear that she preferred to continue her conversations on matters of state with Melbourne and not to involve Albert.

Just the same, Albert provided early proof of his intention to create a role for himself and to bring energy and focus to his work. One significant indication of this was his agreement to become President of the Society for the Extinction of Slavery and for the Civilisation of Africa, which had been established in 1839. Then, as now, members of the Royal Family took on honorific roles to add lustre to an organisation and to help it attract wider support. Albert was clear that he wanted to be more than an ornament. At London's Exeter Hall in June 1840, within a few months of marriage, he made an anti-slavery speech in front of several thousand people, including the greatest luminaries in the land.

'I deeply regret,' Albert said, 'that the benevolent and persevering exertions of England to abolish the atrocious traffic in human beings ... have not led to a satisfactory conclusion. I sincerely trust that this great country will not relax in its efforts until it has finally and for ever put an end to a state of things so repugnant to the principles of Christianity and to the best feelings of our nature.' Sir Robert Peel responded to the Prince. These were honourable and courageous words and they showed Albert's personal courage too, for he was not yet twenty-one years old and was moreover speaking in English, a language in which he was not proficient. Most importantly, it provided evidence to all observers that the new Prince Consort was there to work, and to show what he could do.

At home too Albert was demonstrating a will to succeed. He wished to be the formal head of his Household, even if his wife was the formal head of the nation. At first, neither the Queen nor Baroness Lehzen acceded to his wish. Lehzen ran the Household and Albert complained he hated Lehzen, referring to her variously as a 'hag' and the 'House Dragon'. His dislike of her was fully reciprocated so that although he was content in his marriage, 'the difficulty in filling my place with the proper dignity is that I am only the husband, not the master in the house'. Matters soon moved in Albert's direction. Within two months of the marriage, Victoria was pregnant and Parliament agreed, in a decided and rapid change of attitude to the Prince Consort, to pass a Regency Act. Under its terms, in the event of Victoria's death Albert would act as regent until their child came of age. Meanwhile, his coolness under fire had already been noted and admired not least because in June 1840, in the first of many assassination attempts, he and the pregnant Victoria had been shot at by a gunman during a carriage ride on Constitution Hill and he acted with courage. Albert was building his position.

All this took time and such a state of affairs must have been quite humiliating for a proud man who held a traditional view of manly duties and whose wife had promised to obey him in their wedding ceremony. In a sign of the tiny duties which, at the beginning of the marriage, *were* permitted him, the Queen recorded that 'Albert helped me with the blotting paper when I signed.' She remarked to Melbourne that Albert was keen always to discuss matters of state, while 'when I am with the Prince I prefer talking on other subjects'. By November, Albert had received a key to state boxes of papers but this was a small first step rather than full entry into affairs of state. This entry came at last because Albert quietly made himself invaluable.

Victoria's close relationship with Melbourne had the effect of creating a prickly, almost hostile relationship with the Prime Minister's opposite number, Sir Robert Peel. This led to the first and most serious constitutional row of her reign, when the Queen refused to allow Sir Robert, when offered the deal of forming a government in 1839, to substitute a number of Ladies of the Bed-chamber. By convention such ladies were selected from the great Tory or Whig families, depending on who was in government.

The situation rapidly became a crisis. Peel, deciding that he did not have his Sovereign's confidence without this tangible sign of it, refused to serve as Prime Minister. The episode became known as the 'Bedchamber Crisis' and is the last time that a Monarch's whim prevented a government being formed. When the same situation arose in 1841 following a General Election which had given Peel a majority, Albert recognised the greater constitutional dangers even if Victoria herself did not. He stepped in to make discreet contact with Peel to suggest a resolution. Albert's arrangement was designed to save his wife's face. Peel would indicate which ladies he would like to see depart, at which point the Queen herself would ask for their resignations. It would, in other words, not be *Peel's* work but the decision of the Queen, maintaining her dignity but also ensuring her visible support for the government of the day which had just won an election.

Albert's developing role was also helped by Melbourne's political defeat. The Queen had become so close to this Whig stateman that arguably there was little room for Albert to develop a political or constitutional role. With Melbourne now out of office Victoria was suddenly in urgent need of a private secretary, a confidant, a friend. Albert was there to fill the gap and Melbourne himself now recognised this fact and encouraged Albert's promotion. The political stars were in alignment too, for Albert's waxing role was further enhanced by his friendship with Peel, who became something of a father figure to him as Melbourne had been to Victoria. As Victoria and Melbourne had discussed the issues of the day while out riding so now Albert and Peel debated philosophy and German literature as they hunted together in Windsor Great Park. Albert now had what he had hitherto lacked: an English mentor. Peel also brought the young Prince into his political confidence. He began sending Albert confidential memorandums on the issues of the day such as a response to the 1834 Poor Law, which was not working especially well.

There were dangers implicit in such a relationship. As Victoria's close links with Melbourne had caused observers to frown, so Albert's all-too-evident partisanship in favour of Peel caused occasional problems and sometimes Albert erred. This was especially noticeable during the repeal of the Corn Laws. The Prince's appearance, in January 1846, in the public gallery of the House of Commons to listen to Peel's opening speech in favour of repeal has been mentioned before and was a great error. At a time when politicians knew their history well, the Prince's appearance would have been deeply shocking and it is little surprise that Lord George Bentinck attacked him for it. The Chamber of the House of Commons is forbidden to the Sovereign. The only one to have attempted an entry was Charles I when trying to arrest the five members. For the Queen's Consort to visit and offer tacit support for the radical policy of Peel was a mistake that Albert would never repeat. He kept his support at a distance, confiding his thoughts to his diary and writing privately, often at considerable length, to Peel offering counsel and support.

Albert's influence grew, not by Royal command but because he demonstrated that he was an able and intelligent man, who was willing to put in the necessary work. If anything, Albert worked too hard. As her de facto private secretary, he provided notes for the Queen on all important papers. In both Buckingham Palace and Windsor, Victoria and Albert had their desks set side by side so as to be able to work together more conveniently. He drafted letters for her and filed all her papers with brisk efficiency in an almost cartoonish German stereotype. These papers, now a dauntingly voluminous archive, consist of hundreds of bound volumes detailing correspondence, meetings, even press cuttings. Such work must have been immeasurably time-consuming and those volumes illustrate Albert's appetite for work. This may have been his nature but it also made him indispensable to Victoria. After all, she was a person who would never willingly delegate any aspect of her work, a tendency demonstrated later in the reign when she refused to pass on any part of her role to her heir, the future Edward VII. With Albert, she was willing and eager to work hand in glove for the very good reason that she loved and trusted him.

There would be further battles in store, ones that Albert had to fight and win in order to assert his importance and position. The issue of courtly extravagance is a good example. This was a pressing and notorious problem but one to be handled delicately. As Peel noted, a measure of extravagance was in some ways *expected*. A great many people welcomed the sight of a generous and munificent Court, even if this generosity was taken to absurd extremes. All candles at Court were replaced daily, even unused ones, which were sold off as 'palace ends' with the money going to servants. Equally silly was the Red Room wine payment. This existed because wine had been served to the Guard in the Red Room at Windsor during the reign of George III and the payment continued even though the actual practice of serving wine had ceased.

These and countless other minor frauds were carried on throughout the Royal Household, much to Albert's chagrin. As long as Baroness Lehzen continued in charge, however, he was able to do nothing to stamp them out but when the opportunity arose to dispense with her services he seized the chance. Victoria gave birth to a girl, the Princess Victoria, in November 1840 and for some time the Household ran along as usual. In the spring of 1841, however, the child fell ill when her care fell to servants and physicians appointed by Lehzen and Albert soon became convinced of their incompetence. He pressed for change and for control over the situation. Victoria resisted but as Vicky's health declined further, the Prince confronted his wife, declaring that if she persisted in her support of Lehzen and if Vicky died as a result, it would be Victoria's responsibility.

By now alarmed and fearing that their daughter would die, Victoria relented. Albert assumed charge of the nursery and Princess Victoria's medical care and the child's health improved. Soon after, Lehzen departed for Germany, retiring on the grounds of her health. She remained in touch with Victoria and was given a generous annual pension of £300, which she enjoyed for the remaining thirty years of her life. It is important to note that Albert wanted control not merely for its own sake, nor to assert his position, nor for the avoidance of the chronic waste and extravagance he saw all around him but to introduce what he considered healthier and more hygienic conditions for his child. Of the Royal couple's nine children, all survived childhood. This was unusual in Victorian Britain.

Not that Albert felt satisfied by being only a state adviser and domestic moderniser. In this context his presidency of the Society for the Extinction of Slavery was not an isolated example but should instead be seen as part of a pattern of major and expanding public endeavours. He became President of the Fine Art Commission, which was charged with the decoration and beautification of the new Palace of Westminster, following the fire that had destroyed the previous building in 1834. The Prince worked closely on this scheme with his friend and counsellor Robert Peel. The master vision for the building was to turn it into a treasure house of art as much as into a crucible of political life. Augustus Pugin worked to bring this master vision scintillatingly to life.

The Prince played a key role in this great endeavour. The original idea was to create a palace of frescos chronicling British national life. The damp climate put paid to this founding vision, for the frescos would not adhere correctly to dank, chilly stone. Instead it was decided to paint the pictures in oils on fabric. It was understood that this would be an enormous national undertaking, of years' duration. It is interesting to note that this aspect of the process of decoration, which was still underway when Albert died in 1861, then lost much of its impetus and was concluded as late as 2010 when the

Armada paintings, based on sixteenth-century tapestries destroyed in the fire, were hung in the Prince's Chamber within the Palace. One of them had been created in the nineteenth century but it is important to record that completion of the remainder was made possible only by means of a generous donation by the American philanthropist Mark Pigott OBE, who is worthily commemorated in one of the paintings.

Prince Albert would continue to display this distinctively hands-on approach throughout his career. In 1852, upon the death of the Duke of Wellington, Albert succeeded to the mastership of the venerable Trinity House, a corporation dating back to 1514 which worked, and continues to work today, for the safety and welfare of mariners, among other charitable and maritime functions. Albert used his first speech at the corporation's Annual Banquet to call for more charitable support for retired or superannuated warriors, and for greater preparedness for war. He noted that the United Kingdom did not operate conscription to its armed forces, unlike its continental neighbours. The clear implication of his speech was that this was a risk. The Trinity House speech demonstrates the growth of Albert's advocacy and the development of his vision of his role over the intervening years. From questions of painting and beautification, he was offering opinions on issues at the very centre of national life and critical to the nation's security and future. He was happy to adapt what seemed to be merely ceremonial posts to advance his ideas.

*

The Prince Consort is perhaps best remembered, both in Britain and abroad, for his support of the Great Exhibition, that gargantuan demonstration of human culture and technology which ran for six glorious months in 1851. The 'Great Exhibition of the Works of Industry of all Nations' was the Exhibition's official title. The cultural achievements and technological prowess of many peoples were on display beneath the splendid glazed roof of the Crystal Palace in London's Hyde Park but this was pre-eminently a *British* showcase, a stage for *British* glory. It afforded the nation the opportunity to gaze at its own achievements and its own modernity and, what was even better, to have these achievements absorbed and wondered at by a collection of visitors and a new contemporary media.

Without doubt, this was Albert's dream and his vision made manifest.

The idea that the Prince merely lent his support to the Great Exhibition falls far short of the truth. Without Albert's drive and determination the Exhibition could simply not have happened, and, without the maintenance of this support, the multifarious difficulties encountered during the development phase could not have been overcome.

The idea of an exhibition had grown in Albert's mind over many years. As a child, he had taken pleasure in visits to the fairs of nearby Frankfurt. Later, he watched as the idea of 'expositions' of national industry took wing across Europe. In particular, he had along with a great many other people observed the success of the Paris Exposition, held on the Champs-Élysées in 1849. The news of the Parisian spectacle was carried to him by his friend Henry Cole, a leading light of the newly created Public Record Office. Cole was a man with quite as much energy as Albert himself and he is credited with everything from the introduction of a British reformed postal service and the creation of the penny post to the invention of the Christmas card. One of his prime interests was industrial design and with the backing of Albert as its first patron, he was instrumental in granting a royal charter and patronage to form a Royal Society for the Encouragement of Arts, Manufactures and Commerce. Three modest exhibitions followed in London in 1847, 1848 and 1849 and it did not escape the attention either of Cole or Albert himself that attendance at the last of these reached an impressive 100,000 people.

Cole had delighted in the Paris Exposition but he noticed too the failure of its organisers to allow for foreign exhibition space which he saw as a golden opportunity. Back in London, he related to Albert his notion of creating an international exposition, one that would be a great deal larger, more complex and more ambitious than anything Paris could put together. Albert was especially attracted by this explicitly international dimension and taking Cole's idea, he proposed that this new event would take place in 1851. It would be quite different, a vast exhibition, the largest the world had yet seen. A Royal Commission for the Exhibition of 1851 was put in place and now the scene was set.

'Nobody,' Albert declared, 'who has paid any attention to the peculiar features of our present era, will doubt for a moment that we are living at a period of most wonderful transition, which tends rapidly to accomplish that great end, to which, indeed, all history points – the realisation of the unity of mankind.' Albert's pride and ambition were evident here for all to see but so was a sense of idealism. The Exhibition, *his* Exhibition, would bring the world into a greater and closer union, with Britain as that union's focus and centre.

The scope of the exhibition decided on by Albert was amazingly ambitious. So too was its daunting time frame but Albert was not to be discouraged. To set the ball rolling, he sent Cole and John Scott Russell, who was the Secretary of the Society of Arts, travelling around the country to see what interest there might be in the project. Albert gave them a personal letter of introduction which inevitably opened most doors and Cole reported that 5,000 eminent people were willing to back the Prince's idea. To put it into practice a Royal Commission was established and funds had to be raised. The financier Lionel de Rothschild, a scion of the famous banking family, was one of the treasurers, figures from a wide range of industries were commissioners and soon the funds were flowing in.

It set to work quickly, as it needed to, for it was only formed on 3 January 1850 and fundraising steamed ahead as the House of Commons had resolved that the money ought to come from the voluntary contributions of individuals, rather than from the public revenue. The first subscriber was the Queen, who donated £1,000, Prince Albert £500, the Prime Minister, Lord John Russell, £100, Sir Charles Wood, the Chancellor of the Exchequer, £100 and many others, including Lionel de Rothschild himself, who gave £500, ten times more than the Governor of the Bank of England, who only managed £50.

Fundraising, as it happened, would be the easy bit. As the opening day approached, the critics took to the warpath. The first proposed site for the Exhibition was Leicester Square, in the heart of London's West End. This site was then judged too small and the venue was moved to Hyde Park, causing MPs to fret publicly about the fate of the park's trees. The Ultra Tory Colonel Charles Sibthorp became an unlikely tree hugger, as he denounced the Exhibition scheme as 'the greatest trash, the greatest fraud, and the greatest imposition ever attempted to be palmed upon the people of this country'. He disliked what he saw as its essential *foreignness*; he also, though the war over the virtues of free trade had been lost, voiced a fear that the Exhibition would be a catalyst for a flood of cheap imports that would damage the domestic economy.

Punch magazine, then in its heyday, saw scope for much satire. It called for the turf in Hyde Park to be sold off to help pay for the cost of the building. It was, after all, about to be pulverised by hordes of visitors and turned to mud. Unkind cartoons rained down on the Royal couple, who were correctly identified as the driving force behind the Exhibition. This did not much please Albert, who was sensitive to ridicule. *The Times* thundered energetically against the project, predicting that Hyde Park would become the 'bivouac of all the vagabonds of London'. The newspaper was so extremely and notoriously hostile to the scheme that 150 years later the *Daily Telegraph* was able to identify a thread in history and tease *The Times* about its opposition to the creation of the Millennium Dome.

In the end and in spite of this fundraising industry, the costs associated with establishing the Exhibition did overrun. The overall cost amounted to £169,998, a tremendous sum at this time and at least a third higher than expected. On the other hand a number of other mistakes were sidestepped smoothly. The Building Committee of the Royal Commission initially came up with a proposal to create a neoclassical building to be composed of nineteen million bricks and topped by a dome designed by Isambard Kingdom Brunel. It was not ugly but restrained to the point of dullness and so unpopular that even Albert feared an exhibition housed in such a building could not succeed. It was the great crisis of this entire project.

Fortunately, the inspirational landscape gardener Joseph Paxton came to the rescue. Paxton was responsible, as the Duke of Devonshire's head gardener, for major works in the park at Chatsworth. Paxton had become interested in greenhouse design. He had taken on the conservation of the estate's dilapidated glasshouses and the design and creation of innovative new models.

Now, with the Great Exhibition looming, Paxton initially sketched out an idea on a piece of blotting paper at a meeting in the boardroom of the Midland Railway which he then published in the *Illustrated London News.* It was a plan of a revolutionary light-filled structure of glass, wood and steel. It was to be a building of beauty and one of the most innovative designs of the nineteenth century. The Exhibition, at a stroke, had a home, an enormous home with 293,655 panes of glass. It was 1,848 feet long, not quite managing the 1,851 feet Paxton had hoped to achieve for symbolic reasons, but nonetheless three times the length of St Paul's Cathedral. Four and a half thousand tonnes of iron and thirty-nine miles of piping were used. Six horses raised the seventy-two-feet-long girders which had been tested to hold fifteen tonnes each into place and 2,000 men worked on the site, incidentally drinking 250 gallons of beer, or a pint each, when Albert visited. The Great Exhibition was inaugurated by Victoria and Albert on 1 May 1851 and now *The Times* rapidly changed its tune, exulting, in words that Albert himself might have selected, that this London morning was the first 'since the creation of the world that all people have assembled from all parts of the world and done a common act'. The Royal couple stood centre stage, the Archbishop of Canterbury led a prayer of thanksgiving. The building itself was filled to overflowing with the evidence of British technological prowess: cotton-spinning machines and printing machines, locomotives and telegraphs, steam turbines and steam hammers, carpets from Axminster and ribbons from Coventry. Parts of the displays were lit brilliantly by the British stained glass that lined the upper galleries. And as if to welcome all comers with emblems of the energy driving the British industrial miracle, a twenty-four-ton lump of coal and a one-ton ingot of Sheffield steel had pride of place inside the Crystal Palace.

As Albert had wished, there was a strongly international flavour to the exhibits. The great Koh-i-Noor diamond, lately presented to the Queen by the East India Company, made its first appearance on British soil as did Ireland's eighth-century Tara Brooch, which had been rediscovered only in the previous year. There were rugs from Tunisia, statues from Belgium, carvings from Austria, a fire engine from Canada and a display of Colt firearms from the United States. France focused on luxury, despatching Sèvres porcelain, Limoges enamel and silks from Lyons. Chile sent gold and Russia malachite and porcelain vases.

The scene was memorialised by contemporary painters. David Roberts' *The Inauguration of the Great Exhibition, 1st May 1851* provides a tremendous image of the sheer scale of the Crystal Palace, with its curving roof, mature trees, wide galleries and balconies, crowds and swarming scenes of industry and pleasure. Franz Xaver Winterhalter's painting *The First of May 1851* portrays this moment as pivotal for the nation and the Royal Family. The aged Duke of Wellington offers a casket to Victoria, a birthday gift to the infant Prince Arthur, she holds in her arms, but Albert stands behind the Queen, gazing into the distance to where the Crystal Palace gleams under a sunburst. Most impressive of all, Henry Courtney Selous' *The Opening of the Great Exhibition by Queen Victoria on 1 May 1851* places the Queen, the Prince and their growing brood at the centre of an extraordinary tableau, as the galleries of the Crystal Palace rise tier upon glorious tier behind them.

The Exhibition was a triumph, which is not to say that tensions were absent. Issues in the world outside spilled into the Crystal Palace. For example, Albert's relationship with Palmerston, which was not strong in any case, became worse as a result of what was perceived to be the Prince's championing of Prussian ties with Britain. Albert was not explicitly able to support Prussia but he could use other channels. Later, he and Victoria would marry their eldest child Vicky off to Prince Frederick William, future heir to the Prussian throne, in an attempt to cement the relationship between Prussia and Britain. Meanwhile, he merely used the Great Exhibition to push forward

Prussian exhibits, Prussian diplomats and thus Prussian interests, much to Palmerston's vexation. Nevertheless, Victoria could say that the Exhibition's opening day was 'one of the greatest and most glorious days of our lives'. Enormous crowds turned out on that first day. The only error on the first day was that a Chinese man in traditional robes was thought to be part of the ceremony but even that was a happy mistake in retrospect. Vast crowds continued to come, with over six million visitors making their way to Hyde Park before the Exhibition closed in October. Given that the total population of the United Kingdom was twenty-seven million at that time, of whom 6.5 million were in Ireland, these figures show that the event was a triumph. Thomas Cook's eponymous business, which started with trips for teetotallers,* brought 150,000 visitors to the Crystal Palace. In fact, cheap rail travel was as essential to the event's success as it had been to the construction phase. Fortunately, there was almost no crime and new-fangled public lavatories were laid on at a penny a time.

Albert could be forgiven for gloating in a letter to Frederick William of Prussia. He was able to reply smoothly to the King, who had been fretting about his security were he to attend the Exhibition. Albert replied that the monarch was quite at liberty to worry if he chose to do so, before mocking the expert opinions being circulated in Berlin. Such opinions were, as is so frequently the case, misconceived, suggested the Prince:

---

* The first trip was from Leicester to Loughborough to attend a temperance meeting.

Mathematicians have calculated that the Crystal Palace will blow down in the first strong gale; engineers that the galleries would crash in and destroy the visitors; political economists have prophesised a scarcity of food in London owing to the vast concourse of people; doctors that owing to so many races coming into contact with each other the Black Death of the Middle Ages would make its appearance as it did after the Crusades; moralists that England would be infected by all the scourges of the civilised and uncivilised world; theologians that this second Tower of Babel would draw upon it the vengeance of an offended God. I can give no guarantee against these perils, nor am I in a position to assume responsibility for the possibly menaced lives of your royal relatives.

Best of all, the Great Exhibition made a profit, a princely £160,000, which was invested in what would become known as *Albertopolis*, an area of South Kensington that housed world-class museums, including his namesake the V&A. It was also used to fund awards for industry, science and engineering which likewise continue to this day. There was a profit of a more immediate kind, for the first legacy of the Great Exhibition was to make the Royal Family immensely popular. People knew how hard Albert had worked on the project, even at the cost of his own health. The other commissioners and committees had done their bit but many questions were referred to Albert for final appeal. He had to exercise every skill he possessed as a diplomat too, such as halting mad schemes like the idea floated that the Hyde Park site ought to be surrounded by eight-feet-high railings for extra security.

All this was on top of the Prince's already heavy daily workload.

*

As popular as Albert now became, it was by no means all plain sailing for him. Neither Victoria nor Albert was especially enamoured of the colourful Palmerston, the second of the two key statesmen to figure in the early part of Victoria's reign, and this dislike also came with difficulty attached. Palmerston's attempt on the virtue of Miss Brand had sealed this dislike at the beginning of the enforced relationship between Palmerston and the Royal couple. Later, the tension was emphasised by what was perceived to be Palmerston's high-handed treatment of Victoria, especially his disinclination to await authorisation from the Queen for despatches sent in her name. Victoria and Albert were also appalled by the way in which Palmerston's support for radical causes in Europe during the 1848 Year of Revolutions was laid at their door. Palmerston was after all the Queen's minister and was acting notionally in her name. However, he was a popular politician and Albert was aware of the difficulties that would accompany a public falling-out.

The Prince was, however, not one to avoid a confrontation, especially when the dignity of the Queen appeared to be at stake. On the face of it Albert won the first round in 1850, during the Whig premiership of Lord John Russell. Albert agreed to a request for a meeting with Palmerston and read the politician the riot act, informing him that, although disagreements over policy were not insignificant, what mattered most of all was the failure to follow proper process and what was perceived to be Palmerston's arrogant treatment of the Queen. Palmerston agreed to a memorandum written by Prince Albert with the advice of Baron Stockmar, a German physician who had advised King Leopold of the Belgians and who was a regular confidant of Albert.

The document was intended to regularise the professional relationship between the Sovereign and her senior ministers. It declared that 'The least the Queen has a right to require of her minister is: 1) That he will distinctly state what he proposes in a given case, in order that the Queen may know as distinctly to what she has to give her royal sanction. 2) Having given once her sanction to a measure, the minister who, in the execution of such measure alters or modifies it arbitrarily, commits an act of dishonesty towards the Crown, which the Queen has an undoubted constitutional right to visit with the dismissal of that minister.' Unfortunately, in fairly short order, Palmerston ignored this agreement and behaved as he had always done. This behaviour led, eventually, to his resignation in 1851. This was an apparent success for the Prince. In fact, this event damaged all the parties concerned and worse was to come.

Palmerston's hostility along with the general suspicion of foreigners led to the lowest point in Albert's public life. He had counselled against any form of intervention in a developing stand-off in eastern Europe between Russia and the Ottoman Empire, much to Palmerston's irritation, for the politician judged that an assertive role would prove to be in Britain's interests. In 1854, perhaps not coincidentally, gossip spread that the Prince was under formal investigation as a foreign agent. This was possibly started by an article in the *Westminster Review*, a liberal-minded quarterly with close connections to Palmerston, which pointed to the 'high interests' of the Coburg family. In other words, implying that the Crown was being unduly influenced by Albert's German heritage.

The gossip was spreading at a difficult moment. The Crimean War had broken out in the previous autumn, with Russia and Britain on opposing sides, and national unity was expected and demanded. It was perhaps inevitable that the non-British elements within the Royal Family would be scrutinised at such a time, particularly the relationship, actual and suspected, between the Coburgs and Russia. The *Daily News* wrote that 'above all, the nation distrusts the politics, however they may admire the taste', of the Prince, and by 1855 it was rumoured that both Victoria and Albert had been arrested and put in the Tower of London for treason. 'You jolly Turk,' ran the unpleasant Crimean-inflected ditty, 'now go to work, And show the Bear [Russia] your power. It's rumoured over Britain's isle, That A... is in the Tower.'

These rumours and the deep unpopularity which resulted were a heavy burden for both Victoria and Albert yet it is interesting that relations with Palmerston now began to improve. By the late 1850s, Palmerston was speaking in glowing terms of Albert. This in turn helped to make him more popular in the country at large and it is clear that Palmerston began to accept that the Prince could make a contribution to political life. Albert's last major act before his death in 1861 was to intervene in a dangerous diplomatic incident between the United States, then in the throes of its civil war, and Britain. The so-called Trent affair began with the boarding of the eponymous British ship by American forces and threatened to spark a conflict between the two powers. Palmerston initially intended to send a robust message but Albert, whose health was now failing with alarming speed, moved to soften a despatch that would have raised tensions further. '... Her Majesty's Government,' he wrote at the end of November 1861, 'are unwilling to believe that the United States Government intended wantonly to put an insult upon this country and to add to their many distressing complications by forcing a question of dispute upon us ...' Albert's words did much to defuse the anger that had been growing rapidly and alarmingly between the two sides.

Albert was dead within weeks.

*

Prince Albert's discreet influence left a clear mark on the monarchy itself. It is a commonplace that the character of our contemporary monarchy came into existence during the reign of Victoria, thanks in no small part to the family-centred life of the Royal couple during the years of their strong and happy marriage. It does not follow, however, that Albert set out to mould the constitutional monarchy into the form that now exists. It was rather less conscious an endeavour than this. If anything, what emerges from the story of these years is the profoundly unorthodox family situation in which Albert found himself. He had to fight and manoeuvre to play the masculine part that any other Victorian pater-familias would have taken for granted and it was only with the passage of time and several energy-sapping

209

pregnancies that Victoria permitted him sight of state papers or to make a contribution to policy discussions. He then was obliged to manoeuvre against and confront politicians who tended to be older and vastly more experienced than he. He was only twenty years old when he married Victoria.

Ultimately, he became the Queen's closest adviser but only after 1848, a period of unrest and international tension of the sort that Victoria had had hitherto no experience and a moment when the realisation came, at last, that she needed an adviser she could trust completely. It is here that the benign influence which Albert brought to bear becomes most visible. He was concerned to protect the dignity and pride of the Queen herself but he also understood that the road to the Crown's greatest influence lay through diplomacy. As the great constitutional expert Vernon Bogdanor wisely notes, 'The consort's influence was generally employed in the direction of conciliation' and this habit more than anything else (and to some degree against Albert's own political inclinations) led to the emergence of a more apolitical monarchy.

Albert wanted to ensure, above all else, that the Queen's government could be carried on regardless of political interests so in the period between 1846 and his death this meant that the Crown had to accept the Prime Minister who could carry the Commons. Whether the Sovereign liked or disliked this politician on a personal basis was, and it must be, immaterial. This climate fostered the stable, deeply rooted monarchy, one that was above political currents, reproach and danger. It formed in turn the basis for Bagehot's dictum that the Sovereign had 'the right to be consulted, the right to encourage, the right to warn'.

Bagehot also wrote within four years of Albert's death, 'it is only during the period of the present reign that in England the duties of a constitutional sovereign have ever been well performed.' This was essentially the great achievement of Albert's public life. He set the tone for a constitutional monarchy. As Professor Bogdanor writes, 'Since Victoria the changes in the role of the monarchy have been changes in degree and not in kind. There have been no fundamental alterations to the monarchical model as it had evolved by the end of Victoria's reign.' When so many of the world's monarchies have disappeared since the era of Victoria and Albert, the longevity and sturdiness of the British institution is remarkable and this is because Albert managed to establish a monarchy that was acceptable to the political class and popular with the people.

It is worth concluding with what could be called a 'domestic monarchy', the image of Victoria and Albert as not only a Royal couple but a normal one too. After all, politicians come and go. Monarchs and their families, by the Grace of God, endure and have more opportunity to create and cultivate relationships with the societies within which they live, with their subjects. Naturally, Britons were interested in and concerned about their relationship to the Crown and here Albert was successful too. Victoria and Albert produced the image of a normal family in an exalted position. Sir Edwin Landseer's famous painting *Windsor Castle in Modern Times* exemplifies the success of this image: the Green Drawing Room at Windsor is just grand enough to please, without being too grand, and it is nicely informal, containing as it does frisky canines and a small Princess Victoria playing with a dead bird, the spoils of the day's shoot. A garden beckons from the open window

and, most strikingly, Victoria manages to look simultaneously queenly and subservient. She gazes adoringly at her
energetic husband, who is fresh from the field.

Victoria and Albert's tally of nine children and their
habit of spending a great deal of time together naturally
indicate the truth of a happy and successful marriage
but the Royal couple managed to create a sense of
normality about their homes too. Both the Italianate
Osborne on the Isle of Wight which was purchased in
1844 and remodelled by Albert in subsequent years, and
the baronial castle at Balmoral, rebuilt from 1853, with
a good deal of direction from the Prince, manage to be
impressive without undue ostentation. This relatively
low-key culture of Royal life brought respect and affection. Moreover, Victoria and Albert eschewed excessive
security and in spite of repeated assassination attempts
the pair projected an air of approachability and began
to travel around Britain in ways that their predecessors
would have found unimaginable.

Royal ceremonial began to improve too, to general
approval. Victoria's coronation had been chaotic enough
with the elderly Lord Rolle living up to his name and
rolling down the steps, 'rolled right down', the new Queen
wrote later, after he had paid homage to Her Majesty.
By the time of Victoria's death, assiduous practice had
made perfect: the coronation of Edward VII's reign was
an exercise in perfection and acted as a showpiece for the
monarchy. This, in turn, became all the more important
as the methods of distributing pictures improved. Not
merely Court ceremonial but simple family scenes could
be readily circulated and the image of Albert, Victoria
and the children is one that is still easy to conjure up

in the mind's eye. This was not all by design, nor was it entirely to Albert's credit, but his was the major role for twenty-one years.

Albert's virtues were hard work, dutifulness and also inspiration. His handwritten letters to senior ministers such as Palmerston could run to a dozen pages or more and he drafted endless letters for the Queen to rewrite when they had to be despatched in her name. A man who liked early nights and fell asleep at parties must nonetheless have worked long into the night to produce all this correspondence. Nor did the work ever end. Even at Balmoral or Osborne, Albert kept working, sending and receiving papers or making local visits of any relevant works. Duty was Albert's watchword. He never shied away from what was required, be it another formal speech at a dinner or making the Household a little more efficient.

Most crucially, Prince Albert was not the frightful bore of some historical accounts. He was reserved, he did not seek to display emotion in public but he possessed the inspiration that genius requires. The Great Exhibition was the clearest example of this but his friendship with leading scientists and artists showed the range of his interests. Even when almost overwhelmed with work on the Exhibition, he had time to suggest Tennyson for the position of Poet Laureate against the instincts of Lord John Russell, the Prime Minister, who seemed not to have heard of the poet. Albert's main contribution to the nation was that he left the monarchy in a much safer state than he found it and he survived the manifold criticisms that were made of him, primarily for being German. Albert fought the good fight, finished the course and kept the faith. He was a truly virtuous Victorian.

Disraeli: The One-Nation Conservative

Benjamin Disraeli, first Earl of Beaconsfield (21 December 1804–19 April 1881), is remembered for many striking and wildly varying aspects of his life and long career. He was a master of statecraft and his political cunning and oratorical skills knew few rivals. He was the writer of long novels, an ability which raised eyebrows in the political world. His close friendship with Queen Victoria caused envy and no little resentment and arguably saved the British monarchy from sinking into an abyss of unpopularity. He was one half, with William Gladstone, of a great and profound political rivalry and there seems little doubt that the energy this rivalry generated did neither gentleman nor their respective political parties any harm. He blazed a trail as the first person born Jewish to occupy Downing Street and as the first member of an ethnic minority to hold one the great offices of state.

Disraeli was hopeless with money but happily he married well, in the process providing himself with the support necessary to build a lasting political career and to secure his reputation for posterity. Critically, his was the decisive influence in consolidating the modern British Conservative Party in the aftermath of its troubled birth and it was his work that helped position the party both as a friend of the British citizen and a supporter of the British imperial adventure. He is remembered too as an incorrigible self-publicist whose ability to work on his own reputation knew no bounds. While a disastrous relationship with money is never an asset to any ambitious politician, he was profoundly self-assured and this confidence enabled him to navigate the choppiest of waters and stay dry and untroubled through it all.

He was a conundrum, both to contemporary observers who watched his career narrowly and with pursed lips and to historians today. How could such a complicated individual climb to the top of the Victorian greasy pole?

*

Benjamin Disraeli was born into middle-class circumstances off Bedford Row in Bloomsbury, in the early nineteenth century, when it was still being laid out as a neighbourhood of handsome squares and terraces north of London's West End. He was the second child of the Jewish scholar Isaac D'Israeli, whose parents had moved from Italy in the middle of the eighteenth century, and his wife Maria Basevi, whose family also had Italian-Jewish antecedents. It is of no little significance that Benjamin Disraeli would later take some trouble to romanticise the roots and lineage of his father's side of the family. They were Sephardic Jews and merchants but Disraeli, in a sign of the discomfort he felt at his lingering status as an outsider within the British elite, liked to claim that they were rather more grand, in social terms, than was the case.

The elder D'Israeli was a man of letters but for his son's career the most significant event of his life and that of his family came in 1813. In that year, a simmering quarrel with his home Bevis Marks synagogue in the City of London culminated in Isaac D'Israeli's decision to remove his five children from the synagogue and instruction in the Jewish faith. Four years later, in the summer of 1817, he and his wife agreed to have their children baptised as Anglicans. This was a decision momentous enough in its own right but its ripples would run through the remainder of the life of Benjamin Disraeli. Until 1858, Members of Parliament were required to swear an oath of allegiance 'on the true faith of a Christian', meaning that at least nominal conversion was necessary. This parental decision was thus a pivotal moment for their son. Quite simply, it made his future possible.

His younger brothers would be sent to Winchester but Benjamin did not receive this considerable advantage from his parents and was instead despatched to a series of rather less exalted London schools. This was presumably with the best of intentions. The young Disraeli had delicate health and his parents would have wanted him closer to home but this issue of his education evidently was a touchy one in Disraeli's later life. He blamed his mother for what seemed to him the most unwise of decisions. He then trained as a solicitor – and it was at this point that he and his siblings changed their surname from D'Israeli to the less complicated Disraeli before securing admittance to Lincoln's Inn and in 1824 to the stock exchange, where he began exploring the world of speculative commodity trading.

This move came at what appeared to be a most auspicious moment. The disintegration of the Spanish Empire in Latin America opened the continent's mineral wealth to the world and Disraeli was eager to have his share in what was a rapidly expanding world of commodities. He had little money of his own to fund such a financial adventure so he entered into a financial partnership. He wrote pamphlets extolling the virtues of the investment opportunities in the Americas and teamed up with law clerk Thomas Mullett Evans and with Robert Messer, a stockbroker's son, to purchase shares in both the Colombian Mining and Anglo-Mexican Mining Associations. Alas for Disraeli and his partners the shares in both companies began almost at once to fall sharply while the Lord Chancellor started to examine the actions of those individuals seen as promoting 'bubble' investments, threatening them with prosecution under the South Sea Bubble Act.

By the summer of 1825, Disraeli and his partners had lost over £7,000, at the time a vast sum. It was the beginning of a pattern of debt accumulation for Disraeli. His debts to Messer were not repaid until 1849 and for many years he was obliged to rely on his father's pocket and on the cultivation of wealthy friends in order to make ends meet. Poor and unwise investment is not a particular sin, and the most intelligent people can fall victim – Sir Isaac Newton, for example, had joined the South Sea Bubble in 1720, just before its collapse – but Disraeli threw his weight behind an enterprise without doing due diligence on it. He publicly extolled the virtues of companies he ought to have known were worthless. That he did so to boost the value of his own investment and to save himself from further losses is an activity that would now be illegal and subject to fierce regulatory penalty. This disagreeable episode stands as one of the early debits against Disraeli's name and his detractors have used this to denigrate his reputation.

Disraeli's dire financial straits led directly to the development of another thread in an already distinctive life. He took to writing novels, noting within the burgeoning ranks of middle-class Britons a wish to peep into the more exalted lives of the aristocracy. Fulfilling such a wish might make some money and a first novel was duly forthcoming. *Vivian Grey* was published anonymously in four volumes between 1826 and 1827 and it sold well too but soon the critics noted aspects of the book that did not please. The writer purported to tell a story of aristocratic life, the reviewers complained, but that story was littered with errors and solecisms, revealing the writer to be a fraud and outsider rather than the insider telling a story of a world known well. Which was the truth, for Disraeli did not yet move in exalted circles and such criticism must have stung. It did so even more when Disraeli was unmasked as the author and his reputation received lasting damage. Not that the criticism he received stopped him writing. One novel followed another for the rest of his life, with *Sybil, or The Two Nations* (1845) perhaps the most famous.

His need for funds also meant that Disraeli borrowed from almost anyone willing to lend to him. Thus he developed a friendship with Benjamin and Sara Austen. Benjamin Austen was a lawyer for whom Disraeli had worked and Disraeli was said by uncharitable observers to have flirted with Sara Austen in order to extract loans from her husband. These loans, which ultimately had to be repaid by Isaac D'Israeli, were not inconsiderable. At Christmas 1833, Austen lent Disraeli £1,200 and in 1837 the two fell out permanently. Nor did these regular transfusions stop his finances deteriorating, even though he applied to his father for two more loans and was chased around Buckinghamshire during a by-election in 1837 by his creditors. By 1841, Disraeli was at least £20,000 in debt from his own extravagancies and from the high interest on past loans. His income was not large enough to sustain such levels of debt. Even his entry to Parliament in 1837 as one of the two Tory Members for Maidstone did not help his case, for MPs in those days did not draw a salary and Disraeli's finances remained in a parlous state until his marriage.

Marriage, however, would not come until 1839 and in the meantime his private life continued on its strikingly unconventional course. He had taken a tour of pleasure to southern Europe and the Levant in 1830–31, in the company of his sister's fiancé William Meredith. The tour had to be truncated when Meredith died of smallpox in Egypt and Disraeli himself returned to England requiring treatment for an unpleasant disease. The tour nonetheless expanded his horizons and alerted him to the wideness of the world and to the pleasures that might be taken from it. His private life was for some time thereafter more Regency than Victorian.

Take his affair with Henrietta Sykes, the wife of the wealthy Berkshire landowner Sir Francis Sykes whom he first met in 1834. This was carried out openly for two years, in a way that could have been catastrophic for his future prospects. The connection between them would give psychiatrists a field day, for Lady Sykes signed off a letter to Disraeli as 'your mother'. Sir Francis, who had a mistress of his own, was mainly unconcerned by the affair but on one occasion he banned his wife from seeing Disraeli again. However, this order was promptly rescinded when Henrietta called at the house of her husband's mistress and found him there with her. This led to an accommodation.

However, Lady Sykes's visits to the D'Israeli family home at Bradenham near High Wycombe, where Benjamin Disraeli continued to live with his parents, scandalised polite Buckinghamshire society. Later, Sir Francis would bring proceedings for 'criminal conversation' against the prominent Irish painter Daniel Maclise, whom he had caught *in flagrante delicto* with his wife. Although the case did not go ahead, the thought that a similar case could have seen Disraeli pursued through the courts before his political career had even taken off shows what a risk he was taking. Disraeli, characteristically, turned the episode into a novel, barely troubling to offer a disguise. *Henrietta Temple* was published in 1837.

Disraeli also needed money to fund his political ambitions. Prior to his success at Maidstone, he had stood as a Radical in the elections of 1831 and 1832, declaring that the Tory faction at Westminster was old and worn out, yet he could and would not be a Whig. His politics at this time, however, defied easy categorisation. He favoured the extension of the franchise, yet he also favoured protectionism. From 1834 onwards he began gravitating decisively towards Tory politics. In the following year, he stood as a Radical for the last time on his home turf of High Wycombe and in the same year he stood for the first time as a Tory, for the constituency of Taunton, where he incurred the enmity of the Irish leader Daniel O'Connell, who had misunderstood a newspaper report and concluded that Disraeli had been maligning him. O'Connell was well able to malign in return, dismissing Disraeli as 'a reptile ... just fit now, after being twice discarded by the people, to become a Conservative' and continuing for some time in the same vigorous vein. Mutual mud-slinging followed but all publicity is good publicity and the quarrel did Disraeli no harm. He did not win Taunton but he came close and he propelled himself to public notice for the first time. His victory at Maidstone followed a few months beyond two years.

When marriage at last took place in 1839, it brought a degree of order and stability to Disraeli's life and it also provided vital cash. Mary Anne Lewis was twelve years older than her suitor and was the widow of the rich parliamentarian Wyndham Lewis, an associate of Disraeli with whom he had shared the Maidstone parliamentary seat. Later, Disraeli freely admitted that he had courted her with her money in mind: 'When I first made my advances to you,' he told her, 'I was influenced by no romantic feeling' and the fact is that he found her money not merely useful but essential for his political career. Fortunately for both husband and wife, Lewis had tied his estate up carefully. Mary Anne Lewis had no control over her assets in those days before the passing of the Married Women's Property Act of 1882 and this was just as well. There is every chance that Disraeli, given the opportunity and his record, would have run through it all quite quickly.

Yet there was money available, enough for Disraeli to pay an estimated £13,000 off his debts. He also showed signs of real devotion to his wife, 'whose sweet voice', he wrote in the dedication to *Sybil*, 'has often encouraged, and whose taste and judgment have ever guided, [its] pages; the most severe of critics, but – a perfect Wife'. She certainly was devoted. Once, having caught her hand painfully in a carriage door, she held her tongue rather than put her husband off his speech. Such was her support for him that Disraeli praised her habit of having supper ready for him following late-night sittings at the Commons as being 'more like a mistress than a wife'.

This was the stability that Disraeli needed and craved. He did not stop his flirtations with other ladies and he continued a correspondence with a number of close female friends but Mary Anne was his great support. She was an unusual lady, spirited, plain-spoken and a chatterbox, although not as educated as she could have been. Disraeli said she 'did not know who came first: the Greeks or the Romans'. She was also that priceless political asset, a popular wife. People liked her and she made it possible for Disraeli to achieve his ambition. It is difficult to imagine how he could have pursued his career without her moral as well as financial support. Marriage released his energies entirely for political ends and, once Sir Robert Peel became Prime Minister in 1841, Disraeli went to the centre of events.

*

Benjamin Disraeli's relationship with Peel caused the greatest damage to Disraeli's reputation. Although skilled with language, Disraeli attacked Peel with an excessive degree of vituperation against the policies and strategies of a gentleman who was older, who had earned the respect of many colleagues and the friendship of Prince Albert, who possessed a wealth of experience and who was a statesman of some standing. Disraeli's boldness ruffled feathers at Westminster and bestowed on the younger man a reputation for excess.

The relationship had begun fairly well. In the election of 1841, Disraeli switched seats from Maidstone to Shrewsbury. He harboured from the first ambitions for ministerial office but these were not met by the new Prime Minister. Disraeli waited his moment on the backbenches with something that might have resembled patience. Moreover, he thought he shared with Peel a fair amount of common ground at this time. Peel did not flourish his changing opinions on the question of free trade until 1845 so there was, for the moment, little in the Prime Minister's words to vex Disraeli. He instead used his time networking and cultivating a reputation for foreign policy nous. He also began to develop an overtly paternalistic political philosophy, the forerunner of what later became known as 'one-nation Conservatism'. His opinion was that the Tories must pressure landowners to ally with the working class against the rising mercantile middle classes. The landowners could protect the workers from exploitation by business and could claim their loyalty and defence of the status quo in return. He would in time have the chance to put this philosophy into practice.

As Peel began to show his hand, so Disraeli identified a new enemy, the Prime Minister. The parliamentary confrontation between Peel and Disraeli over the question of the repeal of the Corn Laws and the scaling back of British protectionism is among the most celebrated and notorious in the annals of Westminster. Peel himself was an effective operator and Disraeli was never able to offer a convincing reply to Peel's question, why was he 'ready as I think he was, to unite his fortunes with mine in office'? He responded to Peel's remark in the Commons with an outright lie, claiming that he never sought office, even though he had written to Peel to beg for a position both for himself and on a separate occasion for his brother. Nor can there be any question of a misunderstanding. Disraeli's phraseology was unequivocal and untrue. *Hansard* recorded these words:

> I can assure the House nothing of the kind ever occurred. I never shall, it is totally foreign to my nature, make an application for any place ... I never asked a favour of the Government, not even one of those mechanical things which persons are obliged to ask ... and as regards myself I never directly or indirectly solicited office.

He then went on to say that if offered a ministerial position, he might have accepted but 'with respect to my being a solicitor for office it is entirely unfounded'. Remarkably, Peel was believed to have had Disraeli's letter asking for promotion in his pocket and there was no satisfactory explanation for his failure to use it. It has been speculated that the gentlemanly Peel found it distasteful to read the contents of a private letter into the public record and in the House of Commons, yet the strength and inaccuracy of Disraeli's rebuttal were surely sufficient to excuse any use of private correspondence.

Disraeli's conduct in this instance was flawed on every count. He had had no reason, beyond pious hope, to expect early preferment from Peel. There were many better claimants and his direct lies would, if exposed, have easily derailed his whole career. His credibility in Tory circles would have collapsed, not that at this point he had a great deal anyway. As with his youthful financial speculations and his relationships with married women, so his words in the Commons constituted a reckless gamble that was within a hair's breadth of being catastrophic. Imagine the scene with Peel's hand hovering over his waistcoat pocket, the elder statesman wondering whether he ought to pull out the evidence of Disraeli's dishonesty and cashier him and declining to do so. Consider the irony of it: following his escape, Disraeli went on to destroy Peel.

This question of economic reform has already been considered from Peel's point of view and needs to be examined from Disraeli's side too. Disraeli's ferocious attacks on Peel only in part stemmed from chagrin at ambition stymied. For the most part, they emanated from the great clash stamped through the politics of the time: protectionism versus free trade. It is crucial to remember that there was much at stake. For its proponents, the system of protectionism was a noble cause. It was bound up with greater issues of patriotism and national security and there was every reason to advance such a view.

The Corn Laws had been an intrinsic part of national life for two generations. The University of Warwick estimates that in 1841, in spite of developing industrialisation and urbanisation, the agricultural economy still represented 22.1 per cent of British GDP. In 1814 the Committee of the House of Commons had determined that the fair price for corn was eighty shillings a quarter. Its deliberations had been much influenced by the contemporary economist Robert Malthus, who argued that domestic production was needed to ensure supply in times of scarcity and that no sovereign nation should find itself at the mercy of foreign countries cutting off their food supply. If the eighty-shilling minimum were not kept, the theory went, then wages would have to be lowered or jobs lost, reducing purchasing power and hitting the manufacturing sector as well.

The free trade advocate and political economist David Ricardo* argued that such theories did not stand up to scrutiny. Foreign governments would not cut off supplies when they wanted and needed the money and the benefits trade brought them, and the British, he added, ought to use their superior purchasing power to effect positive change. At this time, however, Malthus proved the more convincing economist. The 1815 Act accepted the eighty-shilling protection level. Above this amount there would be no tariff and below it importation would be banned. The system did not please even its proponents but systematic government tweaking maintained its utility as the years went by and saw to it that cheap corn from expanding agricultural areas elsewhere in the world did not flood the market. The key line for supporters was that imports of grain were to be readily available during the poor harvests of 1828–31, while imports were pegged back during the bumper years between 1832 and 1835.

---

* It is fascinating to speculate on how much Ricardo influenced Peel as they served in the Bullion Committee together in 1819.

Unfortunately, a combination of bad harvests and a manufacturing recession in 1836 led to the resumption of pressure to change or repeal the Corn Laws. The Anti-Corn Law League was founded in Manchester in the autumn of 1838, with a London meeting in the following year. These meetings pushed a simple and attractive message: 'cheap bread'. The use of new campaigning techniques and the greater ease of communication, via the penny post and the railways, enabled the Leaguers to disseminate this message with great efficiency, and even the resumption of good harvests in the first half of the 1840s could not now remove the growing pressure for a fundamental change in the system.

The dramatic point to be made is that both the protectionist and the free trade sides could offer compelling arguments in their favour. After all, both Ricardo and Malthus were convincing and valued economists and their names resonate to this day. Malthus's basic proposition, that we may run out of food if the population continues to grow, is widely accepted and although the historic record shows that mankind can cope with its own increase, still some people worry that we will be unable to feed ourselves. It was not in 1846 wholly irrational or merely opportunistic to be on the same side of the argument as Malthus who represented the mainstream political view at least until 1840 rather than Ricardo.

Moreover, as is so often the case with economic policies, many politicians had not especially strong views against received wisdom. Lord Melbourne's famous description of collective responsibility, quoted by constitutionalists throughout the ages, was based on the issue of the Corn Laws: 'Now, is it to lower the price of corn, or isn't it? It is not much matter which we say, but mind we must all say the same.' In the specific instance of the Corn Laws, however, it should be noted that Melbourne's view *did* settle on a position and in 1839 he remarked that repeal was the 'wildest and maddest scheme that ever entered into the imagination of man'. As for Peel, his political trajectory provides an example of how received wisdom can change as the tides change eventually. He entered the 1841 election committed to retaining the Corn Laws before executing a sharp political turn. He had observed the success of reducing duties in other areas and this appears to have convinced him of the benefits of removing them on corn. In addition, the disaster of the Great Famine in Ireland led Peel to feel the need to soften the tariffs at once and then to acknowledge to the Cabinet and himself that he could see no prospect, once they were suspended, of reimposing them. This decision by Peel has been thoroughly vindicated by history but it does *not* follow that opposition to it was automatically vexatious and opportunistic. The joke at the time was 'Why are the Tories like walnuts? Because they are troublesome to Peel.' That was the fraught context of the 1840s in a nutshell and it left a good deal of scope for politicians to act on the basis of principle. This may be hard to believe about *Disraeli* but not about his ally, Lord George Bentinck, who went on to become the main figure of the anti-repeal Tories in Parliament. Bentinck was no natural leader. Until he rose to speak against repeal, he had not uttered a word in Parliament in the course of eighteen years. He was irked by the sense that his leader Peel stood revealed as a liar and a cheat and that he, Bentinck, had therefore been elected to Parliament on the basis of a lie. His rigorous moral code shone through as he opposed repeal in spite of the personal advantage it would have brought. He said, 'I keep horses in three counties, and they tell me I shall save £1,500 a year by free trade. I don't care for that; what I cannot bear is being sold.' He had even been offered office by Peel so had no sense of personal slight, and to concentrate on politics he sold his horses, one of which went on to win the Derby, depriving him of his life's ambition. This country gentleman now threw his lot in with Disraeli to oppose repeal. He provided what seemed a calm, stout English foundation to the movement, bringing in allies who were wary of Disraeli himself but who would follow a man with aristocratic gilding and the patience to do the quiet but necessary organisational work. Disraeli could now set to work on his rhetorical prowess and we must do him the justice of remembering that he might genuinely have believed in the arguments against the repeal of the Corn Laws. After all, their repeal did little to help relieve the famine in Ireland.

On 22 January 1846, Disraeli rounded on Peel in the Commons. In his speech, he underlined his own consistency, noting that 'to those opinions I have expressed in this house in favour of protection, I adhere. They sent me to this House and if I had relinquished them, I should have relinquished my seat also.' He called for the repealers to listen to 'the unequivocal expression of the public voice'. He then moved to attack Peel for his inconsistency in supporting the Corn Laws 'by eloquent panegyrics on the existing system – the plenty it had caused, the rural happiness it had diffused'. He also mocked Peel for his previous changes of heart over Catholic Emancipation and parliamentary reform.

Then he began to abuse the Prime Minister. Peel, he said, 'might as well at once adopt the phraseology of Walpole, and call himself a sole minister, for his speech was rich in egotistic rhetoric'. He expressed his bitterness at Peel's present arguments. 'What were the means, what the machinery, by which the Right Hon. Gentleman acquired his position, how he obtained power to turn around upon his supporters and treat them with contempt and disdain? ... Would his sovereign have called on [Peel], if in 1841 he had not placed himself, as he said, at the head of the gentlemen of England ... supporting the "sacred cause of protection"?' Disraeli was scathing about the reality of Peel's change of mind. 'The gentleman who has had the question of protection before his official mind in every shape that ingenuity could devise, during his parliamentary career of a quarter of a century – this gentleman suddenly finds that the arguments in favour of protection to native industry, are not, after all, so cogent as he once thought them; he discovers that the principle of protection cannot be supported ... The future of which they are thinking, is indeed posterity, or only the coming quarter day ... What I cannot endure is to hear a man come down and say, "I will rule without respect of party, though I rose by party; and I care not for your judgement, for I look to posterity" ... The minister who attained as he did the position which the Right Hon. Baronet now fills, is not the minister who ought to abrogate the Corn Laws.'

History has given this battle to Peel. The Corn Laws were repealed yet Disraeli did have a point. Not only did he argue that economically the Corn Laws had worked but in addition Peel split his party. He and his 'Peelite' faction would eventually join with the Whigs and liberal-minded politicians in Parliament to form the Liberal Party. Disraeli would remain with the core Conservatives, weaker and unable to govern independently for a generation. The telling line is perhaps when Disraeli remarked that Peel 'is not the minister who ought to abrogate the Corn Laws'. There is an undoubted virtue in a politician being flexible enough to change his mind but there is also reasonable criticism to be made of one who abandons his previous position on which he stood successfully for election. Sir Robert Peel both issued the first election manifesto and made the first great U-turn. While it is possible that Peel may be regarded as a statesman because he was willing to change his mind, so Disraeli can be thought one because he stuck to his election promises.

*

The recent view of Benjamin Disraeli, much influenced by Lord Blake's biography of 1966, is that he was essentially an opportunist with a disreputable early life and a selfish later one and a man guided solely by personal ambition. Yet to achieve what he did, Disraeli had to overcome greater barriers than any of his contemporaries. In the first place, politics was not exclusively an aristocratic profession but it was dominated by the noble families. Even being a Member of Parliament required property ownership. Although the likes of Peel, Disraeli's grand opponent, and Disraeli's nemesis, William Gladstone, were not of noble stock, they cannot be placed in the same bracket as Disraeli either. They held the priceless advantage of coming from exceptionally successful commercial families and were educated at Harrow and Eton respectively. Disraeli invented a noble history for his family and his imagination must have at least persuaded him, although nobody else, that he was the equal of any number of blue-blooded politicians.

Nor can Disraeli's Jewish heritage be ignored. At least since the days of Oliver Cromwell Britain has thankfully never been a hotbed of anti-Semitism but his identity was nevertheless a drag on his ambitions. Had his father not fallen out with the synagogue and chosen to have his children join the Church of England, Disraeli's Jewish faith would have been an insurmountable obstacle to a political career in the first half of the nineteenth century. Lionel de Rothschild, who made so important a contribution to the success of the Great Exhibition, was forbidden from taking his seat in the Commons because he would not renounce his Judaism, even though he was repeatedly elected. Only in 1858, eleven years after his first election, did the House of Lords relent and permit each House to draw up its own oath of allegiance. This enabled Rothschild to take his seat at last as a Liberal and the first Jewish Member of Parliament.

Disraeli had participated in this long-running debate and it is to his very great credit that he sided with the Liberals, antagonising some of his Tory supporters in the process. He argued not merely in favour of tolerance, but essentially that Judaism and Christianity were equally important, a remarkably challenging view, particularly for him to take in the circumstances of the 1850s. Disraeli's argument could only have highlighted his own sense of 'foreignness' and he never sought to disguise his family antecedents. If anything, he made a virtue of them. He was capable of principle, in other words, and it is against this background that his mistakes must be judged and his successes applauded. It is as if the minuses have been piled up, with the result that his reputation has been overtaken by those of Gladstone and Peel. Yet once it is recognised that it is disproportionate to view his opposition to repeal of the Corn Laws as exclusively opportunistic, his successes can be explored with a greater sense of justice.

The formal foundation and naming of the Conservative Party are correctly attributed to Peel but it was Disraeli who developed both its structures and the policies that allowed it to appeal to the legions of newly enfranchised voters. He hauled the party back from the nadir of its Peelite split and made it electable again. As for his political beliefs, these have been hidden in clear sight, for they went well beyond a desire for self-promotion, imbuing the Conservative Party with a range of values that have been quoted favourably ever since. Unusually, he disseminated these ideas through his novels which flowed with his political ideology. He referred to *Coningsby: or The New Generation* (1844), which tells the story of a character who seems a cross between Lionel de Rothschild and Disraeli himself, as 'the secret history of my feelings', while the full title of his next novel, *Sybil, or The Two Nations*, encapsulates what Disraeli felt to be the abiding curse of British society, one that one-nation Conservatives could help to dispel. His writing attempted to replace a 'progressivist' Whig interpretation of history with his own Conservative version, which in turn attempted to heal the wounds in British society and to bring the two nations together.

Disraeli also invested a good deal of creative and political energy in describing a past consisting of a feudal idyll. He held, or claimed to hold, the view that there had once been a golden age in Britain when the interests of landowners and their tenants went hand in glove. One looked after the interests of the other which in return gave fealty not out of fear but from love. Disraeli's was part of a great common vision which a host of others, including Augustus Pugin, shared. It was a concept of a kinder, gentler and more balanced past, that might be resurrected if the will existed. For Disraeli, there was a personal twist. He not only believed that the golden age was about to awaken but he also had no doubt that he was the man to bring it back to life. In *Sybil*, for example, he wrote that this vision, this golden Toryism, 'was not dead but sleeping ... Yet will rise from the tomb ... to bring back strength to the Crown, liberty to the subject, and to announce that power has only one duty: to secure the social welfare of the PEOPLE.' Such a position, Disraeli considered, needed to be revived because the current situation was so divisive.

Again in *Sybil*, the novel's hero Egremont met a stranger who explained to him the situation. Egremont declared in a pious statement of patriotic sentiment, 'Say what you will, our Queen reigns over the greatest nation that ever existed.' The stranger's question of 'Which nation?' puzzled Egremont, and he listened as the stranger then went on to describe the existence of 'two nations between whom there is no intercourse and no sympathy; who are ignorant of each other's habits, thoughts and feelings, as if they were dwellers in different zones or inhabitants of different planets; who are formed by different breeding, are fed by different food, and are ordered by different manners, and are not governed by the same laws.' 'You speak of –' said Egremont hesitatingly. 'THE RICH AND THE POOR.'

The reader today may find Disraeli's reliance on such verbiage a trifle trying but there is no doubt that this is the clearest possible description of his concerns about the divisions in society, ones which had in part, he argued, come about because of the lack of power of the landed interest and the growth of industrialisation which had broken the historic bonds. In *Coningsby*, meanwhile, Disraeli took the opportunity to shape further his vision of a renewed golden age, on this occasion deploying a dialogue between the hero and his grandfather Lord Monmouth. To make his point, Monmouth, who expected Peel to make him a duke, is rebuked by his grandson, who declares, 'What we want, sir, is not to fashion new dukes and furbish up old Baronies but to establish great principles which may maintain the realm and secure the happiness of the people. Let me see authority once more honoured; a solemn reverence again the habit of our lives; let me see property acknowledging, as in the days of faith that labour is his twin brother, and that the essence of all tenure is the performance of duty ...' His grandfather was not inclined to listen to this lecture but he was not the hero of the novel. It is difficult not to admire the boldness of a politician who was able to write a bracing novel as a thundering manifesto.

The essential point of all this is that Disraeli needed to encapsulate a view of the world that would win the approval of his divided party and that his achievement was to do so. After all, he set out an amazingly attractive proposition which cast the anti-Peelite faction as historic heroes abandoned by an awful leader who was really nothing more than a Whig in disguise. He had remarked of Peel that 'the Right Honourable gentleman caught the Whigs bathing, and walked away with their clothes'. His view was of a gentle and paternalistic Conservative Party which brought the two nations together. Is it too much to suggest that even as early as the 1840s Disraeli had seen the future for the Tory Party in the light of a widening franchise? That he had recognised that the Conservatives had to unite the classes to survive and that the first step was to persuade the landed class that its interest was to be the protectors of labour?

If Disraeli had such foresight or even saw the glimmerings of the way democracy was developing, the next Reform Act in 1867 suddenly seems much less opportunistic and instead a part of his long-term ideal. For it is undoubtedly the case that the consequences of this Act, which both Lord Derby, the minority Conservative Prime Minister of the day, and Disraeli, the legislation's chief architect, referred to as 'a leap in the dark', were seismic. As a consequence of its passing, some 938,000 voters were added to the electoral role. At a stroke it almost doubled the 1,056,000 roll of existing voters. How did this Act come about?

The usual answer is 'by accident, with a minority government desperate to remain in office willing to give anything away to win individual votes'. Disraeli's authoritative biographer Lord Blake called it 'one of the oddest histories of confusion, cross-purposes and muddle in British political history'. While Roy, Lord Jenkins of Hillhead, in his important biography of William Gladstone, saw Disraeli's primary aim as being to outfox his enemy. Jenkins wrote that '[Gladstone] failed to realise that Disraeli's governing tactic was to defeat any amendment from Gladstone, even if it meant accepting a more extreme one from another source. He had to show that he was winning, and this meant showing that Gladstone was losing.'

The process of the bill was tortuous. The Victorian House of Commons did not have time limits on speeches and did not timetable debates. This meant that any Member could speak for as long as he liked and the fashion of the day was to be long-winded. In addition, party discipline was also less clear-cut than it is today. Members were willing to vote according to their own or local interests and were also prepared to be explicit about this. These parliamentary difficulties had led to the defeat of attempts at electoral reform tabled by Russell's Liberal government, a defeat in which Disraeli played a leading role, and Derby becoming Prime Minister. The Russell bill had been championed by Gladstone and its defeat led to massive protests around the country. Some 200,000 people gathered to protest in Birmingham, for example, and politicians across the House realised that in such a climate reform would be only a matter of time, regardless of the complexion of the government.

As Jenkins noted, it certainly was one of the ironies of history that Disraeli, who would shortly go on to pilot his own radical electoral reforms through Parliament, was the key player in foiling Gladstone's rather less far-reaching plans. To do so, he worked with people with whom he had no natural affinity, such as Robert Lowe, a Liberal politician but one who opposed any further extension of democracy, to defeat Russell and Gladstone. This operation involved a delicate balancing act. Lowe and his supporters were known as the 'Adullamites', in a biblical allusion to the cave of Adullam where David had sought refuge from King Saul, by their enemies on account of their backward hence 'cave-dwelling' political views. They did not want to bring down Russell's government but they were desperate to halt further electoral reform. In the end Disraeli had his way, Russell's government did collapse and Derby formed a new minority administration, with Disraeli installed as Chancellor.

Disraeli's own research quietly demonstrated that his idea of supporting the extension of the franchise would benefit the Conservatives even if some of his fellow party members remained to be convinced. Yet he had no firm plans as to how to go about this, so, with Russell's administration swept away and Derby in government, Disraeli was forced rapidly to come up with a scheme for reform. There have been quarrels about Disraeli's real place in this scheme. Blake argues that it was Derby, with the discreet support of the Queen, who pushed for reform while Disraeli was dragged along. However, looking at the broader context this may not be correct. After all, once the bill was tabled in the Commons, Disraeli gave way consistently to all attempts to widen the scope of reform, until the lists of newly enfranchised voters reached close to the million mark. These are unlikely to be the moves of a reluctant politician. Faced with such wide-ranging reform, however, the Cabinet split and a rash of significant resignations followed.

Disraeli may have been willing to do anything to stay in office but with a majority of seventy against him in the Commons he knew that the odds were stacked heavily against him. He played his hand now with great skill, lowered the standing of Gladstone, divided the ranks of the Opposition and even, diplomatically, rejected the proposals of the Queen that the whole question ought to be decided by a committee of the Privy Council on a non-party basis. In addition, he published his speeches on this subject in order to claim the credit for reform. Eventually, Disraeli's manoeuvres paid off. The Reform Bill received Royal assent in August 1867.

It seems that Disraeli did have a private masterplan, which was to make it appear that *Derby* was the one pushing for reform while Disraeli was a secondary actor, thus making it much easier for him to carry those Tories suspicious of the whole idea. Nonetheless, to win any vote against his bitter political enemy Gladstone must have been a source of joy to Disraeli. There are further pieces of evidence to back up such a theory. Disraeli had an interesting relationship with the reformer and Liberal MP John Bright, who remarked of him, 'He conceives it right to strive for a great career with such principles as are in vogue in his age and country – says the politics and principles to suit England must be of the "English type", but having obtained power, would use it to found a great reputation on great services rendered to the country.' Bright, of all people, had no particular political need to opine positively on the scope of Disraeli's vision and for this reason is worth listening to.

*

In spite of these great reforms, the Conservatives lost the General Election of 1868. Disraeli had, in February of that year, at last achieved his aim of becoming Prime Minister. A gouty Lord Derby resigned on health grounds and Disraeli was summoned to Osborne to receive the all-important invitation from Victoria. 'Mr Disraeli is Prime Minister!' the Queen wrote to her daughter Vicky in Prussia. 'A proud thing for a man "risen from the people" to have obtained!' His triumph was short for the election of that December saw Gladstone's Liberals returned with a large majority and Disraeli retreated to the Opposition benches, to await Liberal mistakes and to spend his leisure time writing yet another novel. *Lothair* was published in 1870.

Crucially, Disraeli used the time to consolidate the organisation of the Conservative Party, both centrally and in the constituencies. It was at this time that Conservative Central Office evolved as the prime organisational power in the party with sub-bodies established to reinforce its power and influence in the country. One such was the National Union of Conservative and Constitutional Associations, that tentacle of Central Office in charge of organising within newly enfranchised urban communities and if possible claiming the loyalty of these communities to the party. The Union was brought to life when Disraeli deployed it to support his two great speeches of 1872, one in the Manchester Free Trade Hall and the other in the Crystal Palace, which now stood at Sydenham in south London. In both speeches, he excoriated Gladstone's Liberal government, describing the front bench as 'a range of exhausted volcanoes. Not a flame flickers on a single pallid crest.' The crowds roared their approval but Disraeli's principal focus in these speeches was not to attack Gladstone, rather to set out the Conservatives' own distinctive stall, to maintain the institutions of Britain, to elevate 'the condition of the people' and to uphold Empire.

At the Crystal Palace on 24 June, he told the crowd:

It must be obvious to all who consider the condition of the multitude with a desire to improve and elevate it that no important step can be gained unless you can effect some reduction of their hours of labour and humanise their toil. The great problem is to be able to achieve such results without violating those principles of economic truth upon which the prosperity of all states depends.

He argued that reforms had indeed been achieved by early Conservative laws *in the teeth* of opposition by the 'blatant and loud-mouthed leaders' of the Liberal Party. He focused on the sense that 'capital has never accumulated so quickly, that wages were never higher, that the employment of the people was never greater and the country never wealthier'.

All of this was a prelude to the main plank of Disraeli's offer of a new social vision. His central theme was that 'the health of the people was the most important question for a statesman'.

It has many branches. It involves the state of the dwellings of the people ... their enjoyment of some of the chief elements of nature – air, light and water. It involves the regulation of their industry, the inspection of their toil. It involves the purity of their provisions, and it touches upon all the means by which you may wean them from the habits of excess and brutality.

Responding to disdainful Liberal remarks that he was obsessed by the nation's sewers, Disraeli turned such scorn to good use, claiming that

to one of the labouring multitude of England, who has found fear always to be one of the inmates of his household – who has, year after year, seen stricken down the children of his loins, on whose sympathy and material support he has looked with hope and confidence, it is not a 'policy of sewage' but a question of life and death.

This was forceful rhetoric, not least because it was true. His view of the multitude 'in possession of personal privileges – of personal rights and liberties – which are not enjoyed by the aristocracies of other countries' was uniting in tone and his vision for the nation was optimistic:

This issue is ... whether you will be content to be a comfortable England, modelled and moulded upon continental principles and meeting in due course an inevitable fate, or whether you will be a great country – an imperial country – a country where your sons, when they rise, rise to paramount positions, and obtain not merely the esteem of their countrymen but command the respect of the world.

It was something else too. It was a manifesto for office delivered two years out from the next General

Election. It is also to Disraeli's great credit that, when the Conservatives were returned to power in 1874 at the head of their first clear election victory in over thirty years, its provisions were to a large extent carried out. Disraeli clearly drove the organisational reform and the policy direction. He set a great many activities in motion but as Prime Minister he has not in recent years been fully acknowledged for what his administration did. His subordinates have been seen as the workhorses, leaving Disraeli perceived as something of a show pony. Is this really fair or does the clock-maker deserve some credit when the clock tells the right time, even if it is wound every week by another?

Under Disraeli's period of office the Trade Union Act was introduced by Home Secretary Richard Assheton Cross. It was more favourable to organised labour than Gladstone's equivalent Act of 1871 had been. Cross also promoted the Artisans' and Labourers' Dwellings Improvement Act, which allowed slum dwellings to be compulsorily purchased by councils and demolished, and provided for inexpensive loans to construct up-to-date dwellings. This was a stepping stone to further enlightened housing legislation, with the result that Robert Ensor describes the Act as 'one of the milestones in English legislation on the housing problem'. A Sale of Food and Drugs Act remained the principal legislation in this area until 1928 and a Public Health Act, which tackled the issue of sewage as promised by Disraeli, remained a central element in sanitary law until 1937. Each of these Acts was excellent law and each one was passed in 1875, ironically leading to criticism that nothing much happened in the rest of this period of government. However, four key social Acts covering labour laws, housing, food safety and public health is a pretty impressive haul for any administration. Most crucially, they link directly with all that Disraeli himself had said throughout his career. He must be allowed to take much of the credit for the passage of such legislation.

As for Disraeli's foreign and imperial policies, these too were successful. They pivot around the decisions which flowed from the Congress of Berlin, which convened in the German capital in the summer of 1878 and in which Disraeli was a prime mover. The Congress brought the six European Great Powers of the Day, Britain herself, plus Austria, France, Germany, Russia and Italy, together with the Ottoman Empire and the Balkan states of Serbia, Montenegro, Greece and Romania, with the intention of delineating the territories of the Balkans in the years to come.

The Congress has been much criticised, for being essentially a stitch-up, with all the main decisions made before it even met and for settling affairs in south-east Europe so poorly that grudges and rivalries were permitted to fester unchecked. These then erupted in the form of the First and Second Balkan Wars and eventually the Great War itself. Blake, who was not a Disraeli sympathiser, was clear. The Congress was by no means a stitch-up. He wrote that it is 'a myth to suggest that the Congress was a mere façade registering decisions already taken in secret between the principal powers concerned'. It can equally be argued that, as a concerted effort to keep peace in Europe, it did what it set out to do. There was peace for another thirty years. This was no mean feat, given the vicious state of affairs in the Balkans in this as in so many eras.

Disraeli, now seventy-three, was at an age when the energy required for such an important event may have been ebbing. Notwithstanding this, he sensibly travelled slowly to Berlin and was full of enthusiasm for the negotiations. He and the formidable German Chancellor Otto von Bismarck came to admire each other. Bismarck famously made the quip 'der alte Jude, das ist der Mann' ('the old Jew, he is the man'), which provides an indication of his opinion of Disraeli. Indeed, it is almost a commentary on the Congress itself, given that Disraeli achieved most of his foreign-policy objectives.

The new state of Bulgaria, before the Congress an expansionist satellite of Russia, was reined in and its Aegean coastline removed. At a stroke, Russian influence in the eastern Mediterranean was trimmed considerably. The Ottoman Empire, a bulwark, albeit a failing one, against Russia in the region was propped up a little longer and Britain took control of the strategic island of Cyprus. Disraeli also scored a point off Gladstone, whose views of the Ottomans, stemming from their massacres of Christians in the Balkans in 1876, were understandably harsh. The view in London was that the Congress was a triumph. Disraeli returned a hero and was offered a dukedom by the Queen, plus accession to the Order of the Garter. He declined the dukedom but accepted the Garter on the second occasion it was offered.

In this period as Prime Minister, Disraeli also delivered on other Conservative plans. He was a clear and public supporter of the monarchy. His support was somewhat ostentatious, for his friendship with Victoria enabled him to float the suggestion that she emerge from the seclusion that had followed the death of Albert and show herself to her people and that she agree to his proposal that she be proclaimed the Empress of India. It is easy to ridicule Disraeli's flattery of the Queen in these years, flattery which he laid on with a trowel, but it is less easy to dismiss the suggestion that he revitalised the monarchy at a time when public support for the institution was low. The friendship between minister and monarch was much observed and commented upon, with the pair featuring in many newspaper cartoons.

The people were understandably cross at the thought that they had a Queen, the so-called 'Widow of Windsor', who was seldom seen. Victoria had been in mourning for the loss of Albert for the best part of twenty years and had forced the Court to mourn likewise. If the Queen was essentially invisible, the thinking went, then what was the point of having a monarch at all? Victoria was, moreover, inclined to be difficult. She resented not being kept informed but she equally resented being overworked. Disraeli gossiped with her, conspired with her and in general worked to bring her cheer. In helping Victoria to take suitable steps Disraeli did his Sovereign and the state considerable service.

The reason for doing this was that he fully understood the role and function of a constitutional monarchy and he knew that the monarchy, if well managed, possessed a magic that could unite the nation. In constitutional terms, he adhered to Bagehot's insight that the uncodified British Constitution required both a *visible* Sovereign, in the words of our present Queen, 'I must be seen to be believed', and one so far above the fray that she was a focus for patriotism. To this recipe, Disraeli further added his own flamboyance. As with the nation, so with the Empire. Victoria could unify both entities and bring them together. Her new role as Empress of India would command the fealty of her colonial subjects to whom she must inevitably appear as a distant figure. Disraeli had theatrical flair, he possessed the impresario's feel for what the people wanted and the determination to put this into action. By 1897 he would have seen, had he lived, the success of his plan as adoring crowds celebrated Victoria's Diamond Jubilee and statues erected to the Queen Empress across the dominions and colonies.

He did not view the Empire merely as a theatrical spectacular. He was also interested in its material reality and he was determined to make it stronger, sturdier and more vigorous. In this, perhaps his biggest coup was the purchase of the shares in the Suez Canal owned by the the Khedive of Egypt, Isma'il Pasha, who ruled from 1863 to 1879, when he was toppled by the British. By 1875, the Khedive was effectively bankrupt and in great need of money. He had mortgaged his interest until 1895 and Disraeli feared that this situation might have allowed the French to take control of the Canal, as they already owned 56 per cent of the ordinary shares outstanding. The Canal, which opened in 1869, rendered the old shipping routes around the Cape of Good Hope at a stroke redundant. It made the route from India to the UK shorter by thousands of miles and many weeks and it facilitated not only trade but also rapid troop shipments in the event of a second Indian mutiny. Disraeli understood that the Canal was the most vital artery of Empire and now brought off a great coup to buy the Khedive's shares and to assume control of the Canal itself. According to Blake's account, Disraeli visited Lionel de Rothschild in a theatrical whirl and requested a loan of £4 million. This unorthodox approach was necessary because Parliament was not sitting so that the normal and cheaper process of raising money was not available at a political moment when time was of the essence. When did Disraeli need the money? 'Tomorrow.' 'What is your security?' 'The British Government.' 'You shall have it.' Disraeli, in other words, was able to leave office in 1880 for the last time with a sense that the nation, the Empire and the monarchy were in good heart.

*

In his whole career Disraeli saw one thing with great clarity and acted upon his knowledge both in theory and in practice. Although he romanticised the aristocracy, not least in his explanation of his own origins, he knew that the democratic society that was developing would *depend on the multitude being successfully engaged*. This in turn involved symbolism, something he understood exceptionally well, hence the time and effort he spent on winning Victoria's favour. In this he differed markedly from some of his predecessors. Palmerston, for example, did not care to engage in such schemes, because he considered that power had passed from the Crown to an oligarchy, even if a popular one. Disraeli *did* care because he realised that the people could have an affection for a monarchy that they were unlikely to feel for politicians and his understanding still provides a backbone of stability to the nation today. Empire fulfilled a similar role. It was an idea all classes could rejoice at and take pride in and was an idea that required practicality and concrete reality to make it work. Most importantly he knew that the condition of the people, of overwhelming significance compared to symbolism, had to be improved regardless of whether they were voters or not.

The vast expansion of the electorate in 1867 fitted with Disraeli's long-expressed views, yet even if it had been as much influenced by chance as his detractors would suggest, he recognised that the millions still disenfranchised needed to see their lives improve. This explains the message contained not only in his early novels but in his speeches and legislative programme too. Add to this the campaigning and administrative reforms he set in place to put the Tories ahead of the game for years to come and a politician for all seasons emerges. The father, perhaps, of the democracy that is enjoyed today.

Gladstone: An Eminent Moralist

At the conclusion of his biography of Liberal Party politician and Victorian statesman William Ewart Gladstone (29 December 1809–19 May 1898), Sir Philip Magnus wrote, 'In the last analysis what Gladstone was is of vastly greater importance than what he did.' These words, written by an admirer, are an interesting reflection on a politician, because politics is usually about doing rather than being. Gladstone was certainly an Eminent Victorian, one of the towering political figures of the nineteenth century, yet his policy successes are much more difficult to pin down than those of his contemporaries. Peel has the repeal of the Corn Laws as his legacy, Palmerston is remembered for a magisterial command of foreign policy and Disraeli trademarked the 'condition of the people' and 'one-nation Conservatism'. Which leaves Gladstone with, as he exclaimed in 1845, 'Ireland! Ireland! That cloud in the west, that coming storm, the minister of God's retribution upon cruel and inveterate and but half-atoned injustice.'

Ireland was a policy that did not work and one that split his Liberal Party.

So what was Gladstone's legacy?

*

Like Sir Robert Peel, William Ewart Gladstone was not born into one of the great families which had dominated British politics since the 'Glorious Revolution' of 1688, and, as was also the case with Peel, the Gladstone family's wealth was self-created. His father was John Gladstone, later Sir John Gladstone of Fasque, a strong-minded, strong-willed and deeply religious Scottish merchant who had settled at Liverpool. His Liverpudlian first wife Jane died in 1798 and in 1800 John Gladstone married Anne MacKenzie Robertson, like her new husband of Scottish extraction. William Ewart Gladstone was the fifth of their six children.

A few years after John Gladstone's second marriage, the family ceased to attend the local Presbyterian church at Liverpool. They began instead to worship within the Church of England, thus signalling their intention to join the Anglican mainstream of English life. William Gladstone himself would end his life a committed High Anglican. The family also left their original home on fashionable Rodney Street close to Liverpool city centre for a newly built mansion on one hundred acres of land at Seaforth, north of the city. John Gladstone was rising in the world and he had many professional and commercial interests. He became a parliamentarian in 1818 and he also held significant global investments, trading as far afield as Russia, India and the West Indies. His sugar plantations in Jamaica and Guyana were worked by slave

251

labour and conditions were brutal. Later, as slavery was phased out across the Empire, John Gladstone, with the assistance of his newly elected son, William, was among the most assiduous of the mercantile class in obtaining generous compensation from the government. When he died in 1851, he would leave over £600,000. In today's money he died a millionaire many times over.

The young William Gladstone grew up in a household where piety, money and politics were the abiding interests of the family. All three spheres remained at the heart of his personality throughout his life, although he concentrated more energy on the nation's finances than on his own. Again, as with Robert Peel, his parents despatched him to one of the great public schools, though in the case of Gladstone to Eton rather than Harrow. It is worth noting briefly the similarities between the two fathers in these stories. They were both driven and highly successful businessman, they were both elected to Parliament, although neither went on to have especially distinguished careers in public life, and they were both highly aware of the benefits that might well accrue from an advantageous and socially privileged education for their sons. It is fair to assume that the energy that drove both men was inherited by their sons and it is certainly the case that the work ethic of William Gladstone was extraordinary and was recognised by his peers.

The younger Gladstone settled well at Eton. He became a happy and conscientious scholar and was much influenced by Edward Craven Hawtrey, the school's dynamic and reforming headmaster and later its Provost. Eton was followed by a degree in Classics and Mathematics at Christ Church, Oxford, where he gained a double first and served as President of the Union. It was during these years of education at Eton and Oxford that Gladstone established lifelong habits of reading voraciously, diarising faithfully and working very long hours.

There was little that Gladstone would *not* read. Over the course of a long life, he accumulated a vast library of over thirty thousand books the contents of each described in his diary. Towards the end of his life, this most ardent of bibliophiles gave most of his collection to what is now Gladstone's Library, which he founded near his country seat at Hawarden in Flintshire, and he delivered the thousands of volumes to the library himself with the aid of a wheelbarrow.

This story captures not only his character as a lover of books but also glances at the great physical strength that matched his mental abilities and that sets him apart from such peers as Disraeli, who sensibly disliked any form of exercise more arduous than the occasional walk. With this vigour, however, came something perhaps a little less praiseworthy: a degree of impatience for those less endowed with energy than he was. He expected others to be similarly industrious. He counselled one of his sons, for example, to 'establish a minimum number of hours in the day for study' and this was to apply in the vacations as well as the term time of his university career.

This glimpse of the elderly Gladstone also reveals the thread of zeal, of evangelical certainty, that ran through the family as a whole. As a young man, he considered becoming a clergyman but when his father opposed the idea, Gladstone seemed to decide that his vocation must be as a politician. He would maintain throughout his life a commitment to these two channels of religion and politics. He would regularly pray for God's guidance and this divine imprimatur had the effect of making him utterly sure of the justice and wisdom of his course. Queen Victoria herself was just one among many who would complain about the effects of such moral certainty.

It can well be imagined that such rectitude could easily be seen as priggishness and would not always recommend him to his colleagues. Lord Jenkins of Hillhead, his most sympathetic biographer, described with some impatience a scene in which Gladstone's rooms at Christ Church were invaded by a crowd of less pious men. Gladstone's reaction was to tell his diary that 'to suffer for Christ was no disgrace'. He resolved to forgive his attackers and pray for them more earnestly so that both they and he could benefit. As for the twentieth-century Labour Prime Minister Clement Attlee, he judged Gladstone to be a 'dreadful' man because of the letter he wrote proposing marriage to Miss Catherine Glynne which contained a sentence of 140 words concerning the Almighty. Miss Glynne obviously cared less than Mr Attlee did about such matters as she became Mrs Gladstone in 1839.

*

This was for the future but the developing character and preoccupations of this profoundly, perhaps excessively moral and evangelical young man may already be seen. It is important to focus for a moment on passages in Gladstone's life that illuminate this religious element, for it is necessary to understand this aspect fully in order to comprehend the man himself. A deeply felt sense of religion influenced not only Gladstone's political outlook but that of British society as a whole in the Victorian period. Throughout the nineteenth century, religious issues were frequently at or close to the forefront of the national debate. The rumbling debate surrounding the Emancipation of the Catholics of Britain and Ireland has been mentioned before and to this we can add tensions surrounding such issues as the disestablishment of the Church of Ireland, in which Gladstone played a role.

As early as 1864, Gladstone had advocated disestablishment, much to the irritation of his Prime Minister, Palmerston. Gladstone saw the measure as both righting a wrong, in that there were very small numbers of Irish Anglicans in a predominantly Catholic country, and as politically opportune, in that disestablishment in Ireland would please British Nonconformists, who formed a significant element in the evolving Liberal power base. Palmerston blocked the measure at this time but only five years later, with Gladstone now Prime Minister, the bill passed through a bitterly divided Parliament. This particular saga usefully illuminates how Gladstone viewed religion. It was never an independent entity but was instead always one thread in a great web of social, ethical and political concerns.

Gladstone's religious preoccupation also affected his personal relationships, not least the tense and tetchy relationship he endured with the Queen. Victoria famously detested him, complaining that he addressed her as though she were a public meeting and describing him as a 'mischievous firebrand, arrogant, tyrannical and obstinate ... a half-crazy and in many ways ridiculous, wild and incomprehensible old fanatic'. She and Gladstone clashed repeatedly over ecclesiastical appointments. These had a distinct political influence through the House of Lords, which was in those days a smaller and more powerful body than it is today, and Victoria continually agitated for appointees who would check the effects of High Anglicanism upon the Church of England, while Gladstone as continually pushed back against the Queen's wishes.

Gladstone's close personal relationships were also affected as a result of his strength of religious feeling. For ten years, he had no contact with Cardinal Manning, one of Lytton Strachey's most unfairly treated Eminent Victorians, who had been a great friend of his youth. He had been an Anglican cleric who converted to Catholicism and became, in 1865, the second Archbishop of Westminster and thus leader of the Catholic Church in England and Wales. For Gladstone, Manning's breach with the Church of England was too much to bear and even after the breach was seemingly healed, the pair were never as close again. When Gladstone's younger sister Helen in her turn converted he was even less sympathetic. 'You are living a life of utter self-deception,' he bawled in ink. 'Not in religion alone but in all bodily and mental habits' and he advised his father to turn Helen out of the family home and cut off her allowance. Thankfully, John Gladstone was kinder and he declined to follow his son's advice. There was no particularly happy ending to this story. Helen Gladstone became addicted to laudanum until she was cured miraculously by Cardinal Wiseman.

The tenor of Gladstone's own private life and leisure time was also bound up with these intense socio-religious feelings and the sense of obligation and duty which flowed from them. In the aftermath of the General Election of 1874, which Gladstone's Liberals lost to Disraeli and the Conservatives, Catherine Gladstone counselled her husband against quitting the political scene. She claimed that observers would blame his decision on a form of religious mania that had led him away from his true public calling.

Even his most sympathetic biographers, however, have not been able entirely to absolve Gladstone of the charge of hypocrisy, stemming from his notorious 'night walks' and practice of self-mortification. Gladstone was given to walking the streets of London in the hours of darkness seeking out prostitutes – 'fallen women' – with the intent of saving them and getting their lives back into good moral order. This habit resulted in at least one blackmail attempt which ended up in court, the details of the case engendering widespread sniggering among society at large.

It was, to put it mildly, *not* a wise practice. His friends were embarrassed by it and on one occasion Lord Rosebery, later himself a Liberal Prime Minister, drew the short straw and was pushed forward to ask Gladstone to stop. Even Gladstone eventually recognised and acknowledged that his efforts were simply not effective. In 1854, he recorded in his diary that of almost ninety prostitutes he had tried to save 'there is but one of whom I know that the miserable life has been abandoned and that I can fairly join that fact with influence of mine'.

Gladstone revealed to his diary all sorts of additional details that help illuminate the religious dimension of his life. In its pages he habitually and faithfully listed his 'days of impurity' and his diaries were littered with little 'whip' signs believed to indicate days of self-mortification. The implication must be that his various meetings with 'fallen' women were not always or entirely innocent, in addition to which he had one or two remarkably intimate links to married women. One such was the splendidly named Mrs Laura Thistlethwayte, a one-time courtesan whom he rescued. His meetings with her, conducted over thirty years to the all too evident consternation of friends and colleagues, were invariably accompanied by an appearance of the 'whip' symbol in his diaries again.

How does all this very peculiar behaviour square with Gladstone's strongly developed sense of Christian duty, his presumed knowledge of the Sixth Commandment and the declaration he made near the end of his life to his son, the Reverend Stephen Gladstone, that he had never 'been guilty of the act which is known as infidelity to the marriage bed'? This last remark carries with it a definite sense of sophistry. One is reminded forcibly of Bill Clinton's use of careful and legalistic language as he defended himself in the Monica Lewinsky case, and it has led many to believe that Gladstone was not as holy as he liked to appear. This is unfair. His precision with language and his deep religion, which he in earlier life declared had been very much a Bible-based one, provide a different interpretation.

Matthew 5.28 would have been well known to Gladstone: 'But I say unto you, that whosoever looketh on a woman to lust after her hath committed adultery with her already in his heart.' This verse may explain why Gladstone would have referred to 'days of impurity' and embraced the need for self-mortification of the flesh. St Thomas More wore a hair shirt and there is a long Christian tradition of physically atoning for sins which would have seemed much less unusual to Gladstone's contemporaries than it does today.

Of some Christian ideals, however, it is clear that Gladstone was a fine example. He was an impressively charitable individual, believing with his friend Andrew Carnegie that people ought to give money away while alive because it was then that the act of giving made a tangible difference to the life of the giver, whereas once they were dead it did not. Indeed, he believed that such charity was a true moral imperative and he gave away £114,000 in the course of his lifetime. Translated in the value of gold sovereigns, this sum is equivalent to over £25 million.*

Gladstone's religion was real. It was not a hypocritical confection and it influenced his life considerably. He was, as he himself noted, an emotional man. He wrote on one occasion to the unfortunate Helen Gladstone saying, 'The only thing I really dread is the fierceness of internal excitement, and that from experience as well as anticipation, I do dread. May God pour upon it his tranquilising influence.' On his 69th birthday, he confided to his diary that his good health 'appears to me to carry all the marks of the will of God'. And this was the problem. It is not easy to debate or reason with an individual who believes they are speaking with the voice of God. The Liberal politician Henry Labouchère mockingly said that, although he did not mind Gladstone's assumption that he always had an ace up his sleeve, he objected to his claim that it had been put there by Almighty God.

*

---

* These historical exchange rates are not precise but whatever rate is used it was still a considerable amount.

William Gladstone began his political life as a Tory in line with a pattern in which Victorian politicians sail from one political grouping towards another in the course of their careers. He began his parliamentary career in 1832 as the Member for Newark in Nottinghamshire and it is worth noting that in the Commons he opposed the abolition of slavery and reform of the factories laws. The early Gladstone was, in other words, not quite the liberal hero of popular lore.

He was quickly elevated to a ministerial rank, holding a position with responsibility for war and the colonies in Peel's first ministry. By 1835, however, he was out of government and now we begin to see the form of a more familiar Gladstone take shape. He was a vigorous opponent of the Opium Wars with China, condemning Palmerston for the role he played in the first conflict and deploring the immoral trade in opium in general in language that listeners would soon find all too familiar. He lived in dread, he said, 'of the judgments of God towards England for our national iniquity towards China'.

In Peel's second administration, Gladstone returned to ministerial office and busied himself with improving labour legislation, before resigning in 1845 in protest at the 'Maynooth Grant', the decision by the government to increase the annual grant paid to the principal Catholic seminary in Ireland. Here Gladstone's political morality is at its most mysterious ... or dogmatic. The *citizen* Gladstone deplored the grant in and of itself, believing that a Protestant Britain should not have to pay for the training of priests in Catholic Ireland, but the *politician* Gladstone nevertheless voted in support of his government before promptly resigning. Peel was perplexed and cross. 'I really have great difficulty,' he told a friend, 'in exactly comprehending what he means.' With the Conservative rupture following the repeal of the Corn Laws, Gladstone followed Peel away from the Conservatives and with his patron's death in 1850 he emerged as a potent leader of the Peelite faction in the Commons.

Certainty and divine providence remained constant companions in his life and one example of their influence now emerged. In 1850, the Gladstone family travelled to Naples on holiday, principally for the sake of his daughter Agnes. Her health was poor and it was felt that the benign climate of southern Italy would do her good.* Few politicians can travel abroad without finding interest in the local political scene and Gladstone was pushed in this direction by some existing acquaintances. His particular concern was for Baron Carlo Poerio, who had been a minister in the revolutionary government of Naples and Sicily for a short time in 1848, a year during which revolution stalked the continent of Europe. Poerio was found guilty of subversion in 1850 and received a sentence of twenty-four years in chains and Gladstone took it upon himself to visit Poerio in gaol. He was appalled by what he found. As always, he made a detailed note of what he observed in the course of his visit. The chains that were kept on the prisoners twenty-four hours a day; the dark, damp dungeons which served as a prison; and the 'stinking soup' fed to the prisoners. He established that there were between fifteen and thirty thousand political

---

* Two of Gladstone's biographers suggest different daughters, Agnes or Mary. Agnes almost died in 1847, the year in which Mary was born, so seems the more likely of the two.

prisoners in the state, an astonishing number although a figure disputed by the Neapolitan authorities, who claimed that no more than two thousand prisoners were held. It is difficult to criticise Gladstone's righteous indignation and of course even two thousand would be a shocking number. Nonetheless, he did what he could to keep his indignation in check and established from Poerio that his intervention would not simply make matters worse. Assurance received, Gladstone exploded into action.

At this time in Westminster, Lord Stanley was trying to form a Tory government, and, as Gladstone had not yet made an irrevocable break with the Conservatives, he was offered the position of Foreign Secretary. This was a temptation. In such a powerful post he would be in an ideal position to deal with Naples. Instead Gladstone urged Lord Aberdeen by both letter and speech to use his contacts as a past Foreign Secretary to do something. This 'something' turned out to be a letter to the Austrian Chancellor, Prince Felix of Schwarzenberg, asking him to let Gladstone's concerns be made known to King Ferdinand II of Naples. Austria held considerable sway in southern Italy, not least because Ferdinand was married to Austrian archduchess Maria Theresa.

Gladstone published his letter to Aberdeen and it proved to be fairly clear in its condemnation of Naples. 'The present practices of the Government of Naples,' he wrote, 'in reference to real or supposed political offenders, are an outrage upon religion, upon civilisation, upon humanity and upon decency.' He went on to call the conduct 'inhuman and monstrous', adding for good measure that the authorities through the police 'watches and dogs the people, pays domiciliary visits, very commonly at night, ransacks houses, seizing papers and effects and tearing up floors at pleasure under pretence of searching for arms, and imprisons men by the score, by the hundred, by the thousand, without any warrant whatever'.

This letter in turn led to his public report on the prisons of Naples, compiled from first-hand observations. He told Aberdeen,

> as is well known [they] are another name for the extreme of filth and horror. I have really seen something of them, but not the worst. This I have seen, my Lord: the official doctors not going to the sick prisoners, but the sick prisoners, men almost with death on their faces, toiling upstairs to them at that charnelhouse of the Vicaria [the central courts complex of Naples], because the lower regions of such a palace of darkness are too foul and loathsome to allow it to be expected that professional men should consent to earn bread by entering them. As to diet, I must speak a word for the bread that I have seen. Though black and coarse to the last degree, it was sound. The soup, which forms the only other element of subsistence, is so nauseous, as I was assured, that nothing but the extreme of hunger could overcome the repugnance of nature to it. I had not the means of tasting it.

Such language shows the extent of Gladstone's shock and the strength of his moral outrage and not only concerning the quality of Neapolitan soup. It incidentally places Palmerston's meddling tendencies in the shade. It was directed, moreover, at a not-unfriendly nation, which did not react well to the criticism. Nor did its

Austrian ally. When Prince Schwarzenberg replied, some months later, he dismissively implied that the situation in Naples was in fact no worse than that in an Ireland still emerging from its trauma of famine. The affair distressed Gladstone's Conservative and Peelite colleagues but it was manna to Palmerston, whom Gladstone had scolded roundly in the House on account of his interventionist leanings, especially in relation to the Don Pacifico affair.

There were political repercussions to the whole incident and they were of assistance to Gladstone, for they raised his profile immeasurably and placed him in pole position for leadership of the modern Liberal Party, which duly came to pass upon Palmerston's death in 1865. It must be emphasised, however, that Gladstone's Neapolitan agitation was by no means cynical. This was not the well-thought-through product of political calculation, it was instead an emotional response to the deep repugnance he felt towards the horrors he had seen in the bowels of the prisons of Naples. According to Magnus's formula, it matters who Gladstone was, not what he did. The events at Naples met this test in that what he did arose out of who he was, an emotional and driven man who, once certain of a course, would follow it regardless of friends or political calculation. Poerio, incidentally, reaped no immediate benefit as a result of Gladstone's championing of his case. He was released only in 1858 and immediately deported to South America. En route, the ship docked in Ireland and from here Poerio made his way back to Italy, where he would in due course play a part in the Risorgimento.

*

In 1859, Palmerston formed a new government. The composition of this new administration is more than usually significant, for it marked the first time that Peelites, political liberals, Radicals and the remnant of the Whig faction coalesced to form something resembling a liberal – or, rather, Liberal – government. Gladstone put his quarrels with Palmerston aside to serve as Chancellor of the Exchequer and while history naturally tends to focus on his achievements as Prime Minister, it is the case that Gladstone achieved much of lasting value during his time at the Treasury. He is credited, indeed, with giving the ancient post of Chancellor its current character and authority, in effect creating the powerful role that exists today.

He also set about delineating the realms of public and private in a way that stands to his lasting credit. Where materials, paper, ink and so on, were for his private use, they were paid for out of his own pocket even though the distinctions were rather less clear-cut at this point. We have Gladstone to thank for the introduction of today's ethical rules of behaviour within government departments. In his own words, 'it is the mark of a chicken-hearted Chancellor when he shrinks from upholding economy in *detail* [author's emphasis] ... if he is not ready to save what are meant by candle ends and cheese parings in the cause of the Country.'

His aim was to limit the burdens that fell on the least well-off and with this in mind he continued Peel's policy of reducing tariffs. In his first Budget, of 1853, as Chancellor of the Exchequer under Aberdeen, he had exempted 123 articles of goods from tariffs altogether and reduced the rate on a further 135. He left only 48 items subject to tariffs in his 1860 Budget. In his first Budget, he had further proposed the abolition of income tax, although in the end he satisfied himself with reforming it and extending its provision to Ireland. His decision on income tax was grounded on principles of morality. Income tax, deeply unpopular though it was, had shielded Britain from the rigours of the Napoleonic Wars, and it remained necessary in times of peace. 'The public feeling of its inequality,' he conceded in the course of his longest House of Commons speech, which lasted four and three-quarter hours, 'is a fact most important in itself [but] Sir Robert Peel, in 1842, called forth from repose this giant, who had once shielded us in war, to come and assist our industrious toils in peace ... The second income tax has been the instrument by which you have introduced ... the effective reform of your commercial and fiscal system'.

In the end, rather than abolish the tax Gladstone actually extended it for another seven years, albeit in terms which steadily reduced its impact on the individual pocket. It was still meant to be temporary but it has not yet been abolished. He recognised that the demands for public expenditure could only be met by such a levy, particularly if tariffs, which he felt were an unfair imposition on the least well-off, were to be reduced and trade encouraged. Later measures were equally founded in morality and in the case of an emergency levy to pay for the Crimean War guided, it was implied, by God Himself. Gladstone informed the House of Commons on this occasion that 'the expenses of war are a moral check, which it has pleased the Almighty to impose upon the ambition and lust of conquest that are inherent in so many nations',

As Chancellor, Gladstone also developed the practice of putting all financial and Treasury matters into an annual

Finance Bill. This was by accident rather than design and came about in the aftermath of a decision by the House of Lords to reject a bill abolishing duties on paper. This tax raised £1.25 million annually but was resented as a levy on knowledge, in that it made it more difficult for cheap newspapers or pamphlets to be published. At that time every tax had its own bill and the Lords convention was that it could only reject but *not* amend such a bill. In response, Gladstone began the practice, continued ever since, of putting all his Budget measures into *one* bill. This included in this instance the previously rejected abolition of the paper tax. It was understood that the Lords would not throw out a complete Budget and this was the case until 1909, when it rejected Lloyd George's 'People's Budget', with devastating consequences for its authority. This made Gladstone's innovation a constitutionally useful way of marking the Commons' supremacy over the Lords. That Gladstone's Budget box was used by Chancellors of the Exchequer until it became too fragile was a suitable reminder that he set up the system which, for all its growth, is still in essence the same today.

*

Gladstone's career was beset by two difficult relationships. The two banes of his life were Disraeli and the Queen herself who had a profound effect on his work. The dysfunction of these relationships has amusing moments but it also indicates the distinction between the moral and the more clearly political Gladstone.

William Gladstone had met Benjamin Disraeli for the first time at a dinner in 1835 and this marked the beginning of a decades-long relationship of mutually assured detestation. Put simply, Gladstone's moral passion and Disraeli's detached cynicism left no possibility of common ground. They were oil and water. Moreover, Disraeli's later harrying of Peel did nothing to endear him to Gladstone while his ability to run rhetorical rings around Gladstone almost drove the latter mad but Gladstone did not lose every round.

The 1867 Reform Bill provides an excellent example of how the tricky relationship between these two British political leaders leached into national politics, with remarkable results. Disraeli has been accused of taking decisions on the scope and scale of the reforms based solely on what would most annoy Gladstone. Although this is exaggerated, he did seem to refuse any amendment that Gladstone backed. This was a point made explicit by Disraeli himself. In a leaked letter, he wrote, 'If any Gladstone amendment were accepted a dissolution would follow.' In the Commons itself, he said that because Gladstone's amendments were essentially partisan when he 'comes forward with a counter-proposition to the main proposals of the government ... I must say ... that I cannot in any way agree'.

It was in this mischievous spirit that Disraeli accepted one amendment when Gladstone was not in the chamber purely to stop a better amendment drawn up and tabled by Gladstone himself being accepted. In a sense, each side saw dividends flowing from this rivalry, which added something of piquancy to the usual political debates. It did Britain's expanding democracy no harm either. In an age of increasing popular involvement, by means of the extension of the franchise, the growth of newspapers and the extension of the railways, this *personification* of political differences made it clearer to a newer and better-informed electorate that there were serious divergences of opinion.

If the Gladstone/Disraeli rivalry had its benefits, the antipathy between Sovereign and subject most certainly did not. The relationship had begun smoothly enough, thanks to Prince Albert. He had helped to overcome Victoria's hostility to Sir Robert Peel, for whom the young monarch held a deep loathing on account of the Bedchamber Crisis. Albert's solicitous diplomacy had resolved this issue and made the Peel faction, which included Gladstone, an acceptable even encouraged presence at Court and Albert and Gladstone were both acolytes of Peel and liked each other. This was no surprise. After all, Albert's moral certainties mirrored those of Gladstone himself.

With the death of Albert and the onset of Victoria's long widowhood, however, the relationship disintegrated. At first, the Queen described her minister as 'very kind and feeling' in his commiserations but this period did not last long. The perceived wisdom is that Gladstone tended to treat Victoria as his Sovereign and failed to acknowledge her human grief in the black period following Albert's death. After the Queen wrote to thank Gladstone for a tribute he had paid to Albert, remarking that 'Mrs Gladstone whom the Queen knows is a most tender wife, may, in a faint manner, picture to herself what the Queen suffers', Gladstone responded with a letter that, while clearly well meant, was essentially a theological and deeply insensitive tract on the mysteries of the Divine Will. Victoria was far from gruntled.

As time went on, the Queen became steadily more disgruntled. Her complaint that he delivered political speeches during private audiences was acknowledged by Gladstone himself, who reflected that 'unhappily my manner turns every conversation into a debate'. His precise financial accounting almost manufactured a row with the Queen over the issue of the gun metal needed for the Albert Memorial in London. As Chancellor, he would not authorise a small additional expenditure on top of the amount already agreed as it was 'contrary to the rules of good administration ... to ask for more for the same purpose'. In 1866, once Disraeli took over as Chancellor, the House of Commons proved less unbending, smoothing Victoria's ruffled feathers by readily agreeing to the modest amount of additional spending.

They saw too much of each other. As Prime Minister, Gladstone had to be in regular attendance upon the Queen but instead of weekly audiences plus a short annual weekend at Balmoral, as is enjoyed by our premiers in this era, Victorian Prime Ministers were obliged to put in a great deal more time with the Sovereign. Trips to Balmoral often lasted a fortnight. Even Disraeli disliked these because rural Aberdeenshire was invariably so very cold. There were also regular stays at Osborne, frequent visits at Windsor became de rigueur and all these combined with long audiences and even longer letters meant that the Queen and Gladstone were forced into each other's society too often for comfort. The letters in particular were argumentative as well as voluminous. Gladstone would never let a point be lost or accept the blessings of the tactful silence. Both he and Victoria enjoyed arguments and both possessed surprisingly emotional temperaments. This in an age supposed to have epitomised sangfroid.

In correspondence with Vicky in Prussia, Victoria wailed that Gladstone was 'so very arrogant, tyrannical, obstinate, with no knowledge of the world or human nature'. When Gladstone left office in 1874, she confided in her diary that 'I then took leave, giving him my hand to kiss, and expressed my thanks for his services and every wish for his health. It was a relief to feel that this rather trying interview was over.' How different a tone from the clear pleasure she received later the same day when 'Mr Disraeli ... then knelt down and kissed my hand, saying "I pledge my troth to the kindest of mistresses."'

A monarch is permanent but a politician, as Sir Robin Day so memorably put it, is here today and gone tomorrow. Gladstone's poor relationship with the Queen saddened and distressed them both. When he resigned office for the last time in February 1894, Victoria recorded in her journal 'and then Mr Gladstone, who was looking very old and was very deaf. I made him sit down and I said I had received his letter and was sorry for the cause of his resignation. He said very little about it, only that he found his blindness had greatly increased since he had been at Biarritz. Then he talked about the honours for his friends but not many ... then discussed various other topics.' Gladstone himself noted that 'she had much difficulty in finding topics for an adequate prolongation: but fog and rain and [Victoria's] coming journey to Italy all did their duty and helped ... She was at the highest point of her cheerfulness. Her manner was personally kind throughout.'

The ending of a multi-decade relationship of physical closeness but personal estrangement was finally concluded when Princess Louisa arranged for the Gladstones to meet the Queen for tea in Cannes. The Queen noted that they came in for a moment and Gladstone called it ten minutes but it quickly ended.

When Gladstone died Victoria's feelings were restrained. She recorded in her journal, 'Heard at breakfast time that poor Mr Gladstone, who has been hopelessly ill for some time and had suffered severely had passed away quite peacefully this morning at 5. Poor man, he was very clever and full of ideas for the bettering and advancement of the Country, always most loyal to me personally, and ready to do anything for the Royal Family, but alas! I am sure involuntarily, he did at times a good deal of harm.' Victoria's journal entry on the day Disraeli died records that 'I am most terribly shocked and grieved, the Dear Ld. Beaconsfield was one of my best, most devoted, and kindest of friends, as well as wisest of Counsellors. His loss is irreparable, to me and to the Country. To lose such a pillar of strength at such a moment is dreadful! ... I was full of hope that he might be my Minister again.' Perhaps neither Gladstone nor Victoria liked people who treated them as equals and thus clashes were inevitable. Gladstone was *theoretically* devoted to the Queen but he was equally desperate to persuade her that he was right and here we can glimpse the human frailty of a gentleman too accustomed to lecturing and being listened to, too accustomed to regarding women, even his Sovereign, as the weaker sex and unable to change his ways. The Queen in the end was capable of a degree of fairness. In her final note on Gladstone, she recognised 'the power of his oratory, he had a wonderful power of speaking and carrying the masses with him'.

*

The mutual detestation between Gladstone and Disraeli has already been noted. Chalk and cheese seem as twins in comparison with these two dominant figures of the mid-Victorian political scene who spiced their political rivalry with a talent for mutual and gratifying needling. Disraeli, as we know, was especially good at being rude and, although we have a persistent image of the Victorians as bound by rigid rules of decorum and politeness, their politicians could be appallingly rude in ways that would be ruled out of order today and Disraeli was especially the master of the jibe.

In the aftermath of the General Election of 1868, this particular political rivalry set to work with a vengeance. Gladstone was now Liberal leader and Prime Minister. Disraeli, having all too briefly held the reins of power before the election, was now leader of the Opposition. Receiving the news that the Queen's driver was on the way from Windsor and that he would be asked to form a government, Gladstone said only, 'My mission is to pacify Ireland.' At first, however, he focused on social and labour reform and on reform of the Poor Laws in order to emphasise the virtues of individual self-reliance. He assisted in the process of professionalisation in the armed forces by banning the sale of commissions, this a delayed reaction to the scandals of the Crimean War, in which some gentleman soldiers, with no experience or aptitude for their task, had led soldiers poorly. He also condemned Disraeli's vision of a philanthropic and benevolent government and of an alliance between land-owners and the working class as so much quackery. He warned anyone who would listen that the Conservatives would, given half a chance, 'delude you with fanaticism, and offering you a fruit which, when you attempt to taste it, will prove to be but ashes in your mouth'.

Gladstone's reforms were of a piece with the morality of individualism and independence that he espoused. Disraeli promised houses, fair wages and a generally better life, which in the 1874 General Election the people accepted. He had added to the tensions surrounding the election by labelling Gladstone a shoplifter, this on the basis of Gladstone's offer to voters of a post-dated cut in income tax. Disraeli talked of a person who:

> entered a jewellers and asked to look at a costly trinket ... the customer threw a quarter of an ounce of snuff into his eyes, and when the unfortunate tradesman had recovered his sight and his senses he found his customer had disappeared, and his trinket too. And so it is that Mr Gladstone throws gold dust into the eyes of the people of England, and, before they clearly ascertain what it is like or worth, they find he has disappeared with a costly jewel as the price of his dextrous management.

The Times disapproved of such language but, as Gladstone privately referred to Disraeli as the 'Artful Dodger', it is clear that the insults were far from one-sided and that they demonstrate the limits of Gladstone's ostentatious morality, once he found himself in the political bear pit.

Gladstone was out of Downing Street but his loss of power provided him with the chance to busy himself with his favourite occupations, looking about the nation and the world, identifying moral flaws and cogitating on how they might be mended – by him. He was after all a politician and a politician hungry for renewed power, so he was not unwilling to use moral outrage to his political advantage. This was certainly true of his response to a foreign-policy issue which helped to bring focus to the duel between these two skilled politicians. As noted above, Disraeli was applauded for the skilful diplomacy deployed at the Congress of Berlin, which had convened to settle contentious European issues and international borders in the Balkans. The Queen was pleased, public opinion was pleased and even some historians have been pleased, acknowledging the period of peace in Europe that followed the deliberations in Berlin. Gladstone was not pleased, because the Congress had played out against a specific context of massacres perpetrated by Ottoman troops against Bulgarian Christians, massacres which were well known to the British government and to Disraeli.

Disraeli was content to see the Congress bolster Ottoman power as a bulwark against Russia and thus prevent the encroachment of Russian influence in the eastern Mediterranean and this was his bottom line, massacres notwithstanding. Gladstone, however, was scandalised by this example of what he regarded as cold-hearted realpolitik. The Balkans thus provided a morally charged issue with which he could pursue a deep-seated rivalry with his Tory enemy that was close to mutual loathing. Magnus suggested that Gladstone at one point was thought by his friends to have a 'black hatred' towards Disraeli, a hatred which caused him to discount any respect he might have felt in this case for the balancing act of British foreign policy.

He had himself been Prime Minister, after all. He had insights in this specific context and he knew that British foreign policy had, in the years following the Crimean War, always favoured the Ottoman Empire over Russia. This meant overlooking certain aspects of Ottoman rule in their European territories, specifically the harsh treatment of the mainly Christian population of the Balkans. Successive British governments had acknowledged that the Ottomans must be supported. The alternative was to watch Turkish power crumble and Russia and Austria extend their spheres of influence into this strategically vital region. Few envisioned the option of independent nation states and it is certainly the case that Disraeli was content to favour the Turks. Britain *must* turn a blind eye to bloodshed. Russia *must* be kept at bay.

But Gladstone set realpolitik aside. He issued a pamphlet entitled 'Bulgarian Horrors and the Question of the East'. It proved to be a sensation and sold over forty thousand copies in a few days. The pamphlet was a personal appeal by Gladstone, rather than the Liberal Party, and it was a propaganda success backed by almost anyone who mattered, except the Queen, who was almost as anti-Russian as she was anti-Gladstone. The pamphlet's power lies in its moral authority and it exudes a sense of genuine horror.

There have been perpetrated, under the immediate authority of a Government to which all the time we have been giving the strongest moral, and for part of the time even material support, crimes and outrages, so vast in scale as to exceed all modern example, and so unutterably vile as well as fierce in character that it passes the power of heart to conceive, and of tongue and pen adequately to describe them. These are the Bulgarian horrors.

The Turks, declared Gladstone, were 'the one great anti-human specimen of humanity. Wherever they went, a broad line of blood marked the track behind them.'

He deployed his fury to castigate the government for its dissembling answers in Parliament and its lax view of Turkish behaviour, most especially in claiming that the persecuted Bulgarians were to some degree the aggressor. He forensically went through questions and answers to show how the government in general and Disraeli in particular had failed to respond to the facts concerning the massacre and then he set out the specific charges he wished to level against Disraeli's administration. The first was inefficiency of arrangements for receiving information. The second was, even worse, the tardiness of gathering further information about the massacres and the third was the misleading answers which would have left Parliament and public alike believing that responsibility for the massacres lay elsewhere. Gladstone was outraged in particular by the claim that although the atrocities had been committed by Ottoman troops, by agents of the state, there was nevertheless fault on both sides. 'This declaration is a gross wrong inadvertently done to the people of Bulgaria; and it ought to be withdrawn.'

Gladstone's magisterial conclusion has resonated through the decades:

I return to, and I end with, that which is the omega as well as the alpha of this great and mournful case ... I entreat my countryman ... to insist that our Government, which has been working in one direction, shall work in the other and shall apply all its vigour to concur with the other states of Europe in obtaining the extinction of the Turkish executive power in Bulgaria. Let the Turks now carry away their abuses in the only possible manner, namely by carrying off themselves. Their zaptiehs and their mudirs, their bimbashis and their yuzbachis, their kaimakams and their pashas, one and all, bag and baggage, shall, I hope, clear out from the province they have desolated and profaned. This thorough riddance, this most blessed deliverance, is the only reparation we can make to the memory of those heaps on heaps of dead; to the violated purity alike of matron, of maiden, and of child; to the civilisation which has been affronted and shamed; to the laws of God, or, if you like, of Allah; to the moral sense of mankind at large. There is not a criminal in an European jail, there is not a cannibal in the South Sea Islands, whose indignation would not rise and overboil at the recital of that which has been done.

The language is very much of its time, but the rhetoric shows Gladstone at his most masterful. He set out the case against the Turks clearly and he took apart the government's actions and showed them to be not only wanting but far from straightforward. Disraeli was attempting a cover-up, this action being even worse and more malign than the initial policy failure. Then, with soaring rhetoric, he set about shaming people into accepting what he was certain was rightful. This pamphlet in itself reaffirmed his position as the greatest force in the Liberal Party, a politician who could hold the leadership at will.

Gladstone's actions, or rather his language in private, in the course of this episode left much to be desired. He saw fit to deploy anti-Semitic tropes against Disraeli. To his friend the Duke of Argyll he remarked that the Jews of the eastern Mediterranean had always hated the Christians, the implication being that it was therefore no wonder that Disraeli, with his Jewish heritage, would not lift a finger to assist European Christians. This is one of the nastiest thoughts of a self-proclaimed moral politician. The implication was that as Disraeli was a Jew in England so he was not in himself English. Thus no one could expect him to behave as an English gentleman would behave. Disraeli, remarked Gladstone, 'was not such a Turk as I had thought. What he hates is Christian liberty and reconstruction.' When Argyll commented that 'Disraeli may be willing to risk his government for his Judaic feeling', Gladstone replied, 'I have a strong suspicion that ... Dizzy's crypto-judaism has had to do with his policy.' Such unpleasant and racist discourse makes for deeply uncomfortable reading and would have had even greater insidious power in the context of Britain in the 1870s. This was by no means Gladstone's finest moment.

In cold, hard political terms, however, his attacks hit their mark, for Gladstone was now focused on leading the Liberal Party to victory in the coming election and forcing Disraeli from office. Gladstone's work began in 1879 in Midlothian, where he was, ostensibly, campaigning to be elected as the local Member of Parliament. The events in Midlothian were innovative in that they evolved into the first national General Election campaign and before Parliament had been dissolved. As manifestos had started with Peel's address to the electors of Tamworth so the concept and practice of popular electioneering began within this Scottish constituency. Not that this ought to have been unexpected. The reforms of 1867 had increased the electorate so enormously that true campaigning, of the sort we would recognise today, was now necessary. The real surprise is that Disraeli did not innovate first but by now he was old and even less energetic. It was a shock to some, who saw this form of popular election-eering as coarse and potentially dangerous.

Gladstone began his tour on 24 November 1879, trav-elling by train from Liverpool to Edinburgh. Crowds gathered at every stop to hear him speak a few inspiring words against Disraeli. In Edinburgh itself, a vast flag-waving crowd appeared and Gladstone was escorted by a torchlit procession with fireworks and fairy lanterns as he headed to stay with Lord Rosebery at Dalmeny House. It was the sort of reception that today would be accorded to a rock star, not a politician. Gladstone clearly enjoyed the experience, recording that 'I have never gone through a more extraordinary day' but by the end of the fortnight of speeches, such dramatic recep-tions must have seemed almost commonplace. The crowds were huge, and they remained huge. Gladstone carefully made a note of each one, recording the thirty gentlemen who assembled to listen to him on 4 December 'at Sir J. Watson's after dinner', as well as the 20,000 who gathered at Edinburgh's Waverley Market. Each one of these, regardless of context, received the full flow of

Gladstonian oratory and full expression of Gladstonian intellect. In all he addressed 86,930 people, which Lord Jenkins pointed out in his biography was only slightly more than the number of words uttered by Gladstone, a total of 85,840, so nearly one word per person in the audience.

Nor did he patronise his audiences. He delivered complex arguments at considerable length, assuming that his listeners could keep up. At the Edinburgh Corn Exchange he spent seventy-five minutes addressing thousands of people on the details of Disraeli's financial errors and this was only the first of several speeches that day. The speeches were reported nationally and as the total electorate in the General Election in Midlothian was only 3,260 the majority of Gladstone's audience must have been from outside the constituency. Newspapers devoted column after column to Gladstone's words and attacks on Disraeli. Some famous quotations have resonated down the decades. He said of the Zulu War that 10,000 had been killed for 'their attempt to defend against your artillery with their naked bodies, their hearths and homes, their wives and families'. He attacked Disraeli for 'jobbery', a practice that was meant to have died out, for creating a post for a friend, Lord Hampton, as a civil service commissioner at a cost of £2,000 per annum. This he said was 'to do what had been admirably done without that office before, and had not been ... one bit better done since.' He objected to the annexation of Cyprus and defended the rights of the Afghan: 'the sanctity of life in the hill villages of Afghanistan, among the winter snows, is as inviolable in the eyes of Almighty God as can be your own'. This may not be what his listeners believed but he was willing to say difficult things such as reiterating his opposition to protectionism and other short-term solutions.

It is hard to see his speeches as a clear definition of liberalism or even of Gladstonianism because although years before he had opposed Don Pacifico he wanted something done about Naples. It was more a concentrated attack on everything Disraeli had done, on 'Beaconsfield-ism', and was ruthlessly partisan. Equally, it was high-minded and, no doubt in Gladstone's mind, inspired by God but it was important because it made it clear that in spite of his resignation Gladstone was the only leader of the Liberal Party and that he understood the need to communicate to the new electorate. Magnus's phrase that it is about who Gladstone was rather than what he did once again comes to mind and it saw him at the peak of his popularity. It paved the way for people to view him as the grand old man, the sobriquet that was later reversed from GOM to MOG, or murderer of Gordon.

In addition to which, God played His part in Gladstone's campaign. Gladstone's ideas and his energy were inspired by God, because he was God's agent and he was needed at Downing Street. So Gladstone thought, at any rate. His popularity at this moment can be glimpsed in paintings appearing in the years that followed. For example, Alfred Morgan's *An Omnibus Ride to Piccadilly Circus, Mr Gladstone Travelling with Ordinary Passengers* portrays a soulful Gladstone perched amid a crowd of typical passengers on a London omnibus. A wildly improbable scene but a vision which reflects his status as a man of the people. All this, his pamphlets, his speeches, his campaigning, his thunderous denunciations, unsettled Disraeli, and set the scene for Gladstone's victory in the

General Election of 1880, which also marked the end of Disraeli's political career. After all the needling, Gladstone had had the last word.

*

Gladstone's advocacy regarding the state of the prisons in Naples was driven by a sense of moral outrage not accompanied by any particular political gain and his reaction to the atrocities in the Balkans was energised by a similar sense of political morality, though in this case his advocacy brought with it considerable political profit. The extent to which a sense of morality governed his politics in general is apparent, although it is worth noting that it is sometimes difficult to see the coherence in this great moral plan. The Liberals came to power in 1880 determined to step back from the overly imperialist foreign policy pursued by Disraeli yet it was Gladstone who fought and defeated the Boers in South Africa and who asserted British control over Egypt by means of invasion in 1882. Not that these decisions always came accompanied by political advantage. Gladstone's policies in the Sudan, embodied in the shape of Gordon of Khartoum, were both militarily and politically disastrous.

The Irish Question, which dominated the latter phase of Gladstone's long public career, came with little by way of political advantage and a great deal of political cost. Gladstone had been thinking about Ireland for many years and his political career had intersected repeatedly with Ireland, as did so many Victorian careers, before he engaged fully with the country as the central crusade of his political life. When Gladstone assumed the premiership late in 1868, one of his first legislative acts was the passing of the Irish Land Act, designed to protect Irish tenant farmers from unfair treatment at the hands of landlords and to provide for financial compensation in the event of eviction. It was in itself a modest Act. It made no provision for security of tenure and history shows that its effects were even more modest, for its measures were ineffective and widely ignored. It is important to note that the Act passed the Commons with an enormous majority, Liberals and Conservatives alike recognising the need to address the injustices swirling around the ownership and control of land in Ireland. Events in the wider economic world, moreover, also militated against the success of the Act. The agricultural sector went into depression in 1875, with the result that rents that had been affordable in 1870 now became unaffordable and tenants were now liable to be summarily evicted for non-payment.

For all its failings, however, this first Land Act was a sign of things to come. It was an indication that the system was not blind to the existence of a besetting problem in Ireland, that the system of land tenure did not support investment either by landlord or by tenant. It also indicated that British politicians were aware of warnings from history. They were aware that Ireland's Great Famine of 1845–9, described by Lord John Russell as a 'famine of the thirteenth century acting upon a population of the nineteenth', indicated the need for change, investment and reform in rural Ireland. A million people had died in that famine, over a million more had emigrated so this was not an issue that could be simply sidestepped.

Gladstone was as well aware as anyone else of the need for sweeping changes in Ireland. Gladstone being Gladstone, this was much more than an issue of agricultural economics, it was also a question of considerable moral weight. It attracted his eye as a politician, a Treasury boffin and a Victorian moraliser. He had, in addition to all of these factors, been shamed by the remark flung at him by Schwarzenberg of Austria that the state of Ireland was as great a stain on the British body politic as were the foetid prisons of Naples on the face of Europe. This concatenation of circumstances combined with his belief that he possessed a God-given destiny to solve problems so the effect was a desire to act.

He was out of power for the latter half of the 1870s but once he returned to Downing Street at the head of a majority Liberal administration in 1880 his path was clear, and this decade marks the beginning of a new phase in his politics. As he wrote in a letter to his brother Sir Thomas Gladstone in 1885, 'My profound desire is retirement, and nothing has prevented or will prevent me giving effect to that desire, unless there should appear to be something in which there may be a prospect of my doing what could not be as well done without me.' That 'thing' was Ireland in general and the cause of Home Rule in particular.

The germ of the idea must have been in Gladstone's mind for some time before it emerged publicly in 1885. A second Land Act took further steps towards regularising issues of tenancy and ownership in rural Ireland but by now a tide of Irish nationalism was rising and an upsurge of political violence in Ireland focused Gladstone's mind. In particular, the assassination of the

Chief Secretary for Ireland, Lord Frederick Cavendish and his under-secretary, Thomas Burke, close to Dublin's Viceregal Lodge in May 1882, sent shockwaves through Westminster and convinced Gladstone that radical actions would be needed to 'settle' Ireland.

At first he sought consensus, suggesting discreetly to prominent Tory Arthur Balfour that the Conservatives ought to introduce a Home Rule bill for Ireland. The party had, after all, piloted Act after radical Act through the Commons, from Emancipation to the repeal of the Corn Laws to the Reform Bill of 1867, so why not Home Rule too? In December 1885, however, all of Gladstone's cross-party hopes came to naught when his son, the MP Herbert Gladstone, flew the so-called 'Hawarden Kite'. He announced to *The Times* that 'Nothing could induce me to countenance separation, but if five-sixths of the Irish people wish to have a Parliament in Dublin, for the management of their own local affairs, I say, in the name of justice and wisdom, let them have it.' He simultaneously briefed the *Pall Mall Gazette* to the effect that 'Mr [William] Gladstone has definitely adopted the policy of Home Rule for Ireland and there are well founded hopes that he will win over the Chief Representatives of the moderate section of the party to his views.' We cannot know what Herbert Gladstone was thinking in speaking so indiscreetly but the effect was to shatter any possibility of a consensus over the Irish Question. Thereafter, Home Rule was identified explicitly with sections of the Liberal Party, and especially with Gladstone himself.

Gladstone did not succeed in introducing Home Rule, though it was not for want of trying. The issue drove him to the very end of his political career. In 1892, at the age of eighty-two, he formed his last government still with Ireland on his mind. He split the Liberal Party on account of Ireland and he watched the Liberal Unionist faction come into being and complicate the arithmetic of the Commons, also on account of Ireland. At this point, it is worth emphasising that the fate of the Liberal Party was never Gladstone's principal concern, for he was never explicitly a party man. He began as a Tory, became a Peelite, joined and then split the Liberals. Whereas Disraeli was an assiduous builder of the Conservative Party organisation, Gladstone had no such interests. It was policy that drove him forward, policy put through a prism of morality, and Ireland must be understood as one of his great moral political crusades, even if an unsuccessful one. It is only by viewing the relationship between Ireland and Gladstone in these moral terms that it can be properly understood.

One of Gladstone's other failings was in his dealings with General Sir Charles Gordon, almost entirely Gladstone's fault. He agreed for Gordon to be sent to the Sudan, even though others thought it was madness to send an inspired warrior to lead a retreat. Even Gladstone soon realised his error, telling his family that Gordon could lead to the fall of the government and he started receiving troubled messages from the Queen. He had plenty of time to order a rescue of Gordon to be organised but he delayed, fearing, even when he finally authorised such a mission, that it would add 2d. to income tax. Perhaps Gordon and Gladstone were too alike. Both believed that they were on a divine mission and that the Almighty directed their works. Unfortunately, God seemed to give the two of them entirely contradictory instructions hence Gordon's heroic martyrdom which plunged Gladstone into the depths of unpopularity, somewhat unfairly as Gordon directly disobeyed his clear orders. This allowed no respite for Gladstone and the music hall sang out 'the MOG when his life ebbs out, will ride in a fiery chariot and sit in state on a red hot plate between Pilot and Judas Iscariot'.

This must have been a disagreeable time for Gladstone, who had clearly enjoyed the crowds' admiration and now had the reverse. It perhaps shows the truth of William Forster's swipe, 'I attribute his [Gladstone's] not being convinced [of Gorden's being in danger] to his wonderful power of persuasion. He can persuade most people of most things, and above all he can persuade himself of almost anything.' Gladstone had a stubbornness and self-righteousness that were thoroughly exposed by Gordon's insubordination.

*

Current scholarship has favoured Gladstone over Disraeli. Gladstone is seen as high-minded, liberal and far-sighted. Yet so much of what he did failed. Irish Home Rule was defeated, income tax was not abolished, the Liberal Party was left divided and Gordon died while the Sudan was invaded. Balfour in his eulogy, delivered in the Commons on the day of Gladstone's death, said that the erstwhile Prime Minister 'raised in the public estimation the whole level of our proceedings' and perhaps he was right. Gladstone made politics and politicians seem honourable, important and honest. His relative absence of cynicism was no ploy but the genuine article and as his night prowls through London were a real effort to save fallen women, so his political career was devoted to helping mankind. Disraeli's focus on the condition of the people may have been more materially successful and his cynicism rather more an act but history has been the judge of both men. Disraeli's legacy has been scarred but Gladstone's legacy, his failures notwithstanding, has remained unsullied. Perhaps this is the lesson he leaves us, that which Gladstone *was* is indeed of greater importance than what he *did* and that a public and articulated morality is the best tool politicians can have at their disposal for their posthumous reputation.

Gordon: Servant of the People

Too late! Too late to save him,
In vain, in vain they tried.
His life was England's glory,
His death was England's pride.

The scene is one common enough in the annals of Empire: the valiant British officer leading his troops in defence of civilisation and in the face of surely insurmountable odds. Sometimes, these odds prove to be in fact surmountable and a story of valour is forged in the heat of battle and victory. At other times, the context and setting prove too much, even for the doughtiest of warriors. The officer falls in the face of superior numbers and victory becomes defeat. Glory is equally possible and with death comes a story of heroism.

Such was the case with Charles George Gordon (28 January 1833–26 January 1885), better known as Gordon of Khartoum, who was struck down as he led a small British force fighting against all the odds in the Sudan. An image was memorialised by the painter George William Joy, and soldered into the Victorian imagination: General

Gordon's Last Stand portrays a British hero standing upright at the head of a staircase, imperious, dismissive of danger and of his enemies, careless of death. He bids his enemies begone, turns and is struck in the back with a spear and topples from the staircase to his death.

The real circumstances of his death are even more brutal. The consensus is that Charles Gordon was hacked to death and his head paraded around Khartoum on a stick. Yet the image of Gordon on the stairs was caught and endures and, as is the way with the stories of heroes, the real history of Gordon of Khartoum was occluded by myth. He was, for example, another Eminent Victorian unfortunate enough to catch the spiteful eye of Lytton Strachey, with the usual consequences for Gordon's reputation in the twentieth century. Nonetheless, 'Send for Gordon!' He has retained something of his mystique, in spite of the critics.

In this chapter, the aim is to re-examine this British exemplar, this military hero, this globe-trotting servant of the Crown, who gave his life in its service. In particular, to emphasise the forgotten aspects of his story, his deep and unique religiosity; his ability to understand and empathise with the peoples of the lands, from China to Sudan, he visited as part of his ostensibly 'imperial' mission; and the sense in which his life helps to explain elements in this mission that are too frequently ignored or misunderstood.

*

Charles Gordon was born in Woolwich, south-east London, one of the eleven children of Major General Henry Gordon and his wife Elizabeth. The Gordons were a Scottish family and were steeped in British military tradition, with four generations of service to its name. Henry Gordon served with the Royal Artillery and there was never any question but that Charles and his brothers would also enter the armed forces. Elizabeth Gordon had been an Enderby, a family that had made its fortune in whaling in the seas south of Australia and in the Atlantic shipping trade. Travel and an understanding of the great world, therefore, ran in the blood. By all accounts, the Gordons were a stable and happy family. The little Charlie, who was noted from an early age for his 'robust playfulness of manner', was chiefly the charge of Nurse Cooper, a lady who, 'though she loved the boys, [merely] tolerated the girls'. The Gordons were devoutly Christian and religion would play a pivotal role in the later life of Charles Gordon.

Henry Gordon's postings meant that the family enjoyed, or at any rate endured, a peripatetic life. They lived by turns in Ireland, Scotland and Corfu in the Ionian Islands, which, as the life of Charles Napier records, were at this time a British possession. The young Gordon's education was nonetheless English, culminating in his accession to the Royal Military Academy at Woolwich. In the summer of 1852, at the age of nineteen, he joined the Royal Engineers. He had shown an aptitude for the art and science of cartography and his training focused on skills to do with reconnaissance, managed retreats and the sudden storming of enemy strongholds, all tasks necessary for a life and career at the cutting edge of the British imperial adventure.

Even at this early age, Gordon was a man with considerable charisma, a natural leader, even if his strong will meant that he was not invariably held in high esteem by his superiors. He was restive under orders and was apt to follow his own mind, neither of which characteristics was necessarily embraced in the armed forces. Another glimpse of the man he would presently become is in the fact that he had already absorbed the evangelical Christianity of his older sister Augusta and now he adopted a decidedly universal attitude to organised religion, attending a Methodist service one day, a Presbyterian one the next, a Catholic one the next. 'The church is like the British Army,' he remarked to a Catholic priest, 'one army but many regiments.' Gordon never formally adhered to any Christian Church but continued his wide range of Christian experiences for the rest of his life.

It is important to focus on Gordon's religion. Without knowledge of his relationship with God, Gordon the man cannot be fully understood. Strachey certainly lit on this issue, and interpreted it unpleasantly: 'He was Gordon Pasha,' Strachey wrote, imagining the final days of Gordon in besieged Khartoum, 'he was the Governor-General, he was the ruler of the Sudan. He was among his people – his own people, and it was to them only that he was responsible – to them, and to God.' Jeering words from the disagreeable Strachey, yet ironically apt too, for they do capture something of the man and his unique relationship with God.

Augusta Gordon had lent her brother her copy of the eighteenth-century commentator Thomas Scott's *Commentary on the Bible* and this text had immediate and enormous significance for Gordon. 'To me,' wrote Scott as he ventriloguized the Epistle of Paul to the Philippians

1:21, and the young officer avidly read and assented, 'to live is Christ, and to die is gain.' To present-day sensibilities Gordon might seem morbid, if excessively influenced by such words, but present sensibilities are reluctant to contemplate the possibility of death, which Gordon, as with most Victorians, was accustomed to all around him.

That said, Gordon stood out distinctively in his own time even to other Christians. In 1865, as he sat dutifully with his dying father, Gordon wondered:

> whether Christ came for such a wretched, weak sort of religion as that usually followed by the Christian world – a religion of grumpiness, spite, unhappiness, pharisaism, etc. I thought surely, if He did come and suffer, He came for a more effective religion than that; otherwise it must be confessed that as far as our life in this world is concerned, His mission failed in enabling His followers to overcome the world.

From this distance it should be remembered that the England which provoked this reaction in Gordon was almost as alien to him as it is to the twenty-first century. This was a man who served far beyond her shores for nearly all his life, hardly unique in the age of Empire but Gordon's reactions to contemporary British Christianity were filtered through his own experience of the great world. By this time, though only thirty-two, he had already seen a vast swathe of the world, in all its colour and diversity, so it is no surprise that he found standard models of British piety to be narrow and conventional in the extreme. It cannot be surprising, when seen in this light, that he should conceive of having his own personal and distinct hotline to God, one unencumbered by any institutional religion.

This evolution of a private creed, however, was based firmly on biblical teaching. Dressing for dinner one evening, his eyes had fallen on his own Bible, lying open at the First Epistle of St John 4.15: 'Whosoever shall confess that Jesus is the Son of God, God dwelleth in him, and he in God.' This captured Gordon's sense of God as essentially personal and interior and this understanding of the 'indwellingness' of God became the rock of Gordon's faith and the foundation upon which all else came to be built. Later, such books as Thomas à Kempis's *The Imitation of Christ*, with its essentially Catholic message of spirituality, sustained and developed his faith but the simplicity of the message, that anyone could come to and be with God through Christ, he never forgot.

We can also argue that his faith, or this sense of a personal relationship with God, was essential to the coherence of Gordon's life, enabling him to make sense of its travails. 'Man', he wrote to a friend, 'is apt to rest on the Redemption, apart from the liberty which that Redemption gives. God did not redeem us to be feeble and weak but He redeemed us for His service, to joy in Him, to know Him in His thick darkness.' As we shall see, Gordon was to know first-hand much of the 'thick darkness' that the Lord ordained for him.

By the end of his life, his fullest exposition of Christian belief had become idiosyncratic, where, that is, it was not actually patently heretical. He came to believe in the pre-existence of the soul. The body was a 'sheath' in which the soul was placed at birth, to be awoken when union with Christ was achieved. This union could be effected in varied ways according to Gordon's cosmology. Then, once this vision occurred, 'the now raised and quickened soul will grope its way out of its shell', Gordon declared, where 'it will contend with the body, often being nearly extinguished but never quite, till the body gives up the struggle in natural death' and the much longed-for homecoming is achieved. Gordon, as we shall see, almost met his own personal homecoming many times, before he finally achieved that which he greatly desired. There is a strong sense that much of his character was governed by his being so often and for so long denied this supreme goal of homecoming and union with God.

From time to time, Gordon's associates were taken aback or profoundly shocked by his suggestions on the nature of Christianity. Frederick Temple, future Archbishop of Canterbury, was Bishop of Exeter when he learned from Gordon that the progress of Christianity in Africa would be greatly facilitated if its representatives only had the wit to entertain some mild measure of polygamy there. More startling still, perhaps, to the ears of stolidly conventional Victorian Anglicans was the news that Catholics counted as Christians too. On the way to his own Calvary in the Sudan, Gordon repeated his message of Christian union to the men under him and the people he was protecting: 'Catholics and Protestants are but soldiers in different regiments of Christ's army, but it is the same army and we are all marching together.'

Another crucial point to make is that Gordon, irrespective of the 'heathen' field in which he found himself, was never on a *crusade*. At least, not the sort of crusade which, in today's conception of it, sought to pull down rather than shore up. As perhaps his surest biographer of recent times, John Pollock, recounts: 'At one place [during his first stint as Governor-General of the Sudan] Gordon found a mosque had been turned into a powder magazine. "I had it cleared out and handed back with great ceremonies which have delighted the people: it is now endowed and in full swing." Strong Christian though he was, he held that "the Mussulman worships God as well as I do, and is as acceptable, if sincere, as any Christian." Man's dominion was never the thing for Gordon and his mission was never merely his temporal masters.'

What sort of man did this sure faith in God create? The one brought before King John IV of Ethiopia on 27 October 1879, following a month's journey on a mule through the mountains to John's capital at Debre Tabor. "'Do you know," remarked John, eyeing Gordon, "[that] I could kill you on the spot if I liked?" "I am perfectly well aware of it," Gordon replied, "Do so at once if it is your royal pleasure. I am ready." "What, ready to be killed!" "Certainly", Gordon had himself say in reply, "I am always ready to die, and so far from fearing you putting me to death, you would confer a favour on me by so doing, for you would be doing for me that which I am precluded by my religious scruples from doing for myself.'"

Little wonder that W. T. Stead, the famed Victorian journalist, would write to Augusta of her brother's death that it 'had done more to make Christ real to people than if he had civilized a hundred Congos and smashed a thousand Mahdis'. He wished to set an example, in life and in death, and this is what he achieved. To understand who Gordon served and how and to remember how very differently he viewed his life and his mission it is necessary to examine his service to foreign empires which allows a fuller view of the nature of the Victorian imperialism he largely forswore.

*

The Crimean War consisted of rather more than the Charge of the Light Brigade and Florence Nightingale. It was part of a Great Game of politics playing out in the arenas of eastern Europe and the Mediterranean and Black seas, a game of strategy that pitted Russia against Britain and France, with a eddying host of allies on either side. It was the first war of its kind, one waged with such technological innovations as shells, fast rail transport and rapid telegraph-based communications. It was also a war darkened by military mismanagement and it sharpened the call in Britain itself for the professionalisation of the nation's armed forces. A call that would be answered in part in the course of William Gladstone's first administration.

Charles Gordon arrived in the Crimea early in 1855 and his skills in reconnaissance and cartography saw him pressed into service at Balaklava, as part of the brutal siege of the great Russian naval base at Sebastopol. Here, British and French troops had become locked into a bitter, trench-bound war of attrition, this mere months after disaster had befallen the Light Brigade in the same place. Elizabeth Thompson's painting *The Roll Call* captures the horror of Sebastopol and it caused a sensation in Britain. It portrays a muster of exhausted soldiers after a skirmish in the snow, the names of the living and the dead ticked off one by one.

Gordon experienced his share of such military horror. His tasks were by their nature perilous. He was all too frequently under direct enemy fire from the walls of the fortress and he was wounded by sniper fire. In the summer of that year, he was in the front line of a great Anglo-French assault intended to take the city and end the siege and he found himself covered head to toe in mud and the blood of his companions. His reputation for courage under fire was forged at Sebastopol and as a result of his experiences there, he was honoured by both the British and French governments. He followed his experiences in the Crimea with quieter though at times tense service delineating the Russian–Ottoman border in Romania, helping to establish a Commission to manage the economically vital navigation of the Danube and later assisting in the demarcation of the Russian–Ottoman border in Armenia. Here, he embraced for the first time the then new medium of the camera. His evocative and atmospheric photographs of Armenian landscapes and people received much attention and he was elected a Fellow of the Royal Geographical Society.

From late 1858, a spell of home service followed but this was never going to excite such a man. He begged for another foreign posting and as a result came his first visit to China, at first in the Queen's service.

*

The First and Second Opium Wars have been mentioned *en passant*. They were Palmerston's brainchild, even though he had left office by the time the first of these conflicts was concluded in 1842. Palmerston had returned to Downing Street in 1859 thus he was again in charge for a portion at least of the Second Opium War, which had broken out in the previous year. The years between the wars witnessed a rapid expansion of European economic activity in a China revealed now as militarily weak and politically divided but this activity, though profitable in itself, also had the effect of further heightening tension in the region.

The Second Opium War was known at the time as the Arrow War, *Arrow* being the name of a British-registered but Chinese-crewed ship, which had under its previous master engaged in piracy. The seizure of her crew by the Chinese authorities at Canton in October 1856 was taken as a great insult by the British, especially given the fact that the Chinese had hauled down and damaged the ship's British flag. Although the sailors were eventually released, no apology was forthcoming and the incident became a British pretext for war. The real goal was to entrench in fact the hitherto paper concessions Peking had made under the Treaty of Nanking which concluded the First Opium War. A war duly began, with the British bombarding Canton and destroying Chinese ships lying in the city's harbour.

The rising tensions at Canton, however, had not come at an especially opportune moment for the British. The unstable Whig-led government voted down a proposal to take the capture of the *Arrow* as grounds for war and, in the resulting General Election, Palmerston returned to office but in May 1857 the Indian Mutiny caused consternation in London. Troops bound for China were hastily redirected to India and it took a French intervention to bring the European war effort back onto an even keel.

The war was bitter but in spite of various missteps and the lingering effects of the Mutiny, the Europeans always had the upper hand. By the time Gordon arrived at the new British territory of Hong Kong in 1860, the fighting was approaching its end. He was in time, however, to observe one of most notorious incidents in the war, albeit the one which may well have impelled the Chinese authorities to end their resistance. This was the burning of the Summer Palace near Peking in 1860. The Palace is generally considered to have been a wonder of Chinese architecture and garden design. It consisted of buildings and landscapes covering close to a thousand acres and was filled with Chinese art treasures. In September 1860, as an Anglo-French military force approached Peking, emissaries were sent ahead to negotiate the terms of a surrender. These emissaries were instead imprisoned, tortured and killed, so in October Lord Elgin, then the British representative in China, ordered the destruction of the Summer Palace as retaliation. The complex took three days to destroy and some three hundred members of the imperial staff were killed.

Gordon was present as a Royal Engineers commander. He watched the French loot indiscriminately and in an undisciplined manner, the British destroy coolly and systematically. His account was stark and troubled:

We went out, and after pillaging it, burned the whole place, destroying in a vandal-like manner most valuable property which [could] not be replaced for four millions. We got upwards of £48 apiece prize money ... I have done well. The [local] people are very civil, but I think the grandees hate us, as they must after what we did to the Palace. You can scarcely imagine the beauty and magnificence of the places we burnt. It made one's heart sore to burn them; in fact, these places were so large and we were so pressed for time, that we could not plunder them carefully. Quantities of gold ornaments were burnt, considered as brass. It was wretchedly demoralising work for an army.

This is valuable testimony because his words cast a useful light on Gordon's views of the entire event. He is a participant and he profits but it is difficult to argue that he takes part eagerly. He is not only aware of the destruction but aware too of the loss of patrimony and the needless violence. Most interestingly of all, he is aware of the Chinese themselves and of the differences between them. This is no slipshod account, but nuanced history.

The destruction of the Summer Palace left its mark on the man, of this there can be no doubt, for Gordon never allowed troops under his command to loot in any of his subsequent campaigns. Upon the war's close, Gordon organised a poor-relief fund for the local Chinese, much to the irritation of the resident mandarins. It was at this time too that Gordon mounted the pedestal from which no amount of envious slander from Strachey or anyone else has ever been able to dislodge him. For in short and providential order Gordon was to become commander of the 'Ever Victorious Army', in the service of the despotic Manchu regime and against, of all things, a species of evangelical Christianity in the shape of the Taiping. History is never anything other than curious in its ends and instruments.

*

By the time of Gordon's arrival in China, the ferocious and unremittingly savage Taiping Rebellion was in its eleventh year. An odd amalgam of Christianity and local religions, the Taiping had various origins, not least zealous American Methodist missionaries who had laced the Gospel with a species of anti-British propaganda. Its leader, a farmer's son named Hong Xiuquan, had taken to thinking of himself as being the younger brother of Christ. His followers rejoiced in the chance to revolt against the Qing dynasty which had ruled China since the seventeenth century but which now was staggering under the assault of wars, internal rebellion, famine and flood, not to mention an inadequate administration run by the regime itself.

To many Chinese citizens, the Taiping could hardly have brought about an outcome worse than the one to which they had become miserably accustomed. To Taiping supporters outside China, not least among Britons ardent for Christian expansion, there was much to admire in them too. There was some Confucianism and Buddhism for devout Victorian Christians to overlook but there was also a Sabbath kept, hymns sung, idols smashed, the Commandments learned and prayers said. In reality, the scant information which made it back to London illuminated few facts about the Taiping and nothing at all about the inherent savagery of their methods. In taking Nanking in March 1853, to give just one horrifying example, its soldiers had slaughtered some 30,000 of the people of the city and they did not discriminate as to age or sex in the gruesome manner of murder.

In May of that year, the Taiping had come close to seizing Peking itself. In the aftermath of this encounter, its army turned its attentions east and south and by 1861 the Taiping was approaching Shanghai. This thriving port city was home to the greatest concentration of British and foreign residents and businesses in China and now, in alarm and with haste, the merchants of the great entrepôt raised, with the blessing of Emperor Xianfeng, a militia-like army to defend their commercial interests. This militia they named the 'Disciplined Chinese' but the Chinese themselves soon renamed it the 'Ever Victorious Army'. Palmerston had initially insisted that serving British officers not involve themselves in this enterprise and its first two commanders were dissolute Americans.

Eventually, the disparate interests of the imperial Chinese, the British and the merchants of Shanghai coalesced so it was realised that the Ever Victorious Army, if it were to live up to its name, was in need of a professional military commander. One British administrator summed up the situation neatly. What was required was 'a man of good temper, of clean hands, and a steady economist'. The hour and the man came together. Even at this perilous moment, elements within Whitehall grumbled as to the wisdom of British officers taking up roles within a Chinese fighting force, so much so that a directive countering Gordon's appointment was sent from London but the vessel carrying the message was shipwrecked en route. Gordon had meanwhile seized the opportunity offered by providence.

In his very first engagement, Gordon signalled his intent to be victorious. The scent of righteousness was in his nostrils and he won his first victory over the Taiping against a backdrop of the putrefying bodies of earlier, crucified Taiping victims, who had been all too evidently tortured with fire before their deaths. *Gor-don* became *Ko-teng*, *ko* translating as 'offensive weapons' and *teng* 'to rise', as appropriate a name for a commander of sappers as has ever been devised. Immediately, Gordon displayed all the traits which would mark his commands thereafter. He ensured that his men were paid, he banned liquor, he forbade looting and he refused for himself the imperial bounty which was the overwhelming reason why Westerners came to China in the first place.

His experience with the Ever Victorious Army would establish Gordon's reputation among his peers as an individual who could work with the indigenous population and work miracles. As Gordon himself remarked years later to his friend and fellow Strachey target Florence Nightingale, 'I gained the hearts of my soldiers (who would do anything for me) not by justice etc. but by looking after them when sick, or wounded, and by continually visiting the hospital.' This was extremely unusual at the time. Contemporary Western generals struggled to develop a habit of collegiality and empathy even with their 'own' men, to say nothing of local or 'native' troops. In Gordon's expansive heart, however, there really was no conception of division between East and West.

At every stage his humanity shone through. A British deserter from the Ever Victorious Army was ordered to be taken away and shot, ostensibly to prevent his sometime comrades from doing so on the spot. In truth, Gordon had the man shipped away to safety. In the Army's assault on Quinsai, a strategically vital municipality perilously close to Shanghai itself, Gordon rescued a naked infant, who then clung to him for much of the battle. In due course, Gordon sent the child to be fostered at Shanghai and paid for his education.*

As for the campaign against the Taiping itself, Gordon showed his strategic nous and validated time and again the original decision to appoint him as head of this Chinese fighting force. His plans pivoted on the successful capture of the city of Suzhou, immediately west of Shanghai. With the city in sight, Gordon reiterated his proscription on looting and for his pains received an anonymous note from his aggrieved Chinese artillerymen threatening to kill him and all the Western officers with one cannon blast. There could be but one response. Gordon had one man shot and the rest promptly backed down. Indeed, as a scattering of ungrateful, avaricious soldiers deserted the Army, they were as often as not replaced from among the ranks of their captured Taiping prisoners, whom Gordon almost always individually admired. He had no hatred for the ordinary soldiers ranged against him.

Gordon formed the habit, backed by his training and experience in the field, of dashing on horseback, unarmed and unescorted, to reconnoitre the territory and this advance work combined with his strategic thinking to pay rich dividends. His Ever Victorious Army scored one victory after another over the Taiping. This was the life for which Gordon had been born. Soon he was marching behind silk banners inscribed with the names of all his victories but not all aspects of this war were under his control. He favoured clemency if the context permitted and he was keen on victory by

---

* The child, Quincey, as Gordon had named him, would in due course become chief of police on the Shanghai–Nanking railway.

means of negotiation rather than bloodshed, if this might be managed. He gained Suzhou, for example, by parley and he guaranteed the safety of the Taiping who had surrendered to him. Disgracefully, his work was immediately undone when the restored government mandarins sacked the city with imperial Chinese forces and massacred the Taiping leaders who had entrusted themselves to Gordon's care.

There were cultural differences at work. Gordon's attitude was that the judicious deployment of clemency would speed the war to victory. As each victory was achieved without undue bloodshed and with an element of honour, so the next confrontation was all the more likely to be resolved in the same fashion. For the imperial Qing government, however, a show of mercy would only provoke further uprisings. Rebellions must therefore be crushed ruthlessly. False historical accounts would lay the responsibility for such atrocities at Gordon's door, as the leader of the active militia, and these accounts would be spread further by the evangelical American partisans of the Taiping.

In material terms, every temptation was resisted by Gordon. He declined the offer by one of his seedier militia predecessors to march on Peking and make themselves heirs to the Qing dynasty and wealthy with it. With only the better class of missionary his equal in this regard, Gordon therefore contrived to leave China bounty-less and poorer than when he had arrived. He had many times paid his men out of his own pocket. While disdainful of riches, he had a rather more relaxed attitude to racking up debts and borrowing from friends and he refused the traditional imperial bounties pushed his way. He even rebuffed the offer made in the name of the boy-emperor

Tongzhi of 10,000 *taels* of silver. His decision managed to impress the Chinese rather than offend them because of the loss of face.

Gordon even accomplished that rarest of successes with a mercenary army fighting victoriously for a cause inside an antique and tottering empire: he *successfully wound his army up.* The gifted Sir Harry Parkes, the British consul at Shanghai and later the effective founder of Hong Kong, was one of many who felt dismayed at the prospect. That at this moment of triumph for Gordon and therefore for Palmerston's policy of formal non-intervention, he should stand aside? Gordon was unable to tolerate any further Qing abuses of their own people. He told Parkes: 'On these subjects I act for myself and judge for myself. This I have found to be the best way of getting on.' For his troubles he left China a marshal in the imperial army and a wearer of the Yellow Jacket, their equivalent of the Garter. After a brief interlude superintending Chinese artillery training, Gordon went home, having served others as faithfully as he could and, more importantly, as best he felt he should.

During his time in the Far East, 'Chinese Gordon' underscored those aspects of his character that had always been present. Note the inescapable morality play of the great commander who thought as much of feeding enemy civilians as he did of victory in battle, the evangelical impulses of a man who saw that true justice for all lay in recognising that the idea of a new Christian dawn in the East was a false hope and the humanity of a commander who begged for mercy for his defeated foes against their cruel masters. There was no way that this paragon of Victorian manhood could not appeal to the British public.

For all this, however, we must not lose sight of what went on around Gordon, of the large context against which he operated. The collapse of China as an empire and a state would manifestly not have been in Britain's interests. Gordon's work underpinned the success of the cool and sure policy pursued by successive British governments and helped ensure that China did not follow the other empires of antiquity into final, irrevocable dissolution. He returned to Britain in 1864 with the endorsement of *The Times* ringing in the nation's ears:

> The part of the soldier of fortune is in these days very difficult to play with honour ... but if ever the actions of a soldier fighting in foreign service ought to be viewed with indulgence and even with admiration, this exceptional tribute is due to Colonel Gordon.

*

Back in England and stationed at Gravesend, Charles Gordon fell into a routine life. His days began early, with a cold bath followed by an hour of prayer and Bible-reading. His military work could normally be accomplished by lunchtime, which, to the unjust excitement of Strachey and generations of lazy commentators to come, left him ostensibly free for the remainder of the day. He filled these hours with good works for the local poor, not least the boys of the parish, who adored him. Gordon set up his own free or 'Ragged', as they were then known, school. He would pay for the most promising of his charges to get training places on merchant ships and would follow their progress round the globe, with pins on a map showing where he thought their ships were. When he went to whichever church he randomly chose, he sat among the poor and worshipped with them. He permitted the destitute access to his riverside garden and set aside land for them to have allotments. Appalled by the poverty he witnessed during a visit to Manchester, he scratched his name off the one gift he had brought back from China, a gold watch from the Emperor, anonymously sold it and distributed the money for poor relief. It is thought that in his Gravesend years, Gordon distributed 90 per cent of his income to charity.

In a loving if theologically unformed fashion, Gordon came to believe that all would be saved through Christ's redemption. He would visit the dying, of all ages and classes. 'I like to be with them. It brings the future nearer to me, as if you were seeing friends off by a train to a place to which you will eventually go yourself.' This English interlude, pleasant, if in Gordon's own eyes a trifle dull, did not last long and in the autumn of 1871 he returned to Romania, this time to be the British representative on the very Danube Commission he had helped establish in 1856.

Here too he soon saw that something was missing. He happily wrote to the British military attaché at Vienna of his wild travels in search of a correctly demarcated border: 'It is no joke walking over crackling ice with the view of fish swimming beneath you, the great sobs the ice gives, and the wild wail of wolves make it cheerful work. Here you may die without any fuss, for there are but few people about.' As usual he disdained the large pay that came with the post, not least because he saw it as an ever more otiose sinecure. Once more, the ice and the howling wolves notwithstanding, Gordon was bored and it was at this time that an opportunity arose, one he seized with both hands.

In 1872, Gordon attended a dinner held in the wooden summer palace on the Bosphorus of the British ambassador to the Sublime Porte, as the Ottoman Empire was officially known. Here he met Nubar Pasha, a Smyrna-born, European-educated Armenian Christian who was the Egyptian representative in Constantinople. Since 1863 Egypt had been ruled by Khedive Isma'il. He was the leader of a territory that remained nominally under the suzerainty of the Ottomans but which was in fact an autonomous state.

Egypt was *on paper* autonomous but *financially* in hock to French bankers, who had paid for the construction of the Suez Canal. The country was also a key part of international and imperial diplomacy. The Canal provided a rapid route for military might and goods to pass between Britain and India and Disraeli's government was aware that the Canal and Egypt itself were both potential prize assets *and* weak points in Britain's web of global influence.

Gordon's conversation with Nubar Pasha took place at a precise point in this game of strategy and control. Isma'il was determined to create a new Egyptian empire in the valley of the River Nile and it was with this intent in mind that an expedition, sponsored by Egypt and led by the Englishman Samuel Baker, was sent south along the Nile in 1870. It reached Khartoum in February but its control of the river valley remained at best nominal. As Nubar Pasha sat in conversation with Gordon by the Bosphorus, he was aware of the need for a commander and a strategist who could assist in forwarding Isma'il's dream of pushing Egyptian control into what is now South Sudan towards Lake Victoria.

As it happened, Nubar had no idea of Gordon's reputation as a strategist and leader but a conversation developed that would flow in one direction. In 1873, Isma'il formally offered a commanding role to Gordon, who consulted the British government. He could see the advantages of a British presence in the upper echelons of the Egyptian administration and consented with satisfaction. Gordon assumed the role of governor of the as yet theoretical Egyptian province of Equatoria in 1874.

He accepted the job but declined the handsome salary that went with it. After all, he remarked, 'All the coin one takes is wrung out of poor people' and, he might have added, by despots wielding whips. Isma'il himself was at first confused. He thought that Gordon's agreed pittance meant that he must be a spy or intriguer in the pay of the British. Isma'il was not unreasonable to be suspicious of British intentions in general. In 1875, Her Majesty's government would effectively take control of the Suez Canal and in 1879 the British overthrew Isma'il himself. At this time, however, he was convinced by Gordon's bona fides and Gordon set off towards Khartoum. His journey there required all that the Victorian picaresque could provide, camel journeys, desert landscapes, paddlesteamers on the Nile, mutiny, crocodiles, inefficient German servants and naked tribesmen distaining even a loincloth as being emblematic of bondage. All this and more carried the new Gordon Pasha to his glory.

Isma'il had in fact been correct, up to a point. Gordon *did* have an agenda but it was not to seize the Sudan as a British colony. It was to end the scandal of slavery, which, decades after its abolition in the Empire, was still a flourishing trade along the Nile and from which Isma'il himself profited. The very moment of Gordon's despatch to the Sudan had seen a clamour in the British press for him to be sent to the Gold Coast, today's Ghana, on the other side of the African continent. Who could have been better than the master of irregular warfare to deal with the scourge of slavery in West Africa? Gordon could not be everywhere and there was a humanitarian situation developing in the Sudan that had to be managed.

Baker's expedition had stopped the slaving of Africans down the Nile but the result was that, being unable to trade by river, the slavers instead forced their captives on a thousand-mile march across the Sahara, tethered to wooden yokes. At the heart of what Gordon wanted to do in and for the Sudan was to put an end to this evil. These were ethical choices made viable by the fact of British power and fuelled by Gordon's Christian zeal. In fact, the sole embarrassment to the twenty-first-century mind is quite how casually this good work has been allowed to slip out of mind.

Gordon gazed upon horrors in the Sudan. Slavery formed the basis of the region's economy but its human consequences were evil. Right and wrong were at stake and General Gordon, with those who stood behind him, was on the right side. Irrespective of anyone's general views on the intricacies of imperialism, it is clear that the British presence in the upper Nile valley improved matters for the local people. Gordon and his colleagues faced up to the wickedness they saw around them and they acted. To see Gordon at work in the Sudan is to see action being taken which for all its advances the international community seems largely incapable of today. This is to this generation's discredit and still more reason why Charles Gordon's fame should endure with undiminished honour. At this critical and deeply moral moment in the story, it is important to take stock of the greater play of ideas and ideologies that were in movement around the figure of Gordon. His lodestar was a principle of morality and it seems that the guiding principle of the Empire which he served was also founded on morality.

It is safe to say that attitudes to the Empire oscillate wildly between two points. That it was a rapacious monster, which wider still and wider, ate until it was bloated and incapable, or that it was famously acquired in a fit of absence of mind. Neither is true. The story of the Empire is its constant and continuous abnegation by its would-be masters for most of its existence and in most of the places it touched. Put more simply, the British did not want to acquire most of it, most of the time, and once it was acquired the country was mostly not very interested in it. To see the Empire as the men who made it saw it is to see something they largely sought *not* to make. The problem for imperial administrators in London was that on the frontier there were legions of Gordons, to be managed, ordered and controlled as well as possible. They existed to do certain jobs and to manage certain situations, so that British troops would not have to be sent in and in order that certain territories could otherwise be left well alone.

Sometimes circumstances meant that Britain was forced to intervene but the administrators in London worked hard to keep these interventions to a minimum. A map of Africa when Gordon first set foot in it, before the so-called Scramble for Africa which ended the nineteenth century, was one without borders. Such a state of affairs suited the maritime British. They did not want masses of *territory* as they had all the access they needed and were glad that no one else had much territory either. This happy state, for the United Kingdom, prevailed wherever the sea lapped and the Royal Navy went or let others go. The consequence of this was that were many places for such a man as Gordon to go, to do the things his own government did not want to do. Gordon claimed no new realms for Victoria, he undertook an arduous trek into the mountains of Abyssinia specifically to seek peace and not to wage war and he administered precious little of what Her Majesty already possessed.

Time after time, in the course of Gordon's illustrious service abroad his fear of the Foreign Office is evident, as was his concern that his deeds might embroil his own country in unnecessary foreign affairs. The key was to manage events so that British commercial and imperial interests came out on top. A stable Egypt, and a stable China, served British interests well. In both cases, good could flow unimpeded when there was political stability. Let Gordon do his work, and do it well but let him do it in such a way as to avoid the expense and bloodshed that came with an army on the ground. This is central to understanding the motives of the imperial ideology.

*

Early in 1880, Gordon left the Sudan. He admitted that the country, its climate, its internal politics, the strain of dealing with Ottoman and Egyptian bureaucracy, had defeated him. Although he had done his best, he could not even claim to have swept away the scourge of slavery. He had come close to a breakdown and now he took time to calm his mind. He travelled in Switzerland, England and Ireland, from where he wrote to the new Prime Minister William Gladstone on the tensions he observed on the land question. He even reminded Gladstone of his own family's part in the slave trade, to the Prime Minister's perhaps understandable irritation.

Gordon also travelled to South Africa, Mauritius and the Seychelles* and he returned to China where he counselled the Qing in the context of rising border tensions with Russia. He was even offered a position by Leopold II, King of the Belgians, managing the monarch's private possession of the Congo. Belgian activities in the Congo would become the most notorious of colonial activities in Africa and a byword for plunder, torture and rape on a colossal scale so it was well that Gordon declined the offer. Now Sudan again intervened and settled Gordon's fate.

In 1881, an uprising began in the Sudan against Egyptian rule of the region, led by a 'Madhi' named Muhammad Ahmed. In Islamic culture, a 'Madhi' is a self-proclaimed saviour destined to destroy the religion's enemies. The uprising spread along the Nile valley. Simultaneously, Egyptians rose against the British-backed authorities in protest at spiralling taxation, creating a dangerous situation concerning the governance of the Suez Canal. Gladstone ordered British troops into Egypt to guard the Canal. In July 1882, British ships bombarded Alexandria,

---

* He thought the Seychelles the site of the Garden of Eden.

leaving much of the city in flames, and by mid-September British soldiers were on the streets of Cairo.

With Egypt came the gathering imbroglio in the Sudan. Egyptian troops gradually lost control of the situation and by the end of 1883 Gladstone's government had resolved on the withdrawal of all British and Egyptian troops and administrators in the upper Nile valley. It was a complicated operation that would take time to organise. Gordon now intervened on a grand scale. In an interview given to W. T. Stead of the *Pall Mall Gazette*, he advocated massive intervention in the Sudan, to crush the Mahdi uprising and assert control of the entire Nile valley. Stead has a reasonable claim to having invented the political interview as we know it and the opinions he obtained from Gordon were just those the British public wanted to hear from its heroes.

In his interview with Stead, Gordon declaimed that the crisis was:

entirely attributable to a single cause, and that is, the grossest misgovernment ... The [Madhist] movement is not religious but an outbreak of despair ... the natives [had] a right to exist. I waged war against the Turks and Circassians, who had harried the population. I had taught them something of the meaning of liberty and justice, and accustomed them to a higher ideal of government than that with which they had previously been acquainted.

If the rebellion were not ended by force, Gordon said, Egypt itself would soon be under threat, not least from within: 'In all the cities of Egypt, it will be felt that what

317

the Mahdi has done they may do; and as he has driven out the intruder, they may do the same.' British solutions to foreign problems were what Gordon offered and the public loved him.

Gordon's words caused a sensation in Britain and created a chorus of voices demanding that Gordon himself be sent to the Sudan once more. Gladstone was furious. Although he had counselled intervention on behalf of the Bulgarian Christians, he was not minded to intervene everywhere and he and his government suspected (wrongly) that Gordon was a mere figurehead in a larger campaign focused on intervention and a display of British imperial might.

Yet Gladstone was barely in control of the situation and, realising this, he resolved on a limited mission to the Sudan. Gordon would go there and report but the evacuation of British and Egyptian personnel would continue as planned. Gordon departed in January 1884 and he left grave misgivings in his wake. To send such an independent-minded individual into such a difficult and complicated situation was not, many in government felt, a wise move. The British administrator in Cairo, Evelyn Baring, added cautiously that, 'A man who habitually consults the Prophet Isaiah when he is in a difficulty is not apt to obey the orders of anyone.'

Two more differing Britons abroad as Gordon and Baring it would be hard to identify. Baring was worldly, cynical, reserved and hidebound, while Gordon was a Victorian sensation precisely because he was none of those things. Moreover, he despised what he saw as Baring's extravagant Court in Cairo. Baring, he thought, spent his time featherbedding on the back of native toil.

Baring for his part saw Gordon as reckless, self-indulgent and terminally short-sighted. Gordon viewed Baring as the servant of the Egyptian government and the bond-holders to whom they were indebted, while Baring knew that Gordon was proclaiming a tiresome truth in calling himself the champion of the landless peasantry of both Egypt and the Sudan.

In Baring's conception of things, however, what the same peasants needed was better government, *not* a knight errant. Thus it was with understandable misgivings that he contemplated Gordon's progress south along the Nile. Yet Baring's hands were tied. When he wrote his memoirs more than two decades later, he recalled his sincere view that 'during this stage of national hysteria [criticism of Gordon] would have been regarded with a dislike somewhat akin to that which is felt for one who is heard talking flippantly in public of the truths of the Christian religion'.

Gordon arrived at Khartoum on 18 February and at once began the task of evacuating the women and children of the city, plus the sick and wounded, north to Egypt. He declared he would not abandon Khartoum to its fate and instead began preparations for a siege, this despite Gladstone's telegrammed instruction merely to organise and report on evacuations. Telegrams – public telegrams – flew back and forth between Khartoum and London. Gordon requested reinforcements, the government refused to send them and tempers frayed in the course of this most dangerous game of brinkmanship. Gordon admitted his insubordination. He had, after all, no right to remain in Khartoum when his orders were to leave with as many people as he could. For their part, Gladstone and his ministers knew that they dare not publicly dismiss the popular Gordon and knew too that their 'strategy' was distinctly threadbare. In short, nobody in government knew what to do to rescue the situation and nobody bore responsibility for sending Gordon in the first place.

Khartoum was formally besieged on 18 March 1884. The telegraph lines were cut in April but Nile steamers continued to come and go unimpeded until September. In August, the Cabinet overrode the Prime Minister's objections and voted to send a relief force to Khartoum but the force took much time to be assembled. By the end of the year, the people of Khartoum were starving and on 26 January 1885, as the British relief force made its way south along the Nile, the final Mahdi assault on the city began. When the British forces arrived on 28 January, they found the city occupied and Gordon dead. It is estimated that some 10,000 people died in the course of the assault.

*

In the aftermath of Gordon's death, the Queen wrote to Augusta:

How shall I attempt to express *what I feel*? To *think* of your dear, noble, heroic Brother, who served his Country and his Queen so truly, so heroically, with a self-sacrifice so edifying to the World, not having been rescued. That the promises of support were not fulfilled – which I so frequently and constantly pressed on those who asked him to go – is to me *grief inexpressible*! Indeed, it has made me ill.

When we contemplate the Victorian era, the Queen herself is not always to be seen. However, Victoria was both a shrewd and a passionate participant in her age and now the Queen raged on the subject of British humiliation and dishonour and the lack of spirit that had seen Gordon exposed to his fate. As for her view of Gladstone, whom she regarded as the author of this national humiliation, 'Oh!' she exclaimed, 'for a Palmerston or Beaconsfield [Disraeli] to be here now.' In the aftermath of Gordon's death, her messages to Gladstone became a drumbeat, inviting the Prime Minister to take responsibility and resign. To which, evasively and self-justifyingly, Gladstone could only reply, 'The Prime Minister is not altogether able to follow the conclusion which Your Majesty has been pleased thus to announce.'

It is certainly the case that his sanctification by Victoria is a key part of the Gordon legend. His own Sovereign loved him, her embrace crowning the man that the press had already presented to the public as a hero. Indeed, the news of Gordon's death provoked one of the most constitutionally interesting moments of Victoria's reign. She telegraphed *en clair*, that is, publicly, so that all who saw the message as it was relayed along the line would know the Queen's words and might leak them, as they duly did, to Gladstone and his senior ministers, 'To think that all this might have been prevented and many precious lives saved by earlier action is too frightful.'

Victoria's rage, combined with public dismay at what was regarded as official failure to protect Gordon, badly damaged Gladstone's reputation. To be fair, it is worth noting that although there is a feeling that the relief force failed 'for the want of a nail', there is another assessment to be made. Gordon never had the tools to do the job. Always before Khartoum he magically contrived for this not to matter but now, quite simply, his luck ran out. The legend of the siege, embracing the courage, privation, resolution, improvisation, heroism, charity and chivalry of the defenders, is all true. In the matter of military common sense or good political stewardship, however, the fact is that the Barings of this world were right and Gordon was wrong. In short, it was *Gordon's own fault* that he found himself trapped in Khartoum. The story endures. When the city fell and he died, whether by gunshot or spear or in another manner, still we see him standing at the top of the stairs shouting, 'Strike! Strike hard!' That was both what he would have wanted and what the British public required of their hero for whom they erected statues across the Empire in honour. Unfortunately, in logical terms, Gordon of Khartoum ought not to have been in Khartoum at all.

The Madhi died in his bed five months after Gordon. His brutal regime endured another thirteen years and many died during this time, before Lord Kitchener put an end to it in 1898 and caused Khartoum to be rebuilt in the shape of the Union flag. The Sudan was better governed than before. It is most unlikely that this would have happened had Gordon not ignored his orders but nonetheless he did ignore them. As for the outpouring of grief for Gordon's death, this was the penultimate pinnacle of Victorian mourning, prefiguring that which occurred for the Queen herself, sixteen years later.

*

Charles Gordon could have died in battle many times before Khartoum. Such an end would have earned him a memorial: a plaque, a verse, a footnote of Empire, a grateful memory of one illustriously lost so far from home. Instead he died the most famous man in the world. *Punch's* immortal 'TOO LATE!', Britannia, weeping, made up for the fact that the week before the magazine had roared, 'AT LAST!', having erroneously thought that the long, long siege at Khartoum had been successfully lifted.

This was the stuff of Gordon's life, legend and celebrity, bureaucratic incomprehension and far-distant virtue. Those who praised at home were not aware, perhaps, of his actual opinions of the Empire which he served. They did not know that, in his opinion, those over which the Empire ruled would probably be better off ruling themselves, that all humanity was equal before the Lord. Those who praised him were praising a hero, not a man. Nor was his fame sustained. Strachey and others saw to that.

Although Gordon's life ended heroically, although his death was avenged, although these ingredients make his life instantly irresistible as a fable, in the face of all this it is worth remembering what he himself thought. In his Khartoum journals, kept at the end in pencil scribble on scrap paper as his palace held out against the Mahdi's hordes, Gordon reflected, 'The fact is if one analyses human glory, it is composed of 9/10 twaddle, perhaps 99/100 twaddle.' Much scepticism of Gordon was expressed by his own peers, by his British peers at any rate, so it is useful to remember that Gordon could be sceptical too, of glory and heroism, and that he had a firmer grip on himself and his deeds than had many of his contemporaries.

And as with ethnicity, so with class. In marked contrast to so many other Victorians, Gordon was entirely free from class distinction on any subject. Nor was this some mere form of Victorian eccentricity. Instead, it was something greater, a fact which can be in little doubt when we consider again the wellspring of his humility. That he fined junior officers a shilling every time they called him 'Sir' may have rankled with some but it was no affectation, nor a Victorian, immodest self-effacement. This was a man who could refuse an invitation to dine with the Prince of Wales because he wanted to go to bed early and who could muse of a levée at St James's Palace that the uniforms and the decorations were 'a mass of glitter, to be worms in thirty years' time'. He had little regard for this material life at all. As he remarked to his Ulster hostess in a distant Chinese province, 'You have no conception how I yearn for the future life, how I groan over the tugging of a corrupt body after me.'

It is important to understand that this was not fatalism, as some might have it today. It was ardent hope, hungry for what was sure to come. Take that anecdotal indignation at the body to which Gordon was confined. Immediately thereafter, he regaled his hostess with a series of yarns about the hapless captain of the Macau packet. Gordon was not, as the secular mind of today might have it, *morbid*. Rather, he was keen and attentive to what his faith taught and what he saw his life as living out.

As for the doubting and resentment which was begun by Strachey and which has ever carried on with its sour, long, withdrawing whine, Gordon's self-loathing was entirely justified, for he lived in the sure expectation of righteous death and life eternal thereafter. Moreover, Gordon himself was never a Strachey-like scold. A man who could say of himself, 'I knew if *I* was chief I would never employ myself, for I am incorrigible' is a man that we should love and honour for ever. Being the wrong man to send on the wrong mission at the wrong time when everyone knew it was wrong in no way lessens the life he lived in anticipation of his end.

As for the end to which Gordon himself should always be put, it is simply this: to maintain and honour him on the pedestal he occupies. He was brave, faithful and heroic.

Dicey: Call of Duty

Of all the eminent Victorians profiled in this book, Albert Venn Dicey (4 February 1835–7 April 1922) is perhaps the least well known today. Among the colourful and intriguing soldiers, architects, politicians and more, a constitutional theorist does not perhaps stand out. In addition, few prominent Victorians have been hammered by posterity as consistently as Dicey. Like Pugin and others, his legacy was rejected and his ideas debunked comprehensively by the next generation. Speaking for Bloomsbury, Lytton Strachey dismissed Dicey in acidic terms as representative of the 'Eminent Victorians' and Strachey was not delivering a compliment. Such has been the sustained criticism of Dicey that it has taken time and patience for a general reassessment of him to be glimpsed.

Yet it is not truly possible to understand the Victorian era in these islands without also understanding Dicey. As a philosopher of the British Constitution, as a unionist at a time when the Union was questioned explicitly and repeatedly, as an ardent but questioning Liberal, as an upholder of the sacred principle of legal impartiality, in all these areas Dicey's work, writing, thinking and judgement have stood the test of time.

However, Dicey regarded himself as a failure. He was a major figure within the cloisters of Oxford but he failed to become a lion of the Bar and this in turn meant no smooth progression to a political career, no elevation to a higher court, no opportunity to influence and affect the living laws of England. The climate of the time meant that anyone who pursued a legal career was regarded as being second-rate, at a time when the Classics attracted the brightest and best.

An ostensible catalogue of failure, yet what a legacy, all sustained by a sense of duty that was deeply Victorian. He did what he was called to do, for his community and for his expansive sense of nation. The sneers of Strachey and others were born out a reaction against this Victorian dutifulness, out of a feeling that he and his contemporaries could simply never live up to what had been done for them and accomplished before their arrival on the scene.

*

Albert Venn Dicey was born near Lutterworth in Leicestershire. His father was Thomas Dicey, who had enjoyed an illustrious spell as a prize-winning undergraduate at Cambridge, before forging a career as proprietor of the *Northampton Mercury* and Chairman of the Midland Railway, at a time of unparalleled growth in the railway sector. His elder brother, Edward, would establish a distinguished reputation as a writer and journalist. His uncle was John Venn, of Venn diagram fame, who was not only a noted mathematician but also descended from a long line of religious evangelicals. This is an ingredient in the mix which perhaps accounts for the fervency of Dicey's own philosophy and beliefs. Interestingly, given the unsparing and disapproving interest that Bloomsbury later took in his career and legacy, Albert Dicey was related to the Stephen family via his mother Mary. Dicey was a cousin of Leslie Stephen, the father of Virginia Woolf and Vanessa Bell, and of the judge and lawyer James Fitzjames Stephen.

The young Dicey was almost certainly mildly disabled. He was certainly never fully fit. His childhood – he was educated at home as his parents entertained 'grave suspicions' of the public schools – was bookish and quiet. As John Venn later put it to him, 'As a boy I had not your sense of proportion or of historic dignity.' *Historic dignity* sounds like a childhood of dreams and in later life Dicey would look back with gratitude at the stable infancy that life had afforded him. Dicey was the focus of his mother's loving instruction and he was fortunate that she had the gifts gently to draw out the best from her son.

From his father, meanwhile, he gained another gift, an allegiance to classical liberalism, an ideal from which he never wavered. He admired and respected his father, his ideals, integrity and industry, and we can readily see that Thomas Dicey was the sort of sturdy, upright individual the Lytton Stracheys of this world would so obviously resent. Dicey's failure to rebel against his parents was a shocking state of affairs to them. With reverence for his father came a sense of duty which likewise never left the younger Dicey. The household gods were the very ideals that were argued over on the floor of the House of Commons at this time in British parliamentary history. Devotion to free trade, reform without revolution and an affirmation of the free exchange of ideas, for Dicey these were and would remain the supreme virtues.

In spite of the strong current of evangelism that ran through the wider clan, Dicey would not grow up to be a devout Christian. Instead he practised a species of Victorian humanism that we might best call *secular evangelism*, devoted to reason and its many merits. He quietly distrusted religious enthusiasm of any stripe, even to the point of possessing a marked element of anticlericalism distinctly alien in the accommodating English tradition in which he had grown up. Yet he had no divisive urges, even in defence of his own rationalist beliefs. A most important tenet of Victorian culture was its openness to new ideas. Some Victorians accepted a plurality that a more intolerant age would find difficult and Dicey was an exemplar of this expansive attitude.

Dicey therefore was a child and man for whom reason could address and resolve the problems of society. His faith was the intellect and his disapproval was restricted to those who persecuted the beliefs of others. Thus he was able to address and focus on the issues of the day. For example, Catholics being spurned or marginalised, whether in England or in Ireland, was wrong. There was never to be any 'side' to Dicey and this produced a lifelong commitment to doing 'useful work'. This would be its own reward.

Late in life he was able to encapsulate his creed. In a letter in 1900 to his great American contemporary and friend Oliver Wendell Holmes, Dicey wrote: 'We must find satisfaction in making the best or the most out of whatever work one has in hand, and that one's appropriate work is the free development of such faculties as one may happen to possess.'

At Balliol College, Oxford, Dicey imbibed a liberal life. He studied Greats. His tutor was college Master and famous classical scholar Benjamin Jowett, who claimed,

> First come I. My name is J-w-tt.
> There's no knowledge but I know it.
> I am Master of this College,
> What I don't know isn't knowledge.

Jowett was no cobwebbed academic. He is remembered as a great Balliol reformer and his belief in the liberal dictum of human progress and perfectibility supplied Dicey with an ideal philosophical and pedagogical environment. Jowett was an august translator of Plato and Thucydides but the liberal thinkers Jeremy Bentham and John Stuart Mill were the great philosophers imbibed by the young Dicey. Indeed, all his life Dicey remained in communion with the liberal ideal of individualism. This, he argued to the end, 'in its true sense is a source of both greatness and of goodness; and much as we must value all social progress with its accompanying restrictions, we must watch jealously lest these restrictions endanger individuality, and thus destroy that originality which is the very spring of human progress.'

At Oxford, Dicey belonged to the Old Mortality Society, a short-lived undergraduate club intended to permit its members 'such intellectual pastime and recreation as should seem most suitable and agreeable', with a roster of names only the Victorians could hope to see. From the poet Algernon Charles Swinburne to the Belfast-born future Cabinet member James Bryce, probably Dicey's closest university friend, much nineteenth-century liberal life was here. Their cause was 'freedom of thought' and they were indifferent to the theological questions which consumed so many of their intellectual peers. At this point Dicey can be seen as an advanced radical with all the correct opinions. He was in favour of franchise extension, sympathetic to female suffrage and irked by the comfortably somnolent Anglicanism he observed all round him. Later, Bryce noted of his clubmates that all had '*nothing*' in common, meaning that none of them came up to Oxford possessing much by way of connections or material advantages. These young men were self-improvers and their aim was to go out and improve others.

We come now to that element in Dicey's life of which history has tended to approve, that is, his part in our laws. What he achieved here should be understood as being part of the Victorian settlement he wanted to uphold. His scholarship drew out lessons from extant laws, to make their application easier and more efficient, all of which amounted to an effort to preserve what was good. He believed that English law 'will be the lasting monument of England's greatness', above even her empire and arts and parliaments. His own role in this legal context began with his election in 1860 to a fellowship at Trinity College, Oxford.

*

Dicey failed four times to secure academic preferment at Oxford, before Trinity gave him the nod, and he succeeded on this occasion solely because the college allowed him, as an invalid, to dictate his entry, an essay that focused on the Privy Council. The piece won that year's university Matthew Arnold memorial prize and is just as interesting for what it revealed about Dicey's own contemporary opinions in what was now becoming a post-protectionist world. As a supporter of *laissez-faire* economics, he pronounced himself astonished at how much the Privy Council had interfered with trade 'in a way no ruler would now ever dream ... the fact that government interference is an evil is now too well established to need the confirmation of further arguments'.

Dicey now had the security of a university position. He would hold his fellowship until he forfeited it on his marriage to Eleanor Bonham Carter, a member of the distinguished English liberal family, in 1872, and could begin to explore what the world offered. By 1863, he had been called to the bar at the Inner Temple where he came under the sway of the work of John Austin, the founder of English analytical jurisprudence.

Austin insisted on the distinction between the law as it is and as it ought to be. Therefore, he attacked the theory of natural law, which held that 'positive law must reflect a standard of morality'. Austin replied that law arose not from morals but from the need to defer to the power which compelled submission and in turn submitted to nothing above itself. Finally, Austin sought to reduce the law conceptually to a few simple questions on each discrete issue, so systematising the haphazard development of centuries, making the law rational, and freeing it from 'verbal imprecision'. In essence, Austin was arguing *against* any necessary connection between law and morality and *for* the importance of codification and of explication. He was, in other words, a legal positivist. His aim, drawing heavily as it did upon the work of Bentham and others, was to transform the law into a true, delineated and codified science.

Dicey took what he needed from Austin's philosophy while expanding other aspects of his thought and discarding the rest. He appreciated the need to resolve legal questions by stating the fundamental principles which had been derived from close study of the matter at hand. Moreover, Dicey's opinion was that Austin's clarity of thought and method of argument admirably lent themselves to this improved and shared understanding of the law. However, like any good Victorian, Dicey was much preoccupied by issues of morality and in this case he regretted Austin's strict separation of law from morality. He resolved this tension by holding 'the law' to be external, while morality was internal: 'law is concerned with acts, morality with character'. His key insight in this regard was a point that Austin had missed, that it was vital for the public to approve of the law. Without this popular support and respect, the law would wither and die.

A second key conceptual achievement had to do with the issue of sovereignty. This, Dicey insisted, was singular and supreme. It was something which could only reside in the state but for Dicey its sole purpose was to provide for *individual* rights. This was the liberal vision of British freedom of individual liberty based on a strong but reticent state. Moreover, this was specifically something which *had* happened here, it existed in Britain already. Dicey made no intrinsic claims for universality. He was describing English law, in theory and in practice. That it dovetailed perfectly with his mid-Victorian liberalism was doubtless a happy accident, a secular version of providential good luck.

*

In 1865, a rebellion broke out in the British colony of Jamaica. In October of that year, a group of islanders marched on the courthouse at Morant Bay, a coastal town east of Kingston. The demonstration was sparked by the poverty and widespread deprivation which characterised life in the colony. Seven men on the march were shot and killed by armed personnel defending the courthouse, which was then burned to the ground by the protestors. In the ensuing unrest, twenty-five people were killed. The trouble at Morant Bay was not the end of the trouble, for it ignited further unrest across the island. The British governor, Edward Eyre, declared martial law and by the time the rising was quelled more than four hundred people had died.

Eyre's actions led to a debate in Britain, with public opinion sharply divided. Some praised the governor's actions, others deplored them as excessively violent. The episode led to one of Dicey's earliest radical acts, when he joined his cousins Leslie and James Fitzjames Stephen in subscribing to the 'Jamaica Committee', which sought to bring Eyre to trial for what was regarded as his scandalous misrule of the island. The Committee consisted of some of the most illustrious worthies of liberal Britain, including John Bright, Charles Darwin, John Stuart Mill and the biologist Thomas Henry Huxley. Its ultimate aim was to have Eyre tried for murder. The bid failed but the Committee's legacy remained. Dicey never lost his opposition to lawlessness and tyranny, no matter whence it emanated, and his sense of duty to those whom he felt were, or ought to be, under the protection of British laws and justice.

The Jamaica Committee in some ways marked the beginning of the apogee of Dicey's embrace of classic liberalism. For a spell at this time, one sees radicalism and an embrace of the concept of *improvement* as a moral ideal. In his contribution to *Essays on Reform*, published in 1867, the great year of electoral reform, Dicey reaffirmed orthodox liberal opposition to class war. There was no 'balance of class interests' which it was better for politics to seek to achieve. Representation of individuals remained the goal. Dicey was an early opponent of any tendency which would lead to a progressive caste system, breaking society down into groups which individuals were supposed to see as forming their 'identity' before and above their own private one. Yet at this point he railed specifically against the elite, against any idea that class war should be waged from above and that society was best off run by those who knew best. As he noted in his essay, 'Advocates of class representation desire such a political arrangement as would enable a minority, in virtue of their education, wealth, etc. to carry out their views, even though opposed to the sentiments of the majority of the people.'

This was a quintessential liberal assault on what it saw as entrenched Tory privilege. 'Half the evils of modern England,' he noted, 'arise from the undue prominence of class distinctions [and] the fundamental fault of class representation is its tendency to intensify differences which it is an object of political reform to remove.' As his biographer Richard A. Cosgrove put it, a liberal such as Dicey considered that 'Each man was the best manager of his own affairs; citizens ought to be considered individuals first, members of a class second.' His desire, in self-conscious opposition to reactionary Tories, was to have the political class encompass working men, rather than seek fearfully to exclude them.

At Oxford too Dicey articulated his radical principles. He inveighed in moral terms against absentee fellows who consumed funds which could have been spent on education and he lauded the virtues of open competition. Everywhere he saw colleges which were closed corporations, the aim of which was their own perpetuation. This was a moral scandal, for education was the key to the great liberal principles of emancipation and participation in civic discourse. Dicey's views were so advanced in these mid-Victorian times that he even favoured degrees for women, a state of affairs which at length manifested in the United Kingdom in 1878, when the University of London began awarding degrees to female students.

At this time too Dicey worshipped all the conventional liberal heroes, among them the Genoese politician Giuseppe Mazzini, who helped to create the Italy of the Risorgimento; Lajos Kossuth, who led the Hungarians during the 'Springtime of the Nations' in 1848 and whom Palmerston had wanted to entertain at his Broadlands estate, as well as the states of the Union in the American Civil War, for what could be more antithetical to individualism than slavery? He opposed Napoleon III, whom he regarded as a mountebank. On the question of press freedom, Dicey applauded the liberty he observed in action at home, noting the paper guarantees of it abroad but the fact of it in Britain. The liberty of the British press, he felt, lay in its freedom to do things first and perhaps be sued afterwards, without first being *licensed* to do them.

In other ways, however, he began to move towards a more nuanced understanding of liberalism. He remained dedicated to the notion, the Benthamite idea, one which he always had supported, that reason and the human intellect set itself to solving problems so that life could be better and happier. This was the very point of rational legislation, of a more scientific way of doing things. He noted what he regarded as the mistakes that others made by channelling this philosophy to far more interventionist ends. Excessive intervention was, he began to feel, a grave error and to the end of his life he saw that while the good the state did when it acted was habitually visible, the harm it did was not. 'Few are those,' he lamented, 'who realise the undeniable truth that State help kills self-help.' Dicey did not want to free the individual from the prejudices of the past, simply in order to make that individual the helpless ward of the state in the future.

Dicey would continue this move away from radical politics and towards moderation for the rest of his life. In a famous formulation he first rehearsed on his friend Bryce, Dicey summed up his own times in this pessimistic fashion: 'Toryism was a reminiscence – Benthamism is a doctrine – collectivism is a hope.' So the nineteenth century had by this reckoning begun with legislative quiescence, with a sated ruling class, before blossoming into the individualism and freedom of his youth and then, alas, moving mistakenly towards the collective state action of his old age. By 1914, Dicey was mournfully concluding that 'by 1900 the doctrine of *laissez-faire*, in spite of the large element of truth which it contains, had more or less lost its hold on the English people'. This was the world of the Liberal Party's 1906 Trade Disputes Act, which granted freedom from liability in tort to trade unions. Or as Dicey exactingly saw it, elevated one segment of the community to being a legally privileged one, possessing rights others lacked. Whatever this was, it was for Dicey manifestly not liberalism and his duty was to make the case against it.

*

In 1882, after two years of stiff competition, a committee chaired by Conservative politician Lord Salisbury, later Prime Minister, appointed Dicey to the pulpit from which he was to accomplish his enduring work, the Vinerian Professorship of English Law at Oxford. The Vinerian position had first been endowed in the middle of the eighteenth century and Sir William Blackstone had been its first holder with the intention of teaching the Common Law of England, and assist in its evolution. Until that time, only Canon Law and Civil Law had been taught at Oxford and Cambridge, meaning that the most practical application of the law was not taught in a university environment. The Vinerian had altered this state of affairs, in the process becoming central to the study of English law. Now, although it remained in theory a position of considerable importance and prestige, in practice it had fallen into a state of decrepitude.

Leaving London and the great world for Oxford was a move Dicey made reluctantly but dutifully. From his position as Vinerian Professor, he could do what he had always wanted to do, help to change the world for the better. One of his predecessors 'wrote a book ... no one ever read, [another] discharged his duties, if at all, by deputy, while he himself held a judgeship in India'. He could do better than these predecessors, so, while this was neither the position on the bench nor in the Commons' chamber that he in his heart desired, yet he saw himself being obliged faithfully to discharge the role to the best of his abilities. Duty came first and Dicey would maintain this sense of obligation, holding the Professorship until 1909.

In taking up the Vinerian, Dicey was able to demonstrate what the professional teaching of law at university could really do. Rather than muddle through using on-the-job training at the Inns of Court, he could channel the resources and prestige of Oxford to teach the law as a whole and in context. Analysis could be taught as a technique, the law could be understood as a series of rules and exceptions, with their elucidated principles clearly set out and those doctrines' real and absolute limits properly appreciated. Professors, in short, could profess the rationality of principle-based law. There was always a reason to be found, for otherwise the law was unreasonable. What could be more Victorian?

Harold Hanbury, who was one of Dicey's more illustrious twentieth-century successors as Vinerian Professor

(1949–64), praised Dicey for being 'one who revived a tradition, always a more difficult feat than to create a tradition'. Yet the manner in which Dicey taught was secondary to *what* he taught, and here Hanbury again points, in damning terms, to the fate Dicey has suffered: 'His critics have misquoted him and criticised their own misquotations.' The law of the Constitution as set out by Dicey in Oxford is worth examining. It is a law which has endured, though not without strain, to this day.

Dicey divided British legal development into three parts: the sovereignty of Parliament; the rule of law, a ubiquitous phrase to our ears but one he in fact originated; and the idea of constitutional conventions. Later legal critics, such as the late Sir Ivor Jennings, held that 'Dicey's Constitution was the one his politics produced' but it seems that the opposite could be true. That is, Dicey's politics in large part stemmed from his admiration for the Constitution he accurately described. Dicey further divided his description of the Constitution into 'true laws'. That is, statute or common law and rules which were not technically laws but which were what he called *conventions*, with a force of their own.

The sovereignty of Parliament was 'the dominant characteristic of our political institutions' and it could not bind its successors in that there was no 'basic law' or other constitutional document regulating Parliament. Such a declaration is a mere commonplace now but it was a conceptual revelation in Dicey's own time. Some have argued he asserted this as theory but neglected to show it as historical fact and, even further than this, that his assertion was such as to subsequently *make* it fact, so completely were his dictums accepted in his own time. Regardless, the impact of Dicey is total, for, try as its practitioners might, the law has never since been quite able to shake off what Dicey himself said it was and this in itself is an extraordinary and lasting legacy.

Naturally, Dicey was aware of politics in his accounting of the Constitution and distinguished between legal sovereignty, that is the sovereignty of Parliament, and political or popular sovereignty. There were thus external limits on sovereignty, with the possibility that a law constitutionally passed but repugnant to the vast majority could simply be dispensed with by them. It is important to note that this was only theoretical. However, it was to be a theory which caused Dicey much sorrow during the final, dark stages of the Irish Home Rule crisis. For the time being, Dicey was learning to enjoy the stability, security and authority granted by the Vinerian and learning also to delight in his ability to delineate and explain the unique characteristics and glorious flexibility of the British Constitution. This was an entity which could, unlike its known, codified equivalent, respond swiftly and decisively to the political needs of the nation. Indeed, it was precisely this agility which rendered superfluous any need to codify it, for to do so would be to rob it of its essence.

Dicey's *Introduction to the Study of the Law of the Constitution* became an instant sensation, being both understandable to the lay reader and inescapably influential on generations of jurists. In essence, it told a story about Victorian Britain which immensely pleased Victorian Britons. 'The Rule of Law', for example, meant that here we had simply *regular* law, rather than *arbitrary* or even *discretionary* law. After all, nothing offended

Victorian sensibilities more than inconsistency and unfairness. 'Englishmen,' Dicey declared, 'are ruled by the law, and by the law alone; a man may with us be punished for a breach of the law, but he can be punished for nothing else.' This, British Victorians could reflect happily, was a blessed state enjoyed almost nowhere elsewhere in the world outside the Empire.

There was, Dicey went on, a glorious equality before the law. There were no legally privileged classes or state officials. This was a contrast to what prevailed even in western Europe, to say nothing of the rest of the world. To add to the happy Whiggish exceptionalism of this tale, continental Europeans enjoyed every sort of right on paper, as they still do, in virtually every mainland country. These rights emerged from the fancy principles of their individual national constitutions, habitually phrased in the most idealistic terms as to the specific rights the piece of paper in question guaranteed. In Britain, no such abstract rights were listed. Instead, actual rights sheltered in the precedent of the law and in the ability of the courts to protect them from the state. Dicey liked to point to the Habeas Corpus Act, 'which declared no principle and defined no rights but was worth a hundred constitutional assurances'. In Dicey's Britain, rights were held from the past, not bestowed graciously by politicians today who might take it into their heads to remove those same rights tomorrow.

For British officials, unlike so many of their counterparts abroad, could not claim as a defence against charges of breaking the law that they were 'acting under order of authority'. In other words, it was not possible lawfully to obey an unlawful command, so the official was personally liable in law for his own lawbreaking. It is hard to think of a better deterrent against state excess. Indeed, the state, in Dicey's conception of it, which was to say, as he taught judges to understand it, had at every turn to be aware to behave lawfully. All government spending, for instance, had to be assented to by Parliament. Ministers were legally responsible for every act *they* took on behalf of the Crown. This lawfulness was not and in many cases still is not the defining characteristic of other states. Something exceptional took place in the United Kingdom, implied Dicey, and the Victorians, thanks to men like Dicey, the books he wrote and the teaching he handed down, acknowledged what they had and spread the good news accordingly.

*

Dicey and James Bryce travelled to the United States together in 1870, and in good, industrious Victorian fashion this trip spurred the writing of two celebrated books, Bryce's *The American Commonwealth* and Dicey's *The Law of the Constitution*. Bryce was also ensconced at Oxford at this time, as Regius Professor of Civil Law. The three volumes of *The American Commonwealth* would profoundly influence the drafting of the Australian Constitution in the mid-1890s. As for Dicey, he too absorbed much from his American experience. He made friends for life in the course of this trip, including the Irish-born Edwin Lawrence Godkin, influential editor of the *Nation*, who kept Dicey financially buoyant during an expensive journey by way of many book reviews; Charles William Eliot, who was President of Harvard

University, the law school admired so much by Dicey; and Oliver Wendell Holmes, who practised law at Boston and who was still some years from occupying a seat on the Supreme Court. Dicey also learned first-hand much about the American principle of federalism, which governed the relationship between the individual states and the American government, and he studied the United States Constitution, which preserved much that was good in law and government while also preserving that which was less good, in the process allowing and indeed sustaining weak government.

There were, then, a great many observations to make and lessons to learn, perhaps the chief of which was absorbed at the state convention of New York's Democratic Party. Here, Dicey was able to watch Tammany Hall politics in full spate and here he saw the real corruption which perverted the lofty republican ideals in which American democracy was cloaked. As a result, he gained, to put it mildly, prime insights into what was wrong with politics and politicians and he never quite shook off his distaste for party machines. Inevitably, Bryce watched the same political show and overcame his repulsion to recognise US conventions as an ultimately encouraging riot of popular participation and it was Bryce who would succeed in politics.

Dicey, however, recognised that party wirepullers *could* negate democracy by 'managing' it in this way. This much was evident in Tammany Hall and the same lesson could be applied elsewhere. In general terms, American federalism left Dicey with an abiding certainty that a people and its Parliament was the correct way of ordering a state and that a constitution supreme in itself was a mistake. Time has proved Dicey correct. It has become a cliché to talk of the 'black-robed legislators' of the US Supreme Court, substituting their judgements for what would in the United Kingdom be democratic political decisions, and this was a danger Dicey clearly foresaw as being inherent in the US system.

Avoiding what he saw as being the dangers plainly evident elsewhere, in this case the weakness and division so glaringly on display in the United States, was for Dicey merely one more of his 'obvious things'. He would return from his visit all the more convinced of the superiority of the British Constitution, and all the more determined to protect it. He soon concluded that there was no more obvious danger to its integrity than that posed by the prospect of Irish Home Rule.

✻

Dicey, as he surveyed the changing political landscape of Britain, had now definitively shifted his political ground. Radical blood still coursed in his veins but its heat had been tempered by years of surveying and teaching the law, watching the changing politics of the times and assessing the strengths of the Constitution. In particular, he could see that the constitutional form of the United Kingdom was about to be tested to its core. The question was whether the country's arrangements would hold.

The test would come because of Westminster parliamentary arithmetic and political affairs in Ireland. In Victorian times British and Irish politics were thoroughly meshed together, the ability of Britain to influence the political and economic scene in Ireland and the Irish ability to challenge the stability and security of British politics. From Daniel O'Connell's 'monster meetings' and their impact on the question of Catholic Emancipation, to the fall of Peel's government over a matter of Irish-specific legislation and to a host of other questions, challenges and dilemmas, the Irish Question was never very far away.

From the 1870s, a new political dispensation was developing in Ireland. The Irish Ascendancy, a waning force even during the time of Peel's spell as Chief Secretary to Ireland over fifty years earlier, was now a spent force. Irish nationalism was rising and it was gaining a solid footing in a country where the tentative process of land reform begun by Gladstone was helping the rural Catholic Irish, while at the same time a new educated Catholic urban middle class, with financial clout and money to spend, was assuming control of the levers of economic power in Ireland. Add to this a post-Emancipation Catholic Church in Ireland that was now in a position of dominance, its influence embodied in the new ecclesiastical architecture of Pugin and others, and it was clear to all observers that Ireland was in the process of changing. With this new flourishing mood of nationalism came a wish for a restored national Parliament in Dublin, to replace the ancient assembly that had dissolved itself following the passing of the Act of Union. This demand, however, stopped well short of outright independence for Ireland. There was a rising tide in favour of 'Home Rule', of a measure of devolution or self-government for Ireland, under the Crown.

For a watching Dicey, such a change to the country's constitutional arrangements was anathema and now he resolved, on setting out from Oxford, to be the guardian of the Union. Here was the family vein of evangelism once more on display, though as he remarked to his fellow Liberal Unionist, the former Lord Chancellor, Lord Selborne, it was more the case that exacting self-knowledge was the order of the day: 'You will say that I have wandered into a kind of religion rather than politics. I cannot separate the two. Fervour of feeling is essential to vigour of action. You will never triumph unless you make a kind of religion of your politics, or turn your politics into a kind of religion.' He was as good as his word, for no meeting place was too distant, no congregation too small during these years for Dicey.

Dicey had no animus against the Irish, against Ireland or against Irish Catholicism. He was opposed to religious prejudice, which ran counter to his deepest impulses. This in turn meant that he was sympathetic to the position of the Irish in Britain itself and sympathetic to their call for equality. He found the English Protestant prejudice against Irish Catholics disagreeable. Similarly he viewed elements in the politics and culture of the Catholic Church in Ireland as equally unsatisfactory. His thoroughgoing liberalism led him to support reform and relief wherever it could be extended. What began, gradually, to emerge from Ireland after Emancipation in 1829 in the form of Isaac Butt's Land League and then, under the leadership of Charles Stewart Parnell, a disciplined and powerful Irish Parliamentary Party (IPP) at Westminster, was something quite different. It was Irish nationalism and this ran counter to the Constitution so could not be supported.

The young Dicey sympathised with liberal-nationalism when he saw it, as in Germany, Hungary, Italy. This had been his creed. Yet he watched nationalism uniting states in all of these instances, making them stronger and more secure. He had been on the side of the Union during the American Civil War and now, with his own Union under attack, as he saw it, from within, he was steadfastly on the unionist side again.

For all that Dicey admitted clear instances of British misrule in Ireland and wished to see an amelioration of conditions there, his ultimate answer was always that Ireland must be governed in the same way as the rest of the country and that its politicians had a duty to make this happen. Such faults as existed came about when Ireland was not governed as an intrinsic part of the United Kingdom. Any economic woes she had should be dealt with fairly and promptly, because if Irish prosperity was the issue, then that prosperity could be assured by staying within the Union. Irish economic sorrows, though they blighted many lives, were never the whole issue and a pure feeling of national identity underpinned the movement.

Intimidation, violence, boycotting and crime all accompanied the cry for Home Rule in Ireland. At Westminster, the parliamentary obstructionism perfected by Parnell and his followers destroyed the old self-restraint and self-management of the House of Commons. There were major consequences as a result of this behaviour. In response to Parnell's disruption of its proceedings, the government took control of the business of the Commons. Outside Westminster, there was disorder and rising tension too. When Gladstone's government sought to face down the agitation of the Home Rulers in Ireland, it deployed the usual coercive methods. None of this could appeal to

Dicey. He believed government coercion was worse than any parliamentary obstructionism. If there were trouble in Ireland, he argued, it came about precisely because of misgovernment. Hence, when in 1881 Gladstone's regime seized and imprisoned Parnell, inevitably Dicey objected. He could do no other.

Equal rule was the cry maintained by Dicey, equal rule that derived its force and moral power directly from the glories of English and British law. Even for Dicey there were some exceptions. He lowered his legal and moral standards by arguing for the ending of jury trials in Ireland in areas where it was understood that a jury would refuse to convict even the obviously guilty.* Yet he was able to sustain his arguments by deploring the system itself. If the legal system was failing in Ireland, it was because of problems in unionist ideology. Whereas union with Scotland in 1707 had preserved the best of that country's institutions, in Ireland no similar process had occurred.

Where Dicey saw far further than most of his contemporaries was in understanding what would *not* work. He gazed at all the various fiddly schemes erected by a variety of cranks as 'solutions' to the Irish Question and saw them as so much evasion and self-delusion. The choice was stark, it was separation or Union. He even allowed a certain admiration for the open and by implication honest separatists. To Dicey, the notion of 'Home Rule' simply would not work. The Constitution would be divided against itself, sovereignty would be ripped apart.

---

* This argument was also applied during the more recent Northern Ireland Troubles, and resulted in the Diplock courts.

After all, what would be sovereign? The British nation, the British Parliament or the 'Home Rule' Parliament in Dublin and the nation it sought to govern? Home Rule might come about, but the matter would be no nearer being settled. Why, upon attaining Home Rule, should the very people who had sought it be satisfied? What sincere basis was there for believing that Home Rule *would* or *could* have set a boundary on the march of a nation?

By the mid-1880, therefore, Dicey was convinced that Home Rule could not be regarded as a middle way between the destruction of the Union and its preservation. It would simply be the destructive element with deceit heaped on top. Dicey understood what nationalists understood, perhaps because he was one. He was a unionist-nationalist. His unionist-nationalism had the Union as the object of his patriotism while Irish nationalists had Ireland as the object of theirs. There could be no meeting point between these two propositions, as they could not both be true simultaneously. Either the whole United Kingdom was together the nation or Ireland was a nation alone. The propositions were identical but exclusive and a certain fatal political unwillingness to face up to this hard reality was to be the source of much trouble to come.

Dicey understood the psyche of nationalism but he certainly could not foresee what proved to be the great trauma of his life. He, no more than anyone else, at the time or since, could anticipate the William Gladstone of early 1880s coercion becoming, in short order, the William Gladstone of mid-1880s Home Rule. A policy universally excoriated by almost all British politicians suddenly and without minimal explanation became the

policy of the British Liberal Party. This was a policy
which, as Dicey was always at pains to point out, meant
the *end* of that particular state.

There was nothing in Ireland which led to Dicey's
unionism. There was no ancestral tie, no lure, no pull.
His wife was a Bonham Carter there were no encumbered estates or fond childhood memories. Dicey was a
unionist because he thought that unionism provided the
best context and dispensation for everyone and that any
change to it of the sort encompassed by Home Rule could
only leave everyone worse off. He noted too the contrast
between, on the one hand, this Anglo-Irish dispute and,
on the other, political disputes as they worked themselves
out in other states. This was one of the key elements to
Home Rule. It happened in Britain. Had what Irish nationalists proposed, sundering the state in which they unhappily found themselves, been proposed anywhere else, it
would have met with a pointedly non-British response.
The British did not give the answer the United States
gave to the Confederates or which the unified Germans
gave to the Bavarians or Hanoverians. These disputes
had happened within recent decades and must have influenced Dicey. Germany, the United States and Italy had all
pressed themselves together mere years before Charles
Stewart Parnell proposed that Dicey's country should be
undone and they had spilled a good deal of blood in the
process. His reaction, eminently constitutional as it was,
is also entirely understandable.

William Gladstone adopted Home Rule in 1885, in part
to gain the support of the Irish Parliamentary Party in
the Commons and so preserve his government, and the
price for this support for Home Rule was a split in his

Liberal Party. He lost the support both of what could still be termed the 'Whig' element of the party under Hartington, the future eighth Duke of Devonshire, and of many of the radicals clustered round Joseph Chamberlain. Dicey went too. He and his fellow Liberal Unionists found that this was not a crisis of their making. It had been forced on them by Gladstone. There are shades here of Peel's dealing with his Conservative Party, for these disparate Liberals together took the view that they had not stood for election or supported the party with Home Rule remotely in sight as a Liberal objective. It was not a policy they could follow, so they were obliged to step back from the party they loved. It is worth noting at this point that James Bryce, his Belfast birth notwithstanding, remained loyal to Gladstone at this tense time and that he and Dicey managed to remain friends through all the years of Home Rule tumult still to come.

Upon his departure from the Liberal Party, Dicey immediately joined the Liberal Committee for the Maintenance of the Union. In due course, after nearly thirty years of separate but fused existence, the Liberal Unionists and Conservatives would formally merge in 1912 as the Conservative and Unionist Party but this was far into the future. Now, and for the first years of their existence apart from the Liberals, the Liberal Unionists excited every reaction from fury to comedy. Oscar Wilde caught something of this peculiar moment in British history in *The Importance of Being Earnest*:

LADY BRACKNELL: [*Sternly*] What are your politics?
JACK: Well, I am afraid I really have none. I am a Liberal Unionist.

LADY BRACKNELL: Oh, they count as Tories. They dine with us. Or come in the evening, at any rate.

Hartington and Chamberlain were, in their very different ways, professional parliamentarians but Dicey, the adornment of Oxford, was not. Alistair Cooke and John Vincent in their classic study of the period, *The Governing Passion*, go too far when they lift Dicey into that cadre of 'chiefly underemployed journalists, academics and members of the upper classes whom for one reason or another life had excluded from a political role'. Such a cadre did indeed become a feature of late Victorian life but it is unduly harsh to include the Vinerian Professor in their number. Dicey emphatically *had* a political role in the life of Victorian Britain. He wisely stepped out of the cloistered politics of the university precisely so that he could take his place in the public square, where he was more than welcomed by the leaders of political unionism. They benefited from his partisanship, his intellect and his constitutional expertise. His was valuable support to have.

As any Victorian sage would, Dicey wrote a book, *England's Case against Home Rule*, in defence of his cause and it became a bestseller. This was a book speaking to the faithful and not embarking on a fruitless effort to reconcile the irreconcilable. Moreover, the book marshalled Dicey's argument against the weak case made *for* Home Rule. Dicey rehearsed all the arguments everyone had always used in opposition to Butt and Parnell before Gladstone's conversion to their cause but he also despaired of the soft-headed, well-meaning Englishmen who canvassed solutions which were no solutions at all and hopes which were misplaced. Many sought to answer the demand for Home Rule by offering Ireland the measure of local government possessed by England. Dicey saw at once the absurdity of such arguments. He recognised that they would sate no Home Ruler.

Dicey was also all too aware of the part that cynicism was playing in the debate. In particular he saw clearly that there existed English MPs who were weary of the Irish Parliamentary Party and frustrated by their politics of obstruction. They would be glad to see them gone for good from the chamber. Such cynicism was immoral in Dicey's eyes. As he put it scathingly, 'Cowardice masks itself under the show of compromise and men of eminent respectability yield to the terror of being bored concessions which their forefathers would have refused to the threat of armed rebellion.'

He was also aware of the issue of Ireland's northern province of Ulster. The north-east of Ulster formed the country's industrial heartland and Protestant unionists made up the bulk of the population in these prosperous areas. Dicey was perspicacious in seeing immediately the lethal flaw Ulster constituted for nationalism. If the prospect of Irish secession from the Union was contemplated and conceded, what principle militated against Ulster's secession from Ireland's secession? It is a backhanded tribute to note that Irish nationalists did not even try to answer the 'Ulster Question'. They knew what they were about and what they wanted. Dicey, in contrast, never lost sight of what breaking the Union would mean for those who had been loyal to it but who were now to be denied the rights they once had.

The First Home Rule Bill was, for Dicey, pure Gladstonian chicanery. It had the effect of degrading British sovereignty, by proposing the creation of another body separate from the British Parliament and a body which could not help but think of itself as sovereign too in the sphere it claimed for itself. The bill rendered Parliament a practical nullity, whatever Gladstone claimed, and plainly its passage would do nothing for those to whom equal British justice was owed too. Home Rule, Dicey predicted, would not secure the place of beleaguered, unpopular, law-abiding minorities such as the unionists of Ulster. As for the complex position of Irish unionists in the rest of Ireland, this, after the partition of Ireland in 1921, was something Dicey himself would live to see. Dicey was clear that the maintenance of the Union equalled the maintenance of the law for all and the rights and freedoms conferred on all by the law. It says much about the unpopularity of the cause to which he attached himself that to this day Dicey's memory is supposed to be tarnished by it.

It also says something about the teleology of history and historians that Dicey is reckoned to have been 'negative' in his stance, when he was defending the status quo, while those who assailed the status quo are seen blandly as being a positive force. History may not always be written by winners but it is invariably written for them. Dicey stood by what existed already, while others sought to destroy it. He saw himself as the guardian of the Union, freed from petty party squabbles to make the case for it, but he was gloomy about its fate. He understood that to lose one great part of the state was a grim prospect. Any government could potentially bring this about and this, he was to come to see, was the great problem in the British Constitution. It could be undone, were ever statesmen foolish or venal enough to be minded so to do. Another charge which was made in his own time against Dicey and which has been amplified ever since is that he was a 'catastrophist', speaking the language of doom and dissolution. He did, because this is simply what he foresaw. It is an odd thing that markedly more violent and fear-laden arguments from his opponents have not likewise been tutted about for a century. In defending the Union, Dicey did something history and historians find hard to forgive. He stood by a cause that lost and made gloomy forecasts that were broadly right.

Sales of *England's Case against Home Rule* did not delude Dicey. 'One check on vanity,' he wrote to Eleanor, 'is that though the book is a success, the day when a book could have real effect on politics is gone ... The voters don't read books and the book-reading classes are, I suspect, ceasing to have political interest.' As the Home Rule crisis developed, Dicey refined his arguments to their essence and concluded that the problem of Home Rule was a question so fundamental no compromise could be attempted. This was not an easy matter for the English heart to contemplate. Yet it was true both for Dicey's nationalist opponents as for him. What was the nation? Was it the Union or was it its parts? While the Union could be four nations in one, Ireland outside the Union could only be herself. These propositions were irreducible. It had to be one or the other.

In June 1886 the First Home Rule Bill was defeated in the Commons courtesy of Liberal Unionist votes and a Tory government came into office with this faction's lusty support. The constitutional arrangements of the United

Kingdom seemed secure again but Dicey was adept at taking the longer view. The Vinerian Professor continued to pay attention to what the Home Rulers wanted *beyond* Home Rule. This was both in the sense of what they freely admitted and in terms of their unspoken, ultimate goals. In 1891, the *Spectator* called Dicey the 'keeper of the Liberal Unionist conscience' and he remained consistent in his vision. Thus, when Gladstone returned to office the following year and again failed to pass Home Rule, but this time thanks to the House of Lords, Dicey's arguments were the same.

In 1894, after Gladstone had left office for the last time, Dicey wrote to his friend Leo Maxse, editor of the *National Review* and lodestar of all which was most Tory, in pungent terms: 'The attack on national unity is to me very like an invasion being an attack on the life of the nation, & I feel as I should about an invasion, that the one paramount duty of every man is to repel it.' The Lords had stopped Home Rule again in 1894 but Dicey could see the walls crumbling in the future. It was in anticipation of this blow that Dicey contributed his next great interpolation to the Constitution. The Vinerian Professor became the father of the referendum in British politics. Although it did not happen in his time, his case for referendums in British political life is as persuasive now as it should have been then.

*

In Dicey's view, the role of the referendum in Britain stemmed directly from the decline of the House of Lords. Its standing had begun to sink in the mid-1880s, in the context of the First Home Rule Bill, when the movement of Liberal peers to the Conservatives led suddenly to a loss of a precious balance in the chamber. The Lords was now overwhelmingly unionist in nature and while this might be viewed in many quarters as desirable, such a unified power base could not be and was not positive in terms of its standing in the country. That it was of one such firm view on the issue of the hour put it at risk of contamination by party politics, rather than being, as it ought always to be, somewhat above the cut and thrust. It could not in such circumstances discharge its developing role of making the Commons think again and pointing that House back towards the people who had sent them there.

Dicey observed this new constitutional danger. He could see clearly that the country's constitutional arrangements had to be strengthened to deal with the risk of potential short-term Commons squalls inflicting lasting damage. He could also see that, while the Lords itself needed reform, its ultimate power of bringing about a General Election must remain intact. None of this happened. Rather, from Dicey's standpoint, the worst thing possible occurred in 1911, in the wake of the rejection by the House of Lords of David Lloyd George's so-called 'People's Budget'. The Liberal government of Herbert Asquith, dependent once more on the votes of the Irish Parliamentary Party, pushed through the Parliament Act, which removed the Lords' veto and placed the prospect of Home Rule on the table once more. The Parliament Act had stripped the Lords of its most valuable power, while at the same time doing nothing to reform a chamber that was chronically in need of it. The result was a risky imbalance in Britain's constitutional arrangements and this saga converted Dicey to the referendum as a necessary mechanism in the life of the country.

In essence, he now discovered the great merit of the referendum, a mechanism at which he had once sniffed as fit only for the Swiss. It was a fine safety net, for when the party system could not handle an issue, it could be taken out of the parties' hands and put in those of the people. As he more neatly put it, a referendum could become 'the People's Veto'. Writing to Prime Minister Lord Salisbury in 1892, Dicey made his case thus:

> Constitutional devices can rarely do much positive good; they may however ... avert some evil arising from unnoticed though very real alterations in the working of the Constitution ... I have long been convinced that the Referendum [must] sooner rather than later be introduced into the Constitution in order to guard the rights of the nation against the usurpation of national authority by any party which happens to have a Parliamentary majority. The principle of the Referendum has two great merits. It is at once honestly democratic in theory & conservative in practice.

It provided a 'check on tyranny' and history was to vindicate this analysis, in that polities in which referendums are a feature of life tend towards long-term stability. The people have a habit both of knowing best and being prudent and there is much to be said for modestly and respectfully deferring to their wisdom.

In language which will be familiar, Dicey observed that even the greatest of issues were apt to get lost in the muddle of a General Election, when a ragbag of controversies would randomly veer this way and that, with neither particular rhyme nor reason as to why anything should be any more or any less prominent than anything else. The beauty of the referendum, always assuming, as Dicey never for a moment contemplated could be otherwise, one respected it, was that it focused on the great issue at hand. The thing which had proved itself to be beyond the party system would not be beyond the clear-sighted judgement of the people.

Unfortunately it was not to be. Referendums were not sensibly, prudently and harmoniously introduced into the national life as Dicey wished. The party system alone confronted the crisis of Home Rule and failed in the process. Dicey watched in horror as the situation in Ireland spun towards civil strife, as opposing sides armed themselves and drilled in preparation for war, as the *popular sovereignty* that Dicey had parsed long ago at Oxford now took hold among the unionists of Ulster in the face of the looming reality of Home Rule.

*

In terms of his reputation, it is to the credit of Albert Venn Dicey that he remained a democrat. When across Europe national unity was threatened in the late nineteenth and early twentieth centuries, the posture of the democrat was not universally adopted as a response.

Decline and disenchantment pervaded the end of Dicey's long life and not just because of the fate of the Union for which he had fought heart and soul. Rather it was because he realised that something had been lost in his lifetime. Historians have pilloried his political opinions as having become those of a fossilised reactionary, abandoning the lines of his radical and academic youth. Instead of disapproving of Dicey, however, his political commitment is worth admiring and it is worth noting that he fought the good fight willingly because he recognised its overwhelming importance.

The elegiac quality to what Dicey's life reveals about Victorian Britain is that he knew what he had lived to see, which was the loss of the true and fair liberalism of his youth. He had sought only to defend the state against violent and unreasonable schemes, he had loved Parliament only to weary of parliamentarians, in thrall to their parties as they were but had not been in his youth. Where progress once had meant only ever more freedom to do good, he lived to see a time in which socialism and collectivism rose in significance and where the state made it its business to decide what was good and what was not.

From his chair as Vinerian Professor of Common Law at Oxford, Dicey reconstructed the prestige of the position he held and performed the role of secular oracle on public controversies. His opinion, however, was that he had simply done his duty, in this as in his other roles. He felt himself to be a 'prophet of the obvious', who lacked originality or inspiration. 'Throughout life,' he said of himself, 'I have to an excessive extent, as I quite admit, followed the habit of expressing obvious thoughts on obvious matters, of which to my own knowledge I am by no means a complete master.' This, his legal scholarship, was earnest hard work and it is for this that he is still applauded and was where his influence remained greatest. It still remains. It is not sullied by his unionism, which was principled and clear-sighted. He was a messenger whom naïve people wanted to shoot but his constitutional understanding has relevance today. It is his structure of Parliamentary Sovereignty and his understanding of referendums that provide the constitutional authority for the United Kingdom to leave the European Union. It is a sovereignty which ultimately is of the peoples which was not ceded because it could not be. Thank heavens for Albert Dicey.

Grace: The Superstar

On one level, the story which follows steps away from the ground so far trodden in this book. No House of Common debates, no Royal interventions, no military battles or diplomatic skirmishes, no bitter political rivalries and certainly no shadow of revolutionary France, no glittering edge of a guillotine.

Instead, the story of a cricketing life.

As every Englishman knows, there is more to the game of cricket than the sound, satisfying though it is, of leather on willow. More than any other sport, cricket at its best captures the soul of the nation. Fair play, etiquette and gentlemanly behaviour. It also exemplifies the reach and influence of English and British power around the world, for where the Empire went there also cricket went and there it remains to this day.

The life of William Gilbert – W. G. – Grace (18 July 1848–23 October 1915) is also the story of cricket. He was its most famous English player, with a global name, true star quality and an extraordinary record of achievement and victory. Grace also complicates the story of cricket, and of England, in a way that is fascinating. His life is

363

bound up, not only with cricket but with questions of class, money, etiquette, honour and raw ambition. All of these elements complicate the comforting image people may prefer to have of the game, of shadows lengthening across the outfield as a languorous, sunny English afternoon draws to a close. There was more, much more, to the Victorian game of cricket than this. There was more to England too, and in many ways Grace captures the swirl and tensions and contradictions of this Victorian world better than anyone else.

*

This chapter begins standing behind the stumps at The Oval cricket ground in south London on Tuesday 29 August 1882. Victoria had been on the throne for forty-five years, William Gladstone was her Prime Minister and under his direction British troops had just landed on the beaches of Alexandria, as the Anglo-Egyptian War exploded into life. On the field at The Oval Australia was playing England in the only Test of the summer tour. The skies, on this second day, were heavy and the light poor and a crowd of more than 20,000 had gathered to watch another struggle explode into life before their eyes.

The Australians had won the toss on the opening day, elected to bat and promptly collapsed to 59 for nine wickets. By mid-afternoon, they were all out but when England came in to bat they too played badly. Fred Spofforth of South New Wales, the Australians' most-feared pace bowler, known as the Demon, took seven wickets for 47 runs, with England's famous W. G. Grace out for four. The first day of the Test concluded with England holding a slender lead. The second day saw Australia gradually inch up to 113 for the loss of six wickets. This was how matters stood midway through that second day. It was finely poised and tense, with Billy Murdoch and Sam Jones holding steady against ferocious English bowling.

Now, Murdoch hit a delivery and set off, with Jones running towards the stumps. There being no fielder nearby, the English wicketkeeper, Alfred Lyttelton, made his leisurely way out to retrieve the ball. He threw it to Ted Peate, who dropped it. Jones assumed the ball was 'dead' and stepped out of his ground. Strictly speaking, the ball was still 'live' and now Grace picked it up, broke the stumps and appealed to the umpire for a run out. Because the ball was indeed still 'live', the umpire had no choice but to award the wicket.

If you are not a cricketer this scene requires some explanation, for it goes to the heart of what made the Victorian game so nuanced and coded. Today, Grace would be considered within his rights to act as he had done but on that late summer day in 1882 the situation was more ambiguous. For some observers, Grace had committed the cardinal sin of gamesmanship. He had violated the game's code of honour, which demanded that he instead warn the Australians that they had made an error and would be punished if they did it again. In this argument, Grace's action simply was not cricket. For others watching the scene that day, Grace had behaved honourably. He had stuck to the rules and that was that. In other words, it absolutely *was* cricket.

Whether it was or was not cricket Grace's breaking of the stumps that day changed the course of the game's history. His actions added another layer to the story of

Grace's own life and to his legacy too. He was playing to win that day and he paid for it. He was barracked for the remainder of the Test, which Australia won by seven runs. He paid for it in other ways. He was sensationally popular at this point in his career, the first global superstar, yet his decision to break the stumps that day at The Oval added to the sense, in some quarters and in posterity too, that Grace was not the gentleman he might have been. This was also the first time that England had lost to a colonial side on home ground and a few days later the *Sporting Times* ran a mock-obituary 'In Affectionate Remembrance of ENGLISH CRICKET, which died at the Oval on 29 August 1882 ... N.B. – The Body will be cremated and the ashes taken to Australia'. The story of the Ashes was born but this was not even the most significant aspect of that Test at The Oval.

It was Grace who had magnified and had maintained right out in the open his own competitive edge and who in so doing had created discomfort and an edge to a game that rather gloried in its gentlemanly image. He was a true professional, hungry and ruthless and he helped to shrug a dead hand from the shoulder of cricket, a weight that was keeping the game back. He achieved something else too, which was to begin a process of dispelling a miasma of hypocrisy that was in the process of staining the name of cricket.

*

William Gilbert Grace was born in the famous Year of Revolutions in Europe and it is difficult not to ascribe a note of interesting coincidence to this fact. His parents were Henry and Martha Grace, who lived at Downend, where the suburbs of Bristol met the fields of Gloucestershire, and he was one of eight children, five boys and three girls. His next oldest brother, Ted, became the E. M. Grace to Gilbert's W. G., both famous and highly accomplished cricketers, with reputations that spread far beyond Gloucestershire. Henry Grace was a doctor and he played a crucial role in all his children's sporting activities. He became interested in cricket, eventually establishing his own team but long before that he had set up a practice field in the garden of the family home and it was here that the Grace children first learned the happily complex rules of cricket. Martha Grace too was steeped in the game, although the tales of her close involvement in her sons' sporting development carry a touch of myth. However, it is certainly the case that she was the first and for years later remained the only lady to be listed in *Wisden*'s chronology of births and deaths of cricketers.

The young W. G., Gilbert to his family, was therefore wrapped up in cricket practice, cricket lore, cricket rules and cricket culture and in family competition. Indeed, it would have been against a context of capable young cricketers that he was first introduced to the game. No doubt there would have been a little sympathetic bowling to him when he was an infant but most of the time he is likely to have been a fielder or even a ball boy, thus helping ensure the smooth flow of the game for the benefit of his father and elder brothers. As he grew older, he would have had a greater share in the batting and the bowling but with so many brothers it is not surprising that there was a need for all-rounders. After all, in a family game specialisation is awkward. In this way he competed and grew competitive and it is this competitive streak that appears and reappears throughout his history of his life.

Did he feel destined to become a professional cricketer? Hardly. His family background was professional, but professional in the sense that a profession ran in the family. That profession was not cricket but medicine. This was seen as the way the Grace boys might make their way in the world. They were a professional family but in Victorian terms, and in class terms, this meant that there was little family money as such and that they would have to earn their living. The young Grace could not conceive of becoming a gentleman cricketer, with private resources on which to draw. This was simply not part of the scheme of his life. In any case, the notion of professionalisation was a fraught concept in Victorian England.

Gilbert grew into a slim but athletic teenager, with a sharp mind. Not that the latter has always been picked up by historians of cricket, some of whom have stuck to the peculiar idea that Grace, because he was apparently born in rural Gloucestershire rather than a Bristol suburb, was in essence a horny-handed son of the soil, an 'instinctive' cricketer, a rustic with a 'simple, almost puerile mind'. This last, astonishingly, was the verdict of the official history of the Marylebone Cricket Club (MCC), published in 1987. He was analytical and creative and this was the case not only in cricket but in all aspects of his life. He ignored the rule book if he could see a better way of doing things. In other words he was essentially self-made and this created problems in Victorian England.

Grace went to boarding school at the age of ten, not to Eton or even Harrow or any of the other illustrious public schools the names of which are sprinkled across the pages of this book, but to Ridgway House near Bristol, which was able to offer sound, solid educations to the sons of local families who could not dream of more illustrious educations for their offspring. Here too the route trodden by Grace and his brothers was neither privileged nor deprived but somewhere in a difficult-to-categorise middle. The Ridgway school fees, though by no means high, were a stretch for the family. Henry Grace was obliged to think always of his income, to answer each and every call placed to him by a patient, and his children were well aware of how hard their parents worked so that the younger generation could have the best possible start in life. It is clear that money, a liking for money and a fear of not having enough of it, all occupied significant parts of Grace's psyche and it is important too to stress that this interest in money was very reasonable.

In 1864, at the age of sixteen, Grace was removed from Ridgway, possibly because his parents could no longer afford the school fees, and spent the next year at home, studying under a tutor. He was destined for a medical career. Until a few years previously, it had still been possible to serve an apprenticeship with a doctor, with his father Henry Grace in this case, before completing a brief formal training course at medical school. This was the inexpensive path followed by Grace's elder brothers but now the regulations had been updated. W. G. himself would have to spend almost three years in formal medical training in order to qualify. He did qualify in the end but it took him nearly eleven years to do so.

The reason was cricket. By now both Ted and Gilbert Grace were recognised as superb young players. They had amassed much experience at local level but there were serious obstacles to the young Grace achieving his ambition of playing at the highest level of the game. For one thing, Gloucestershire at that time was not a county team. There were only seven such teams and each operated strict rules on residency and family ties. Ironically, only MCC itself, the original club and the sport's regulatory body, offered a possible route to the top. Ironically, because the club was a byword in those days for sluggish administration, antediluvian attitudes and a ground at Lord's that, with its field grazed by sheep and its ramshackle facilities, was far from being the best ground in the land. Yet MCC was the only club which did not operate a residency bar, meaning that the Grace brothers could aspire to play at Lord's. What was the problem? There was none on paper but a problem existed nonetheless and it had everything to do with class and with hidebound attitudes that were holding back the game of cricket. MCC was a bastion of amateur cricket, in a world that was straining at the professional leash. Moreover, the gentlemen who sat on the MCC committee were, alas, unlikely to accept the membership applications of the sons of a middling, jobbing doctor from the Bristol suburbs.

As it happened, chance would intervene to smooth the path of E. M. Grace towards top-flight play. A conversation in the summer of 1862 between the Grace parents and an MCC committee member revealed a problem. MCC had organised a cricket festival at Canterbury, beginning the following day, but the team was a man short. Henry Grace proposed that Ted step in, on condition that he also be permitted to play for Middlesex in a county match against Kent the following week. It was a deal and Ted had his foot in the door. The Kent team grumbled at the presence of this non-amateur player in an amateur fixture. It was implied that Ted was socially inferior and that he played cricket for money, which was definitely not cricket. Ted did, however, make the team, played supremely well and he was duly admitted to MCC's hallowed halls.

Regrettably, his presence at Lord's was still seen by many at the club as an embarrassment. He *was* socially inferior, he *did* play for money and his mere presence underscored the existence of what became known as *shamateurism*, the presence of ostensible amateurs who were in fact earning a fee. Ted's presence might have made it easier for his younger brother to join MCC too but it might also have made the process more difficult. In the meantime, the Grace brothers had become symbols of the tensions vibrating at the heart of this archetypal gentleman's game. The Graces had little option but to work with the system as best they could even if this system was problematic. They had no other choice. It was beyond their capacity to overthrow the existing order, even if they wanted to do so. This question of shamateurism endured for and set an undertone to much of Grace's career.

Several years passed, during which Ted proved his worth to MCC and was selected to travel on a tour of Australia but it was not until 1866 that W. G. himself was at last admitted to the club. He had to show his class on the field again and again. This included two staggering centuries at The Oval, until MCC felt obliged to embrace this young genius. The committee's hostility to shamateurism remained as potent as ever but the hypocrisy which surrounded this stance was becoming ever more glaringly obvious. Money was being made under the gaze of all and people could only avert their eyes for so long. At last, an MCC committee member, Robert Allen Fitzgerald, noted in his book *Jerks in from Short-Leg* that the situation was intolerable. It was time 'for the gentlemen cricketers of England to assert their position, not merely as patrons of the game, but as performers'. The word *performer* was unlikely to please some of the more traditionalist committee members, who were already in sharp reaction to events in the world outside, among them banking troubles, factory disturbances and the death of Albert that had caused the Queen to vanish into the shadows of her grief, but Fitzgerald's point was well made. Finally, in May 1869, W. G. Grace became a member of the Marylebone Cricket Club. This was the first necessary step on a road to stardom.

The sense of security that came with club membership obviously served Grace well. In the years that followed, he hit centuries at a prodigious rate. In July, the *Daily Telegraph* wrote rapturously:

He knew exactly where every ball he hit would go. Just the strength required was expended and no more. When the fieldsmen were placed injudiciously too deep he would quietly send a ball halfway towards them with a gentle tap and content himself with a modest single. If they came in a little nearer, the shoulders opened out and the powerful arms swung round as he lashed the first loose ball and sent it away through the crowded ring of visitors until one heard a big thump as it struck against the furthest fence.

It is no surprise that the cricket impresarios began to circle, sensing a profit to be made, and no wonder that Grace, being a professional and in need of money, welcomed their advances. When a proposal was made to tour Australia in the southern summer of 1869–70, Grace was keen to accept. Ted had returned with tales of goldrush Melbourne and Victoria that sounded, as Grace's biographer Richard Tomlinson put it, 'rather more interesting than Bristol on a rainy day in February'. It made perfect sense. There would be no cricket to be had for the whole of the northern winter and Grace had to make money. Nor could MCC realistically object, since it was now paying him euphemistic 'expenses', that is, a fee for each match.

As it happened, the plan collapsed. It was a rainy Bristol that winter but the proposal did Grace no harm. It made it abundantly clear now that he was a paying proposition, thus normalising his stance as a proto-professional cricketer and helped to flush out the remaining opposition. It also emboldened Grace himself to seek appropriate remuneration for what was becoming his full-time occupation. Furthermore, the mere fact of his presence in Britain enabled him to consolidate his position as a star. He was rather more available to journalists and photographers than he would have been in Melbourne, even in the new world of telegraphs and comfortably rapid communication.

At Christmas 1871, Henry Grace died suddenly at the age of sixty-three, thus depriving his son of one of the most significant influences in his life. This made another problem press upon him instantly. It was one which underscores his status as a self-made man and not an amateur gentleman player. He was forced to face the fact that his mother might not now have enough money to live on, that he and his siblings were obliged now to consider the question of finances with even greater seriousness. When fresh proposals were made for lucrative tours of

Canada and Australia, made on the strict proviso that Grace would be on the team, he considered them with more than usual attention.

The story of these negotiations highlights starkly and disagreeably the criticism that Grace faced, then and since, for being in the position of having to earn a living. He delivered an ultimatum to the Australian consortium charged with luring him to Melbourne. A fee of £1,500, plus his expenses, a tremendously large sum at the time and, as it turned out, beyond the capacity of the organisers, meaning that he went to Canada instead. Much of the criticism that was turned on Grace hinges on his Australian demand. It shows that he was greedy beyond the dreams of avarice; that he was grasping, disgracefully so; that he was manifestly not a gentleman and so on. Such arguments fail to take into account just how unpredictable Grace's earnings were and they also fail to recognise just how large an amount of money the Australians were hoping to make out of him. Most of all, there is a heart-sinking snobbery in this scolding of Grace for seeking to maximise his worth or perhaps for failing to be born a gentleman, with his own money already in the bank.

Grace's tour of eastern Canada – a tour of the north-eastern United States, including a visit to the then cricket citadel of Philadelphia, was added at the last minute – contained no great moments of cricket but it did what it was supposed to do. It provided a decent payday for Grace. This was just as well, for he was returning to a fiancée and a marriage plus a tour of Australia which was planned for the following year. More than ever he needed the money to live the life that he wanted and that his bride-to-be may have hoped to enjoy.

*

Grace had become engaged to Agnes Day early in 1873. She was a distant relation and her branch of the family was even less financially stable than his, although the reasons for their economic want verged on the sensational. As already mentioned, Palmerston, the liberal-minded Foreign Secretary in the 1848 Year of Revolutions, had struck up an unlikely and in the minds of British diplomats, to say nothing of the Queen and Prince Albert, decidedly unwelcome, friendship with the Hungarian nationalist leader Lajos Kossuth. Agnes' father William Day, a lithographer, had also crossed paths with Kossuth and he had printed a run of illegal banknotes to assist the Hungarian. When the Austrian authorities discovered what had happened, they sued Day, with the result that the family was financially ruined. Grace and Agnes Day married in early October 1873 and a week later the happy couple joined the team at Southampton, for Agnes had obligingly consented to look upon the southern tour as an extended honeymoon. When they sailed, the team discovered that Grace and the handful of other 'amateur' players were billeted in first-class accommodation for the duration of the two-month cruise to Melbourne while the professionals were forced to endure cramped and smelly steerage quarters below decks. These arrangements proved more evidence, not that it was needed, of the class distinction at the heart of the game.

Agnes has left little trace. It is assumed that she burned the correspondence she had had with her husband, for none has survived. However, it is possible to glimpse a woman with a steely core, one well able to keep a family together and to keep the show on the road. She was certainly the spine of family life. Her unorthodox honeymoon was the first of two tours of Australia, the second with her children in tow. There would be tragedies ahead for the Graces. As so many Victorian families discovered, death was never far away and two of their children predeceased them. Their eldest son William (known as Bertie), who was also a promising cricketer, died after an operation for appendicitis in 1904 and a much-loved daughter, Bessie, died in early 1899 of typhoid fever.

A secure and happy family background is not, of course, a guarantee of an easy and regular temper and it is certainly the case that Grace could on occasion be extremely overbearing. He had a fierce temper and this could sometimes be brought into full flame by something simple or absurd, such as when, in May 1889, he instructed that a notice be erected at the Gloucestershire County Ground at Ashley Down. The notice proclaimed that practice was forbidden because it has been raining, not an unusual occurrence in English summers. Grace then discovered that some young people had disobeyed the notice and had been playing in the nets and he exploded with rage. So extreme was his anger, indeed, that he had to apologise to the club president, writing, not very apologetically, 'I was sorry I had struck the boy, but that nine out of every ten persons would have done the same under the provocation.' The parents were not enormously happy but were persuaded not to take the matter any further. No doubt many forceful characters have been tempted to behave in a similar way but Grace by this point was not merely a forceful character, he was also a promi-nent national figure and an altercation with schoolboys would not have burnished his reputation.

On his several Australian tours, too, his irritation was wont to boil over periodically and this is part of the reason why his reputation in the country was of somebody more aggressive than was necessary. The row with the promotor William Runting, who had organised a match in Sydney between the England 11 and a New South Wales 18 during the 'honeymoon' tour of 1873–4, was sparked by the latter's decision to ask Grace to delay the start of the final day's play because the local team only needed 56 runs to win. A delay, he thought, would make the match more exciting for the crowd. Grace disagreed, vehemently. Reports at the time suggested that spectators had to intervene to separate the two, whose row developed rapidly beyond mere verbal aggression. Interestingly, the altercation actually led to Grace having additional work to do. The match ended earlier than planned, so to fill the remaining hours an exhibition game was rapidly scheduled, starring Grace himself.

His dealings with officials, even those on his own side, were equally high-handed and were sometimes tense purely because he had been thwarted in one way or another. One such incident took place when Grace double-booked himself to play both in a benefit match and for Gloucestershire in a fixture against Nottinghamshire. He resolved this clash in his own inimitable fashion. He simply told Nottinghamshire to change the date of its match and when the county refused Grace refused to back down. He announced that if Nottinghamshire insisted on going ahead, he simply would not play on the date suggested. He was a man who expected to be obeyed and his position meant that he generally would be.

This was an undoubted flaw in his temperament and it would sometimes have negative repercussions. It led to the miserable severing of his relationship with his home county of Gloucestershire. Grace was not good at letting the Gloucestershire committee know when he was and was not available. He had many other cricketing commitments but it was his responsibility to keep all parties informed. Eventually, in 1899, the county wrote to him to ask precisely when he *would* play, to the very great irritation of Grace, who replied coldly, 'I have always tried my very best to promote the interests of the Gloucestershire County Club and it is with deep regret that I resign the Captaincy. I have the greatest affection for the County of my birth, but for the committee, as a body, the greatest contempt.' Not surprisingly the committee found this more offensive than it could bear and Grace never played for Gloucestershire again, even though it was through him that Gloucester became a first-class county. He was well into the twilight of his career at this time but he remained a draw and it was a sadness that his association with his home turf ended badly.

To some extent his temper was born out of his competitive spirit and because he took cricket seriously. It was for him both a life's work and perhaps rather more than a business that his temper could sometimes bear. This competitiveness was also on occasion comical, as in the incident during a Gloucestershire vs Surrey game in 1878, when a fielder threw in a ball which lodged in Grace's clothing. Grace maintained that he could not touch the ball. After all, if he did touch it he would be at risk of being out handled ball. He therefore simply carried on running until finally the fielders managed to obstruct him. Not surprisingly he claimed the extra runs.

Sometimes his competitiveness shaded into courage and set an example to others. When batting for Middlesex against Yorkshire at Lord's on a terrible wicket, it was said at the end of his innings of 66 that his legs resembled beaten steaks. One of the two Yorkshire fast bowlers, Tom Emmett, commented that he did not think that 'WG had a square inch of sound flesh on his body after that innings'. A determination *not* to be out *and* to get as many runs as possible *and* to try to ensure that every wicket that could be gained was gained: this summed up Grace's cricketing attitude and is part and parcel of the Grace legend. He was so successful *because* he was so competitive and the competitiveness cannot be taken out of his nature, but the reflection that this ferocity did inevitably sometimes cross over the line into gamesmanship is hard to avoid. The Australian team watching his behaviour at The Oval that sultry day in August 1882 certainly took this view. Nonetheless, it was an attitude of mind that improved the standard of cricket, not just in the teams in which he played but in the teams that opposed him. The Australians certainly noticed that they raised the quality of their game, precisely because they knew Grace would give them no quarter.

*

The degree to which sport and class were interwoven in the England of the nineteenth century has already been seen. *Gentlemen* were not paid to play and were expected to have an income outside the sport which allowed them to pursue the game. *Professionals* were paid. On the other hand, they were treated much less well than the gentlemen. One of the great fixtures each season was Gentlemen vs Players, an event in which Grace built a remarkable record over his long career. There was another layer in this complicated relationship, for not everyone who pursued a career as a full-time player could actually afford to maintain themselves without financial assistance, without receiving some form of emoluments from the game. In what was held to be a strictly amateur game, however, these emoluments had to be covered up in the form of putative 'expenses'. The point being that these payments bore no relation to actual expenses. Instead, they were simply fees or salaries in a genteel disguise. This was a curious, hypocritical and unsatisfactory state of affair, scoffed all.

Grace squarely occupied this difficult position of needing money while being expected not to earn it. There were periodic outbursts of concern about it. In 1874, Captain Henry Holden, who was the honorary secretary of Nottinghamshire County Cricket and the Chief Constable of Nottinghamshire, wrote to MCC calling for a 'proper definition ... of the term *amateur*', as distinct from professional. Fitzgerald, as secretary of MCC, replied that he was opposed to 'anyone playing as an amateur who is essentially a professional'. His remarks were unfortunately leaked, and led to suggestions that Grace, for it was Grace's position that was on the mind of everyone in the world of cricket, could not reasonably be considered an amateur by anybody.

This row had little effect. This clearly unsustainable situation nevertheless sustained itself. Four years later, the list of expenses for Gloucestershire's match against Surrey at The Oval makes it clear that 'expenses' related to the quality of the player as much as anything else. Hence W. G. Grace received £15, G. F. Grace (Fred Grace) received £11, Walter Gilbert £8, Billy Midwinter, a professional and therefore not given the honorific 'Mr', £10, the umpire £6, the scorer £5 and Dr E. M. Grace (Ted Grace) £20. As it happens, Surrey on this occasion thought the claims bill too high and cut it back by £20 overall. Nonetheless it would have been very hard to justify the difference in fee on the basis of 'expenses'. It was simply a code for a fee or salary which everyone knew. A degree of officially sanctioned humbug was tolerated then, just as it no doubt is today in many walks of life.

The *unfairness* lies in the damage done to Grace's reputation. To add to this unfairness is the sense that his record as a cricketer has never been properly understood. By today's standards, this record certainly is curiously patchy but it must remembered that he was playing within a different system. In the first place, he played fewer Test matches than players today but there were simply far fewer Test matches played. For example, the Australian tour of 1882 included only one Test, at The Oval, and as a result his record stands and falls largely on his first-class record, which is of much less interest today.

Secondly, batsmen's averages have been considerably higher. Grace averaged just under 40, which compares unfavourably with Sir Donald Bradman's 99.6 in Test matches and with the expectation that the highest-level batsman will average over 50. In terms of Grace's bowling, the situation differs again. He bowled more of a side-arm action and took relatively few Test wickets and again this has made him look less compelling than the great bowlers of the present era.

In addition, it is perhaps forgotten that Grace played in the earliest Test matches at a time when it took several months for a team to travel from the United Kingdom to Australia. In addition to which, such lengthy tours had to be financed privately. Inevitably this made them a much larger financial risk, so much rarer events. This is a key reason as to why Grace had no opportunity to play Test cricket at anything like the rate of professional cricketers today and this makes his first-class averages of overwhelming importance. *This* is where Grace's remarkable dominance is shown and any fair evaluation of him must be judged against nineteenth-century standards and conditions rather than those of the twenty-first century. When this is done, his dominance and tremendous talent are unbelievable.

Grace's achievements were stunning. He scored fifty first-class centuries by the age of twenty-seven. To place this in context, it has been calculated by the cricketing authority Irving Rosenwater that in the ten years prior to this, fifty first-class centuries were the *total* achieved by the thirteen next most successful batsmen. This level of dominance truly remains unprecedented and compares favourably with Bradman. Grace's bowling was also remarkable. Aged only sixteen, he took thirteen wickets in a match for 84 runs. This was in the course of a match between Lansdown and United All England at Bath. All of the United England wickets fell to the Grace brothers, though one assumes that his elder siblings must have felt rather outshone on this occasion by their younger brother.

One of Grace's most remarkable feats came just a couple of years later. In 1866, he was playing for England against

Surrey at The Oval. He scored 224 runs, then the highest score anyone had made at The Oval, but that was not enough for Grace. Having batted for hours and run a total of 431 runs, as there were no boundaries at that time, he then hurried to the Crystal Palace in nearby Sydenham for a meeting of the National Olympian Association. He took part in the 440-yard hurdles, which he duly won, before returning to his game of cricket. Such incredible levels of sporting prowess are always unusual but as an all-round athlete Grace was one of the true greats. The prodigious feats continued. In 1868 at Canterbury's summer festival of cricket, Grace scored two centuries in a match, 130 and 102, the first time a batsman had done this since 1817. As he got older and grew taller, the remarkable agility and fitness of his youth were forgotten. The enduring picture of the large and formidable figure of his later years has eclipsed his youthful athleticism.

His first *annus mirabilis* was 1871, when he became the first batsman to score more than 2,000 runs in a season. He totalled 2,739 and an average of 78.25, double the average of the next most successful batsman. He also scored 2,000 runs in the seasons of 1873, 1876, 1887, 1895 and 1896. In all, he scored 1,000 runs twenty-eight times in a season. This remains a record and the only player of recent times who comes close is Geoffrey Boycott, who managed this feat twenty-six times. Even this does not do justice to his dominance. In 1876, Grace scored 1,389 runs in August alone. He noted himself that this was 'greater than any other batsman made in the whole year in first class-cricket'.

His greatest year was possibly 1876. He scored his first triple century, 318 not out for Gloucestershire in a fixture against Yorkshire and the highest score achieved until that date. In the course of that summer, he managed 2,622 runs in eleven-a-side matches and 1,047 in matches 'against the odds', that is, in which teams of eleven played teams of more than eleven. This 'against the odds' match was a regular feature of nineteenth-century cricket, when the stronger team would allow the other side to have more players. It is within this format that many think Grace's ability to place the ball so precisely was honed. Even when there were as many as twenty-two fielders, he managed considerable accuracy and careful shot selection to maintain his prodigious scoring. Naturally, this is something that helped him in ordinary cricket as well. In addition to his first-class triple century, he also scored 344 in a twelve-a-side match. Incidentally, he made 400 not out in an 'against the odds' match although that was not in itself a record, as another player had managed 404 not out.

Nearly twenty years later Grace was achieving similar success. Aged forty-seven in 1895, he became the first batsman to score 1,000 runs by the end of May, a feat achieved by only two others, Wally Hammond and Charlie Hallows, in the history of first-class cricket. Others have scored 1,000 runs before the end of May but they had matches in April to help them. In the same season, he scored his 100th first-class hundred. He was the first batsman to achieve this feat and for his pains was presented with a glass of champagne on the field by the captain of Somerset, Sammy Woods.

The aggregate scores achieved in this latter phase of his career are even more remarkable considering his increasing girth, and the fact that he could not possibly have been so nimble between the wickets. The following year of 1896 was almost as good. He managed a triple century, and his bowling figures were not bad either, for he took 52 wickets for just over 24 runs each. Quite simply, nobody else has ever managed to match such all-round quality and longevity nor placed such a distance between himself and the player in second place.

These achievements also require further contextualisation as the quality of wickets was simply appalling. Lord's only dispensed with its sheep and reluctantly purchased its first lawnmower in 1864. On occasions Grace found himself having to pick gravel out of the wicket on this supposedly hallowed turf. On one occasion, in 1870, the poorly prepared wicket led to tragedy. Grace carried his bat,* scoring 117, while lamentably at the other end George Summers was hit on the head and died, the ball having bounced around erratically against everybody. The rolling of pitches was not agreed until the latter part of Grace's career, when, and partly at his insistence, such elements in the game were standardised and professionalised. In other words W. G. achieved his incredible performance in an era when nobody else could match it on appalling wickets. As an indication of this, in the period in which he scored his first fifty hundreds, all the other batsman in England combined had only scored 109 centuries. Thus Grace had fifty of 159 to his own credit, or nearly a third.

---

* For any non-cricketing reader 'carrying your bat' is applied to an opening batsman who is still not out when all the other batsmen have lost their wickets. It is a rare occurrence last achieved in an Ashes Test by an Englishman by Alastair Cook in 2017/18.

As Grace commanded the heights of cricketing achievement, so he showed his distinctiveness in other ways. He used his brain and his analytic abilities, developing theories as to how to play, which he then tried to put into practice when coaching others. In addition, he knew how to use his charisma to popularise the game. He always wanted to play *attractive* cricket, even when this gave the Australians an advantage. As he told the cricket organiser Lord Sheffield, 'It is the game I have tried to play all my life: it is the game every lover of cricket desires to see played, and it will be a bad day for our national game when it is given up, and a slow defensive game takes its place. Matches are played to be won, not lost.' This commitment to attractive play was essential in making cricket into one of the great national sports, and it was essential too in establishing the ongoing rivalry between England and Australia and it made money, which Grace undoubtedly liked.

There were other elements in building what would become this wonderful rivalry and here too Grace played his part. In the course of his first, or honeymoon, tour of Australia in 1873–4, there were complaints that he had bet on the result of matches and that this influenced his behaviour. There were also complaints about the relationship between the amateurs and the professionals which upset the sensibilities of the egalitarian Australians. On top of all this, Grace's extracurricular activities included shooting three kangaroos, which he presented as a romantic gift to Agnes. This made it seem as if he were not completely serious about the tour and it further antagonised the Australians. David Gower flying a Tiger Moth during the 1990–91 tour had a similar effect.

On the second tour (1891–2), matters were, if anything, worse and the rows even more preposterous. Even the toss at the first Test at Melbourne on 1 January 1892 caused a problem. Grace was suspicious of the penny produced by John Blackham, the celebrated wicketkeeper and Australian captain, for it was so worn that it was too difficult to tell one side from another. The ground was packed, 20,000 people were there for the first day and Grace, who lost the toss, tested the coin just to make sure it was not 'weighted'. This is not a way to charm an opponent, even if Blackham was gentlemanly enough not to object too strongly.

Another of the rows concerned an umpire by the name of E. J. Briscoe in a match between England and New South Wales. Briscoe thought that the English style of appealing was too aggressive and he became irritable as a result. He then refused to give a catch behind the wicket. Grace, in his own recollection, told him mildly enough, 'I wish you would pay attention to the game; we all heard the catch.' Briscoe's recollection of the exchange, however, was that Grace had been rather more forceful: 'You will give no one out. It is unpardonable. You must be blind. We might as well go home tomorrow.' Briscoe then left the field in a huff and the Australian newspapers had a field day. Grace was obliged to defend himself, remarking in Sydney, 'I did not insult Mr Briscoe, nor did I think him a cheat', adding later from Adelaide, 'I did tell Mr Briscoe that his decision was unpardonable, and that he must pay more attention ... I did not insult Mr Briscoe, nor do I think him a cheat, but, I am sorry to say, he is not a good umpire.' With that, he took ship at Adelaide and left Australia, never to return.

The essentially good-natured passions continue between England and Australia to this day, with each side fond of digging the other in the ribs with a rigid index finger when the chance presents itself. The taunting amusement that occurs in England when the Australians are found to have used sandpaper on their cricket balls perhaps derives from the heightened sense of competitiveness generated in Grace's time. It charged up the battery of this rivalry and its currents are still flowing today. It is no wonder that, if looking back at the August day in 1882 at The Oval, the circumstances of the game have never been forgotten. With luck they never will be.

Later in life Spofforth, the Demon, and Grace became the best of friends and perhaps the origins of the Ashes can be traced back a further two years, to a Test at The Oval in September 1880 in which both of these marvellous cricketers played their part with gusto. The witty and wise *Wisden* report is worth quoting at length:

The compiler much regrets that the limited space allotted to the Australians' matches in this book precludes the possibility of giving a lengthened account of this famous contest. He must therefore rest content to put on record the following facts anent the match: That in the history of the game no contest has created such worldwide interest; that the attendances on the first and second days were the largest ever seen at a cricket match; that 20,814 persons passed through the turnstiles on Monday, 19,863 on the Tuesday, and 3,751 on the Wednesday; that fine weather favoured the match from start to finish; that the wickets were faultless; that Mr.

Murdoch's magnificent innings of 153 not out was made without a chance ... that the fielding and wicketkeeping on both sides were splendid; that a marvellous change in the aspect of the game was effected on the last day; that universal regret was felt at the unavoidable absence of Mr. Spofforth; and that England won the match by 5 wickets.

Grace had set the tone by scoring 152 and then wagering Billy Murdoch that he could not beat his score. Murdoch managed to do so by one run, achieving 153 not out while carrying his bat for Australia in the second innings. Grace gave him the sovereign that was owed and Murdoch continued to wear it on his watch chain for the rest of his life. He even held onto this memento after bankruptcy had led to the dispersal of all his other goods. Grace's tribute to Murdoch's innings was marvellous. 'It was,' he said, 'a triumph for him to have not only exceeded my own fine score of 152 by 1 run, but also to have achieved the distinction of being not out, and I take this opportunity of congratulating him most heartily and sincerely in print as I did at the time verbally, on having enrolled his name for ever on the scroll of cricket fame by his gallant achievement.' This is Grace at his most attractive and effective. A great competitor, a generous player, a man who settles his debts, a man who admires skill in others and a master controller of his own image, which was one reason for his enormous celebrity. He was simply very good at what he did.

Grace saw a market for cricket, and for his cricketing prowess in particular, and he wanted and needed to cash in. His competitiveness and skill drew in the crowds and this made it economically attractive for the promotors of games to pay him handsomely. He was also more than a very large cog in a machine. By the 1870s, his position as secure as it would ever be, he would regularly put together scratch teams and take them to play matches across the country. For this, he would be paid as much as £100, most of which amounted to pure profit, in its day no small sum of money for a freelance player. To achieve these amounts he was always a fierce negotiator. When Lord Sheffield first proposed that second tour of Australia in the southern summer of 1891–2, Grace demanded a fee of £3,000, plus expenses, plus the fare for Agnes and their two youngest children. Sheffield agreed, calculating that he could, such was the cult of Grace, make his money back even on such an enormous initial outlay. It *was* enormous. While it is difficult to convert nineteenth-century prices into current values a useful rule of thumb is that in those days a pound had a fixed gold value, with a sovereign being worth £1. Today the value of gold in a sovereign is £225, which means Grace's charge for that second and last tour in today's value of gold would be £675,000. This is less than today's cricketer at the highest level would be paid but it does provide a more accurate flavour of the amounts of money that the leading player in the world was able to charge towards the end of the nineteenth century. Grace was competitive and he liked money but how curious that these days sportsmen are not viewed, much less judged, through the same lens.

For all of his self-confidence, even bumptiousness on the field, he could be a kindly and generous man off it, especially when he was engaged in his other life as a general practitioner. For he did at last qualify from medical school by 1878. Having completed his training he was able to spend time, though not much, ministering to the ill. His habit was to send in the smallest possible bills to his poorest patients and he cultivated a gruff if friendly bedside manner. It must have been slightly peculiar having the most famous man in England swinging his stethoscope at your bedside. His first biographer, Methven Brownlee, noted, 'From early morning until late in the evening you will find WG toiling at his profession, trudging through rain, sunshine and storm as cheerful as if you were playing cricket, so his diligence is not in doubt even if he was no more than a competent GP or at least his medical standing was not as high as his cricketing standard.' Brownlee's *Cricket* (1891) is to all intents and purposes hagiographical and is not wholly reliable but there is no reason to doubt Grace's methodical attention to his medical job on those occasions he was obliged to do it. Such passages supply a useful corrective to the dominant narrative of a man as grasping and ungracious as he was driven.

He also had an important place as a role model. To cricketers he was inspirational. In an edition of *Wisden* in the tributes recorded in 1896, Grace's peer Allan – A. G. – Steele of Lancashire wrote, 'I shall never forget the kindly encouragement I, a young cricketer, received from WG the first time I met him', while George Harris, Lord Harris of Kent, added that 'the old man is the kindest and the most sympathetic cricketer I have ever played with. As I said in proposing his health some years ago at a banquet the Kent County Club gave in his honour, I never knew a man make a mistake in the field but what WG had a kind word to say to, and an excuse to find for him, and I doubt if I could conclude with anything in praise of my old friend which would be truer or more gratifying to his feelings than that.' Invited contributors to a volume who were specially commissioned to celebrate a cricketing life would be expected to offer friendly remarks. In focusing upon Grace's kindness and generosity, especially towards other players, these gentlemen were very likely to be telling the truth.

*

The level of Grace's celebrity is hard to imagine for a cricketer today. Perhaps society is more fragmented, and therefore no individual figure can be so overwhelming, but as Richard Tomlinson notes in his excellent biography, the British Library's online newspaper database produces about 43,000 articles about Grace for the period from the 1850s to 1899, which is more than double the number for Sarah Bernhardt, the most famous actress the world has ever known. Grace possessed an indefinable star quality. This meant that the crowds flocked to see him and *this* perhaps explains some of his eagerness to make money, because others were able to make so much money out of him. To give one small example, in 1873, in advance of a game between the United South and the 22 of South Oxfordshire, the promoter doubled the entry to the cricket ground at Thame from sixpence to one shilling just because Grace was there. The hike did not deter the crowds. Gate receipts were £276 against expenses of £135, increasing the profit from £3 to £141. In other words, a forty-seven-fold increase, thanks to the presence of one man. The same swelling of the crowd at the Melbourne Cricket Ground or The Oval made considerable the profits, which means that Grace's attitude made perfect sense and was entirely reasonable.

Grace's popularity could not only be shown in attendance figures at matches but also through the desire of advertisers to use his image. The advertising campaign for Colman's Mustard epitomises this ability to monetise Grace's image. It survives very clearly today in the public consciousness. In the end, such advertising worked well for Grace even if, in the course of his career, he had not been good at taking financial advantage of such events. When the *Daily Telegraph* in 1895 launched a 'shilling testimonial' to celebrate his career and especially his one hundred centuries, it raised £5,281 9s. 1d. Individual contributions flooded in from across the country. Even schoolboys sent their pocket money to pay tribute to W. G. Grace. This is an indication of his stature, popularity and *visibility*. When he played in his own Jubilee match celebrating his ability to play first-class cricket at the age of fifty, 17,500 turned up to watch.

He became not only the most celebrated cricketer but one of the most popular *celebrities* of the whole of the nineteenth century, conceivably only outplayed by the Queen herself. This inevitably created the myth around Grace and some wonderful stories grew up about the unwillingness of W. G. to leave the crease. On one occasion when he was bowled he suggested to the umpire, 'It's a windy day today', implying that the bails had only tumbled because of the weather. The iron-willed umpire replied, 'Yes, and I hope it doesn't blow your cap off on the way back to the pavilion.' Such a story reflects both the positive and the negative sides of this extremely determined character and it is also the case that such apocryphal stories are only told about great figures.

*

Grace was in some ways the model of a Victorian. This was certainly the case in physical terms, for his strength and fitness was the classic picture of robust Victorian manhood, and he had the confidence and strength to add reality to the image. This would have counted for very little without his genuine brilliance on the field, a brilliance that has arguably never been surpassed. As is the case with many of his contemporaries, a lack of historical context has lessened his stature in recent decades. We have found it too easy to forget that Grace lived in a pragmatic age which has sometimes appeared to later generations as hypocritical. The Victorians loved the outward signs of gentility, epitomised in the form of the amateur who need not be paid, but they also recognised, or most of them did, the need for people to profit from their enterprise, to make a decent living.

This was after all an age of business success whereas our present society, being more tiresomely censorious, is more inclined to criticise Grace for working *with* the grain of the society in which he lived, rather than seek to overturn that society. How could he have tried to do so when the risk was so high? Had he failed to create a new cricketing culture, what might have been the result? Perhaps the greatest player of the day might have found himself banished from the game for good. This would have been bad news for cricket. Instead, this man of ambition and pragmatism and drive, who built a business and a brand in the face of all the odds, who worked with what he had and who stands as the original face of today's cricket, deserves to be saluted. Without him Test cricket may never have started and it was mainly a commercial endeavour.

In this Grace was a businessman. He would most definitely have been keen to embrace T20 or 100-ball games, so long as the ground was full and he was paid 'expenses'.

Victoria: Pole Star

Finally, the book ends with Her Imperial Majesty Queen Victoria (24 May 1819–22 January 1901). The end of the story, its beginning and everything in between. The reference point and the pivot on which the other Victorian lives have turned. The wife and the mother, the Queen and the Empress and the subject of dozens of books and, more recently, films and television series too. An enormous amount is known about this long-lived woman and this long-reigning monarch. This is owing in part to the labours of generations of scholars and historians but in the main to the Queen herself, who left such a legacy in the form of journals, letters and documents, reams of paper upon which she wrote her thoughts and opinions and observations. She opined on the Empire and on its various regions and territories and on Britain itself as well as Ireland. She had firm views on the laws formulated and on the politicians who governed in her name. There had never previously been a public figure who was observed so intently and who observed so intently and who watched so much herself. Who bequeathed such a record and who stamped her presence and her opinions indelibly upon her era.

396

The Queen influenced so many lives. Each of the men whose lives have been traced in this book glanced back over his shoulder at Victoria. Some met her in person, indeed, some spent altogether too much time in her company. Others never met her but all of them regarded her as a reference point, a moral and cultural pole star who guided their work and directed their own sense of identity and purpose. 'The history of the Victorian age will never be written,' sniffed Lytton Strachey but he was wrong there, as he was so often elsewhere. The story of the age has been written and rewritten many times but it revolves around Victoria herself. This is the story of the symbol and of a culture but also a story of the woman herself, in all her guises.

*

A glance at the family tree of the Hanoverian Royal Family demonstrates the strange and improbable nature of Victoria's accession to the throne. There should never have been a Georgian succession crisis. George III had more children, fifteen in all, than any other British monarch and the line of succession should have been so long as to quench any prospect of Victoria finding herself at its head. Yet, for all that there were fifteen possible new families still to come, there turned out to be a surprising dearth of legitimate candidates for the throne. This meant that the British public was treated to an unseemly race between his children as they tried to provide a grandchild to succeed. They tried but largely failed so Victoria, and, as it turned out, the British nation, was the winner.

George III was the third of the Hanoverian line, brought over from Germany to occupy the British throne following the death of Queen Anne, who had no surviving children in spite of at least seventeen pregnancies, she the last of the Stuart monarchs. George III was the first of the truly British Hanoverians, the first to be born in Britain, the first to speak English as his native language and the first never to set foot in Hanover, the principality over which he also reigned. 'I was born and raised in this country,' he said, and 'I glory in the name of Briton.' Victoria herself had a very good understanding of what the Hanoverians were for and just as importantly what they were *not* for. As she noted coolly, it was all to do with

> the duty which is imposed upon her and her family, to maintain the *true* and *real principles* and *spirit* of our *Protestant* religion; for her family was brought over and placed on the throne of those realms *solely* to maintain it.

This was code for the sort of reflections that a Queen could not discuss aloud. That the Hanoverians were, or ought to be, in the business of supplying legitimate heirs to the throne, which in turn meant that the illegitimate offspring that were something of a Georgian speciality, had to be quickly forgotten about.

George tried to ensure a smooth succession by means of the Royal Marriages Act of 1772 but his assiduous efforts almost backfired. The remarkably silly Act drew up the most stringent rules possible concerning Royal marriage candidates. Pitt the Elder criticised the Act's provisions as 'new fangled and impudent, and the extent of the powers given wanton and tyrannical' and the Act almost had the consequence of ending the line. To avoid domestic factionalism, George opposed British and therefore non-Royal wives. Thus, between a slew of illegitimate children and various mad, unhappy, absent, unfortunate or unwilling albeit Royal foreign and lawful wives, the dynasty almost failed.

In the end, only one young princess blocked the unwelcome prospect of the Duke of Cumberland, George III's unpopular and reactionary fifth son, acceding to the throne. Even then this was only thanks to a dashing young German princeling from the pettiest of states. The young princess was Charlotte of Wales, who is the tragic reason we have a Victorian age to look back on. Loved by the people as much as her father, the Prince Regent, was held in contempt by them, Charlotte was heir presumptive, had charm, looks and no brothers. The dashing young German princeling was Prince Leopold of Saxe-Coburg-Saalfeld,* the finest husband the *Almanach de Gotha* could offer.

Sadly, in 1817, Charlotte died in childbirth. She was only twenty-one and her infant son was stillborn. Her husband and her country were bereft. This calamity set in train the disagreeable contest in the course of which various aged Hanoverian roués put aside their mistresses and common-law wives and sought instead someone who could be married. Now that Charlotte was dead and gone, who could marry and supply an heir in short order? This was a game the whole family of Hanoverians could play.

---

* This is the Prince Leopold who became King of Belgium and was close to both Victoria and Albert.

Essentially, they were playing for cash rather than behaving out of patriotic duty so this was the reason for this frenzied drive to sire a legitimate heir. It was not the result of a dream to have a descendant occupy the throne. Rather, success at the game held out the prospect of what most of them sought more dearly than anything else. An heir would bring money, because Parliament had voted an allowance to the father of an heir to the throne and money would bring a rescue from the bankruptcy that was an all too common family trait.

Prince Edward, Duke of Kent, was the fourth son of George III and he won this game. He was in so much haste to marry appropriately that he settled on a comparatively elderly thirty-two-year-old widow for his bride. Princess Victoria of Saxe-Coburg-Saalfeld was the sister of Leopold, and she had two children already from her previous marriage to Charles, Prince of Leiningen. The choice of Victoria demonstrates clearly the extremely narrow field of candidates available to Edward and his brothers by the terms of the Royal Marriages Act. The couple married in 1818 and to save money the Duke took his new bride back to Germany, which was cheaper to live in, and only in the seventh month of her pregnancy did they return to England. Kent was in debt so deeply that he drove the carriage which brought them back to England himself, for he was unable to afford a driver. Victoria, as Queen, would still be settling her father's debts twenty years into her reign.

Alexandrina Victoria, names perceived to be so unpleasantly foreign that MPs for years thereafter petitioned to have them changed, was duly born at Kensington Palace, British-born and an heir at last, although at this point still only fifth in line to the throne. The Duke of Kent died in 1820 and the Duchess, who was still not rich, almost moved back to a cheaper Germany. Only the counsel of the canny Leopold, still an immensely popular figure, which was attested to by the Field Marshal's baton he had been given, the dignity of 'His Royal Highness' which he was permitted to use and, perhaps most galling to the greedy Hanoverians, the £50,000 per annum pension Parliament allowed him, persuaded his sister to remain and to raise the princess in England. Although her succession was not assured, Leopold knew that there was every chance the infant Victoria would ultimately become Queen. How much better for her, for the monarchy and for the country, that she be raised in Britain as a Briton, like her proud although sometimes mad grandfather before her.

This background is vital in itself because it illustrates the vagaries of history. Victoria was only born because a bounty was offered, in effect, to bring her into being. She only became Queen because of a Ruritanian law drafted decades previously and because another princess had died in childbirth the year before Victoria herself was born.

How the destiny of an age, and of a country and of an empire, can turn on chance.

*

Victoria's childhood bears all the hallmarks of an over-written novel. A suffocatingly over-protective mother, a Rasputin-like minder and a swirl of bitter enmity fringed the edges of her cloistered palace life. None of this ought to bode well for a happy future. In later life, with a fine instinct for understatement, the Queen described her childhood as 'rather melancholy'. She was reared under the elaborate and forbidding 'Kensington System', a maze of rules and regulations which involved her isolation from other children and other outside influences, including other members of the Royal Family, the better to render her dependent on her mother and on her mother's ambitious aide John Conroy.

This Conroy was a man for whom the word 'cad' was invented. A long list of other insults was levelled at him by contemporaries and it may safely be assumed that the insults were well founded. The relationship between Conroy and the Duchess of Kent has fascinated Royal historians for generations. Whether he was, within the walls of Kensington Palace, more to his Royal mistress than a domineering servant is not known but he was in control of the young princess's upbringing and watched her every move. The Kensington System facilitated this surveillance. Victoria, until her accession, slept in her mother's room and played with no one other than those permitted by Conroy. These tended to be his own children, who were instructed to join in the spying on the princess and whom Victoria came to hate as heartily as she did Conroy himself.

It is important to emphasise just how complete and appalling this state of isolation for the young princess was and how little the monarch and his court saw of the precious, much-sought-after heiress who after 1830 was heir presumptive. George IV invited Victoria and her mother to dine once. Conroy successfully intrigued so as to prevent mother and daughter from attending William IV's coronation. In fairness to Victoria's mother she was in return scandalised at the rakishness and parading immorality of the late Georgian Court and wished to preserve her child from their contaminating influence. Yet the effect of such isolation and loneliness could only be negative for her daughter. This was a girl in training for the role of Sovereign, who was nevertheless barred from socialising in Royal circles.

Any measure of sense in Victoria's early life came only from Leopold and at some point even his wisdom had to be delivered by letter. The popular prince had first turned down the insecure Greek throne, before accepting that of the new Kingdom of Belgium in 1831, and following his departure for Europe Conroy's pretensions grew further. He tried to force Victoria to sign a document confirming him as her adviser, should she, as seemed entirely likely, accede before she was of age. He constantly intrigued against her uncle the Duke of Cumberland, even going so far as to claim that this uncle plotted to murder his niece in order to obtain the throne for himself, and he pushed for the status of the Duchess of Kent to be raised. He failed to have her made 'Dowager Princess of Wales' but he did succeed in having her confirmed by Parliament as regent-elect, in the event of a minority. In her own household, Victoria's only true friend, at this point in her unhappy childhood, was Baroness Lehzen, an erstwhile governess to the older, now adult children of the Duchess. Even she was not the easiest person in the world to handle but she was dutiful to her charge. Amid this world of dysfunction, the wonder is that Victoria emerged from her childhood as a stable and thoughtful young woman.

It is certainly the case that Lehzen, together with the male tutors assigned to the princess, did a fine job educating Victoria. The two Anglican bishops whom the Duchess invited in 1830 to assess her eleven-year-old daughter were delighted with the child's progress. Victoria, they reported, 'displayed an accurate knowledge of the most important features of Scripture History and of the leading truths and precepts of the Christian Religion as taught by the Church of England, as well as an acquaintance with the Chronology and principal facts of English History'.

Conroy made much of his Royal possession. A capable man if an incurable schemer, he organised carriage tours round much of southern England, in the course of which Victoria was displayed to the crowds as though she were a prize beast. She hated these engagements. They made her ill and tired, and the Court liked them no better, accurately reading Conroy's intention to set Victoria as an opposite pole of interest and power to that of the King. Those who took the trouble to look to the future could see all too clearly the role Conroy was preparing for himself and it was an open secret that the Duchess was comfortable with this state of affairs.

There was a fly in this ointment. Victoria herself, wholly unworldly and inexperienced though she was, was *not* comfortable with Conroy's plans and strategies and she was never, then or at any time, prepared to concede one inch more than her youth and relative powerlessness obliged her to do. She displayed as a teenager a touch of that steel that later her ministers would come to recognise only too well. No stratagem Conroy could pursue would lead the iron-willed princess ever to sign over any future rights to him.

While the Court saw next to nothing of the heir presumptive, there was a final sense of satisfaction felt by William IV, who had come to despise the weak-willed Duchess and her unpleasant sidekick, when he realised his ambition of living long enough to see his niece come of age. He passed the line with just over a month to spare. The King lived until 20 June 1837 which allowed him to pass Victoria's 18th birthday on 24 May and enjoy a final Waterloo Day on the 18th. As eighteen is the age of majority for monarchs there was no reason for a regency, so scheming relations and their friends were irrelevant.

Victoria could now order her own Court, her own Household, her own advisers and counsellors and break free of her mother and of Conroy. Victoria's first act as monarch was to move out of her mother's bedroom and to have the Duchess's suite placed far away from her own. While she could not expel Conroy from her mother's household, she could, in effect, now remove her mother from hers.

At her first Privy Council, the Accession Council, two of her Royal uncles, the Dukes of Cumberland and Sussex, were the first to do homage to the new Sovereign. From the start, this petite, near child-sized monarch behaved as if born to the role. She 'not merely filled her chair', the great Duke of Wellington observed, 'she filled the room'. William IV's last Parliament dissolved on his death. It was only in the course of Victoria's own reign that the practice ceased of dissolving Parliament upon the demise of the Crown. The Queen vowed: 'It will be my care to strengthen our institutions, civil and ecclesiastical, by discreet improvement, wherever improvement is required.'

This was all very well but Victoria was a woman and *this* indisputable fact meant that the first significant event of her reign was the loss of the principality of Hanover. The kingdom from which the dynasty derived its name slipped from its grasp, because in Hanover the succession was determined by the Salic Law, which forbade female succession. Hence Ernest Augustus, Victoria's unpopular uncle the Duke of Cumberland, who had coveted the British throne himself, became a king in Germany instead. The personal union with the British Crown ended.

The reputation of the new Hanoverian monarch has suffered and been blackened by history, explicitly because of his family connection to Victoria herself. This is, as far as it goes, a shame, because he had had an illustrious military career, serving Britain with distinction against revolutionary France. Yet it was an easy matter to set him beside the virtuous eighteen-year-old Victoria and compare the two to instantly unfavourable effect. Plainly the new Queen could not stand accused of having done all that her uncle was suspected of having done. She could not have murdered her valet or fathered a child with his own sister or have been one of the principal opponents in the House of Lords of Catholic Emancipation. Only the last of these was actually true.

Ernest was in fact infatuated by the House of Lords in general. So tender was his devotion to the institution that even after becoming King of Hanover he found occasion to visit London and sit with them. Alas, he did not love his own German institutions so much. One of his first acts on becoming King was to suspend the constitution of Hanover, an act which did nothing for his reputation. No wonder the reputation of Victoria should be so burnished, for it is the easiest thing in the world to compare a beautiful young woman with a rakish, autocratic and allegedly murderous and incestuous older man and find the older man sadly wanting. Certainly one thing is true. Victoria never tried to suspend the British Constitution.

*

Prince Albert, the 'good' German to balance Ernest Augustus's 'bad' German, was famously the man in Victoria's life. He was not, however, the first man to play a pivotal role in her evolution as a queen. The credit for this success belongs to her first Prime Minister, the agreeably cynical Whig politician and noted dandy Lord Melbourne. He was a widower when Victoria came to the throne. There was, therefore, no other woman waiting to monopolise his time and the youthful monarch instantly discovered a rapport with him. Agreeable, solicitous of her comfort and gallant, Melbourne was the opposite of the chilling Conroy in every possible way. The monarch and premier spent hours together, walking, talking and cantering together in Windsor Great Park, as shown in Francis Grant's evocative painting *Queen Victoria Riding Out with Lord Melbourne*. The Prime Minister acted in these critical early years as a combination of counsellor and confidant, affectionate uncle and private secretary. His support, though watched intently by his political critics and the factions within her Court, was vital in assisting the Queen's development of a role and a style. Melbourne became something of a paragon but unfortunately for his many successors, other possibly than Disraeli, nobody in the eyes of the Queen could ever quite match up to her great and dear Lord Melbourne.

She was, in this impressionable phase, under his tutelage, though she was still capable of making errors. Looking back decades later, Victoria, who was never fond of admitting to her own mistakes, nevertheless publicly regretted some early missteps. One was the so-called 'Bedchamber Crisis', the details as mentioned earlier and which had the effect of causing the Queen to become entangled in a potentially dangerous political spat. Another was even more painful, not to say profoundly diminishing to Victoria's standing. This was the Lady Flora Hastings affair, when the Queen took against one of her mother's ladies-in-waiting. She had long disliked Lady Flora, suspecting that she was yet another spy in the service of Conroy and when in 1839 she saw that Lady Flora's belly was swelling suspiciously, she jumped to the conclusion that the unfortunate woman had become pregnant by the dastardly Conroy and dismissed her from her service.

In fact, Lady Flora's swelling was caused by the liver cancer which was to kill her. Soon it became all too apparent that she was dying. Conroy took the opportunity to broadcast the story, not exactly false, that the Queen and her Prime Minister had been blackening Lady Flora's name and the lady herself felt obliged to publish a piece in the weekly *Examiner* defending her honour and blaming Victoria's tutor Baroness Lehzen for slandering her. This was, in other words, a truly appalling incident and few of the principals emerged from it with any honour except for Lady Flora, who died in July. Victoria visited her shortly before her death and years later the Queen continued to report the nightmares that assailed her as a result of her role in this episode.

In the Whiggish account of Victorian constitutional progress, these early outbursts of personal rule were an aberration and one which the Queen cured by taking wise advice, from her Prime Minister, from her uncle and ultimately from Prince Albert. Marriage meant further evolution for the Queen. Victoria could free herself further, in the most respectable way possible, from the mother with whom she continued to have a complex and not entirely unaffectionate relationship. It also led to the displacement of Lehzen. She and Victoria had always been close and their relationship had been all the more critical when set against the context of Conroy's presence and role as architect of the Kensington System. Yet Lehzen's past service would always count for less once a husband appeared on the scene, especially a husband who would assist in producing the heirs that would bar Ernest Augustus once and for all from the British throne.

Prince Albert, who has his own chapter, had a great impact upon Victoria's style and concept of governance. She was strong-willed and apt to do as she pleased and these characteristics never truly disappeared. Albert brought with him from Germany precisely the form of prudence needed at this time by the British monarchy and its head. Each of the German Royals, focused as they were on their own tiny principalities and duchies, grew up aware of the delicacy and fragility of their situation as rulers and Albert passed on this awareness to his wife. Even though the British monarchy had roots sunk deep into the national psyche, this did not mean that these same roots could not be dug up if the context changed. Victoria's strong will never diminished in the course of her long reign but her awareness of this potential delicacy of governance, bestowed by Albert, caused her to rein herself in and to play her part in developing the constitutional monarchy that survives to this day. A sound monarchy that knows its role, its place, its duty, that instinctively steers clear of any political spats.

The wedding of Victoria and Albert in 1840 was the first sign that 'Victorian values', as they have become known, were more truly *Albert*'s values. The Prince wanted only bridesmaids whose mothers were themselves also of impeccable virtue while Victoria maintained a late Regency toleration of human foible. 'One ought always to be indulgent toward other people,' the Queen ruled, '[if] we had not been well brought up ... we might also have gone astray.' The rigour that came to accompany Victorian morality and that is widely believed to have flowed from Victoria herself fortunately came to the Queen via the good offices of her consort.

*

In religion, Victoria and Albert were as constant in their doctrines as they were in one another. Both shared a Protestant faith that was relatively uncomplicated. Neither was tempted by Tractarianism, that form of doctrine that emerged in Oxford in the 1830s and that manifested as a more ritualistic High Anglicanism, or by any form of evangelicalism. For the Queen, her values were simply those taught her by the Bible. She regarded the Tractarian debate coldly. She named it 'ritualism' and pressed for its advocates to receive no preferment within the Church of England. She was, after all, Supreme Governor of the Church so her words must be listened to. She also had significant power and patronage within the Church hierarchy and she was not afraid to exert her influence.

Her opinions showed themselves most clearly in 1868, when she championed the appointment of a solid anti-Tractarian, Archibald Tait, as Archbishop of Canterbury, or rather, as *her* Archbishop of Canterbury. In 1874, she signalled her approval of the Public Worship Regulation Act, which Tait introduced as a private members' bill to Parliament and which sought to stamp out 'ritualist' practices in England. The bill passed, much to the pleasure of Victoria, but it was by no means without its critics. A number of clergymen were prosecuted for what were regarded as excessively 'Tractarian' practices and the law was not repealed until 1965. To involve herself with such a bill was arguably not the cleverest move the Queen made but her conscience drove her. She saw *her* Church as being the very opposite of High Anglican. Indeed, it was often observed that she and Albert were arguably at their most religiously comfortable in the unyielding Presbyterian pews of Crathie Kirk, the small church adjoining Balmoral.

Importantly, Victoria had no tint of sectarian enthusiasm. She vocally decried mistreatment of her Catholic, Hindu, Muslim and Jewish subjects alike. This was because they were *her* subjects. On her own religion, she was privately sure. When in 1874, a member of Gladstone's first administration became the first minister to convert to Catholicism, the Queen's reaction was: 'How dreadful this perversion of Lord Ripon's ... I knew him so well and thought him so sensible.' Yet time after time she would come to the defence of those being persecuted

411

for holding to their faith, whether in Ireland, India or even Germany. She was appalled, for example, at Chancellor Otto von Bismarck's cynical and dishonest *Kulturkampf* against the Catholic Hierarchy in Germany and entirely sympathised with her daughter Vicky, by then the German Crown Princess, in her doomed, liberal opposition to it.

As for Victoria's attitude to the Catholic Church in general, this is inevitably coloured by historical enmities. Hence the Queen is often presented as being a good deal better disposed towards Pope Leo XIII, who reigned from 1878 until his death in 1903, and with whom she shared a taste for Vin Mariani tonic wine than she was towards his formidable predecessor, the Blessed Pope Pius IX, who reigned from 1846 to 1878. Pius IX was frowned upon by liberal Protestants for formalising the doctrine of Papal Infallibility and for reconstituting the English Hierarchy in the aftermath of Emancipation. It was under Pius's direction that England witnessed the enthronement of the first Archbishop of Westminster and such examples of the growing confidence of the Catholic Church in England and Wales led to a sharp reaction and the last bout of widespread anti-Catholic violence witnessed in England. It also led to the ludicrous Ecclesiastical Titles Act of 1851, which permitted only the Church of England to use formal episcopal titles. This was a law of such surpassing foolishness that it was repealed a mere twenty years later but, in its day, it had the natural effect of placing the Catholic Church very much on the defensive.

It is important to glance at this context, for it places Victoria's own relatively expansive attitudes in sharp relief. For all that she was *personally* disapproving of other religious observance, she was also perfectly aware as *Sovereign* that Victorian Britain contained many mansions and they all ought to be respected. Her own religious faith was impregnable and this confidence flowed into her relaxed attitudes to the religious worlds she saw all around her. She deserves a good deal of credit for her leadership on this potentially fraught issue.

*

It would go too far to say that Victoria engaged in a form of *Albertolatry* in the lifetime of her husband but no one could ever doubt the Queen's devotion to him. As we have seen, however, this love did not extend to allowing Albert to play the role for which he yearned. It was a year before the Queen allowed her husband a key to her government boxes and his emergence as chief counsellor and practical intermediary with the government was gradual. For the truth was that, in the matter of power and authority, Victoria was deeply territorial and this was a habit that, like many of her habits, took time to dissipate. Her attitudes could be contradictory nonetheless. While she kept her new husband at arm's length from her power, she was delighted when, following an attempt to assassinate her and coupled with her recent pregnancy, Parliament agreed to designate Albert regent in the event of her death.

The Queen's jealousy and sense of territoriality also figured in her relationships with others. Specifically, she luxuriated in the time she was able to spend exclusively with Albert, exclusive of the nine children the Royal couple had together. Victoria was, as we have seen, the first Queen Regnant to have her all of her children live to adulthood but her famously large brood was for her a mixed blessing and she made little attempt to hide this opinion. While Albert was positively *au courant* in his attitude to parenting – he played, taught and cared for them personally as much as he could – Victoria could be peevish if forced to spend too much time with her offspring. When they were adults, she told them quite freely that they had got in the way of her doing the thing she really liked, which was time alone with their now-deceased father.

'What you say of the pride of giving life to an immortal soul', she said to Vicky of a new grandchild, 'is very fine, dear, but I own [that] I think much more of our being like a cow or a dog at such moments.' Though breastfed herself, Victoria abhorred the practice, much preferring the institution of the wet nurse. Indeed, the Queen, though having the advantage of being a woman, had decidedly Victorian attitudes about her sex in general. Nonetheless she and Albert, the Court and government all conspired in promulgating a most potent and useful story of the Royal Family as being as near an image of family perfection as could be imagined.

Together, in the eyes of the public, Victoria, Albert and their children indeed constituted the model family. In much the same way that model farms had been the effort of the upper classes to show others how things could be done, Victoria's family showed the British people that Hanoverian dissolution did not have to be life *à la mode*. It succeeded so much so as to justify entirely Victoria's boast that 'England is the country of family life'. In terms of symbolism, this was very powerful.

In the course of her long reign, Victoria mastered the art of symbolism. From statues to stamps, young Victoria and old Victoria were symbolically represented in every corner of the globe and in every fashion conceivable. Daughter, woman, wife, mother, grandmother, ruler, Queen and Empress, all these roles she demonstrated on a greater stage than any other personality enjoyed in her lifetime. For Victoria, for example, to compile some memories of her family's time in the Highlands was to write an instant bestseller. There was nothing the Queen did which was not interesting and little which was not held to be in some way exemplary. Yet this was also someone who freely observed, and not merely for effect, that 'we women ... are not fitted to reign'. Is there a paradox here or is it necessary to try to understand Victorians in their own terms?

The changing sense of womanhood was one of the many revolutions witnessed in the course of the nineteenth century. Queen Victoria was intellectually explicit about her response to the ideological clamour which arose during her lifetime, as she put it, 'this mad wicked folly of "Women's rights" with all its attendant horrors'. There was much that was cut off from Victoria simply because she was Queen and not King. 'My whole heart is in the Crimea,' she wrote of the war with Russia. 'I regret exceedingly not to be a man & to be able to fight in the war.'

It is worth reflecting on what it meant to have a queen on the throne at this time rather than a king. In all European monarchies, whether liberal and constitutional or backward and unconstrained, direct exercise of the prerogative was everywhere clung most tightly to in *military* affairs. It followed that Victoria's reign saw the Crown rise above military politics just as much as it rose above party ones, simply because the Sovereign was a woman. This inadvertent change, this evolution, truly is worth noting as a highly significant moment. It certainly did not happen everywhere else. Royal rule over vast armies was very much a later, twentieth-century European concern, not least with William of Prussia, the Queen's eldest grandson.

Victoria, though never greatly bound by the desires of others after she became Queen, chafed at what womanhood meant for her. Although she looked with horror at the prospect of female emancipation, she was not unaware of what the Victorians called the Woman Question and was well able to connect the issue with herself and her own experiences. Marriage, and, more to the point, if you asked Victoria, childbirth, meant that 'the poor woman is bodily and morally the husband's slave. That always sticks in my throat.' It was the human or physical condition to which Victoria was imperiously objecting, and *not* the relationship between the sexes. Of this she approved thoroughly.

If there were an alternative history of Britain, what difference would a King Victor have made to the world over which he ruled? Perhaps he would have been tempted to become embroiled in the military and strategic squabbles in which Britain, as the world's most powerful state, found herself occasionally entangled. After all, the monarchs of far lesser states all involved themselves intimately in their armies and navies. Without doubt this fantasy Victor, even if displaying exactly the same personality traits as Victoria, would have been spared the criticisms she has since suffered, from all manner of otherwise respectable opinion.

Take just this one recent view of the Queen as the end of her reign approached. A most distinguished British historian remarked that:

> the Queen had become very fat, rather ugly, semi-invalid and half-blind ... In general she was callous, insensitive, obstinate, outspoken, capricious and bigoted and quite extraordinarily selfish ... A long unchecked habit of self-indulgence effectively trans-formed the monarch into a monster and her courtiers into sycophantic cyphers ... The result was a court regimen at once tyrannical and tedious, unbearable and unreal.

All of these things might have been true too of the notional King Victor. Indeed, some of them might even have been said by historians a century on from his death. Yet they would not have carried quite the same bite or been said to the same ends as the words above. Victoria inevitably was abused because she was a woman and because she had transgressed in terms of appearance and temper, aspects that no man would have been taken to task about in the same terms.

The best example of Queen Victoria being excoriated in a way unimaginable if applied to King Victor comes with Albert and the loving family life the Royal couple created for themselves. At the time there existed a phenomenon known as the 'Coburg conspiracy', a contemporary para-noia in which various princelings of this obscure epony-mous Royal house conspired in a cabal to run Europe, with Victoria herself being Albert's cat's paw. Nowadays, there are other criticisms, in this case broadly feminist in nature. Victoria is chided for supposedly having let Prince Albert rule in her stead. That far from being her de facto private secretary he became a kind of shadow king, while she retreated, happily, most proponents of this theory at least concede, to the pleasures of mere domesticity.

In truth, Queen Victoria became no less of a woman when she learned to rely upon Albert as a partner and to trust him. In his sphere, Albert performed the roles his age allocated to him but these did *not* include somehow supplanting Victoria as the 'real' monarch, whatever that was meant to mean. The services he performed for his wife were those he did out of duty and love and which she had him do out of desire and need. Victoria wanted him to help her, to help manage the vast burdens of monarchy, which would otherwise continue almost entirely unsupported. We must not forget that Victoria in the first part of her reign lacked even a rudimentary private office. Albert should be applauded by history for having loyally and devotedly served his wife the way he did, while Victoria should be acknowledged for facing her own limitations and having the courage to design her role afresh.

*

At the age of eleven, Albert decided to 'train myself to become a good and useful man'. No one who looks back on the Prince Consort's still-manifest contribution to British public life can doubt that he succeeded. Part of his success came in weaning the Queen off her addiction to the Whigs, embodied so charmingly as they were in the figure of Melbourne, and encouraging her to see the likes of Sir Robert Peel as a figure no less useful and loyal. It can be hardly stated strongly enough that Albert's achievement, in dissuading the Queen from the kind of party allegiance in which all her Hanoverian forebears indulged constantly, was crucial in moulding the constitutional monarchy that is enjoyed today. He left another tremendous legacy to Victoria as monarch. He opted not to follow Wellington as Commander-in-Chief of the Army and this further insulated the Royal Family from active involvement in a potentially divisive political question.

His loss, when it came, was overwhelming. Infamously, Victoria blamed her eldest son for Albert's death in December 1861. The Prince Consort died of typhoid fever or stomach cancer but his demise was attributed by Victoria to the weakening of his spirit brought about by Bertie's near *mésalliance*, or so his parents thought, with an actress in the course of a visit to Ireland. Appalled by the story he had heard, a gravely ill Albert travelled to Cambridge to confront his son. Albert died a fortnight later and Victoria never forgave Bertie for what she took to be his malignant role in precipitating her husband's death. 'I never can, or shall,' she hissed in a letter to Vicky, 'look at him without a shudder.' This reaction is of a piece with the entirety of her response to the tragedy. It is worth noting at this point that the Queen, very untypically by nineteenth-century standards, had had scarcely any experience of bereavement up to this moment of crisis in her life. She had been devastated by her mother's death earlier in the year, for this very reason. She had never known her father, had no siblings and her own children had all survived into adulthood. Death had been remote to her and now first her mother and then her husband had been, as she saw it, snatched away.

Her response was understandably extreme. The stark details of this response stand out as only Victorian ones still can. Albert's watch was wound daily, his clothes were laid out each day, the jug of hot water and fresh towels were brought daily into a room that remained unchanged for twenty years. Victoria slept every night in the company of a cast of Albert's right arm and his nightshirt. All these, plus the infamous 'withdrawal from public life', conspire to paint the picture of a Queen who had abandoned her duties, first under the weight of unbearable grief and then out of something akin to self-indulgent wallowing in the life of the unmerry widow.

Certainly Victoria-the-irresponsible is the spiteful image Lytton Strachey sought to paint. He was very successful in this and the staying power of his jibes is astonishing. The century of sneering at the Victorians is not simply the handiwork of one Bloomsburyite, for Strachey was preaching to a secular choir. There has rarely been a century more resented for its success than the nineteenth. The problem with Strachey's portrayal of Victoria is well put by Matthew Dennison, one of her more sympathetic and acute biographers. What *Eminent Victorians* does to all its victims is simply to doubt their sincerity. This was Strachey's horrible and selfish genius. Thus in Victoria's case, readers are encouraged to watch ironically and coldly as she parades her emotions in a paroxysm of self-indulgence. This is certainly what Strachey did and 'in doing so [Strachey] strips her writing of its power and denies the possibility of her pain'.

Victoria's grief was criticised in her own time. There is, for example, the response to 'Mourning the Prince Consort', a photograph commissioned by the Queen which showed her posed alongside three of her children in a state of what Dennison describes as 'emotional collapse' alongside a garlanded bust of Albert. The feelings were real but the commission was questionable and was duly questioned, on grounds of its over-publicised intimacy. Just as the Queen had been the model wife, now, perhaps too ostentatiously even for an age in which black crepe was sold by the furlong, she was to be the model widow, whether her people wished it or not.

Her grief was in the foreground even at highly inappropriate moments. At Bertie's wedding to Alexandra (Alix) of Denmark at Windsor, the Queen cloistered herself in Catherine of Aragon's closet, perched high above St George's Chapel. This was in 1863, almost a year and half after Albert's death. Seldom would the Queen again open Parliament during the forty years remaining of her reign. Yet Strachey's picture must not be allowed to overwhelm the truth. Desolate as Victoria was, she never stopped doing her boxes. Society went on without her, Bertie and Alix soon became its focus in Marlborough House, but the business of government did not. The Queen continued to work and exercise her prerogative.

What ended instead, and this is why Victoria's 'withdrawal' from public life has such hold on our collective imagination, was a certain way of 'doing' monarchy. To put Victoria's time on the throne in its proper, very different context, after the purchase of Balmoral and

Osborne in the 1840s and 50s, the Royal Family intention-
ally spent easily up to half the year away from view at one
or other residence. Simply put, being Sovereign in 1869
did not mean what it does today. It has been well said
that after Albert's death Victoria opened more hospitals
than she did parliaments but the point is that she *did*
open them. She did not become a hermit in one of her
many residences. Life went on, only now in a different
way. Victoria simply progressed, without the support
on which she had once been able to count. Her sorrow
continued and this is understandable, being a true and
proper tribute to the love she and Albert had enjoyed.

*

As for the work that also went on, a good proportion of
it was entirely supernumerary to that laid down for any
British Sovereign. Its particular quality is best captured
by what Frank Prochaska has brilliantly called the
'welfare monarchy'. This was a monarchy that presided
over, and honoured, the Victorian age of philanthropy.
Victoria and Albert were ardent champions of voluntary
endeavour, which in her reign encompassed many forms
of welfare, including hospitals and schools. *The Times*,
with a flush of entirely deserved patriotic pride, noted in
1885 that London charities alone collected funds worth
more than the budgets of several European states. In
other words, doing good was serious business.

Between people and Sovereign, the real connection
was not the impersonal state headed by Victoria but
rather the good works she directly encouraged and indi-
rectly inspired. Interestingly, while the idea of a 'welfare

monarchy' was intimately tied up with good works, it was not some kind of John the Baptist for the coming of the welfare state. It was instead an end in itself. It was that most Victorian of ends, doing the right thing for its own sake.

The philanthropy stemmed from sincere religious conviction but it also helped ameliorate class divisions. In form, it was often an endeavour led by women, who were denied a range of other outlets. Victoria, as focal point and inspiration, was Royal patron of many more worthy causes than any Hanoverian before her. Moreover, she inspired, or required, if the native inspiration was lacking, as was sometimes the case, her children to discharge the same level of moral leadership in their own activities. This in turn moved others to work harder too and this was the good that social ambition could do. A desire to be noticed by a member of the Royal Family while doing good was not ignoble.

*

However, the poor Prince of Wales was fingered for his father's death, viewed coldly by his mother, regarded by history and again, by his mother, as an unfortunate and regrettable dilettante. He was the heir, as his mother had been before him, but there the resemblance between them, in the eyes of many, ended. Playing cards for money, enjoying the company of more mistresses than any of his great-uncles, named in actual divorce proceedings, Bertie trailed impish scandal and disappointment forever in his wake. Yet, there were strong resemblances between son and mother. He was the open-hearted and passionate son of an open-hearted and passionate mother and not the copy of his father she sought him to be. He shared her loathing of racial prejudice, in such marked contrast to the ideologues of the age, yet it took many years for Bertie and Victoria to reach a detente.

In fact, it took a near tragedy to reconcile the nation and Queen to the Prince of Wales. In December 1871, on the anniversary of his father's death, Bertie contracted typhoid during a visit to Yorkshire. Years later, the writer E. F. Benson, who was yet another professional mocker of the Victorians, popularised an anonymous parody of Alfred Austin, the poet laureate of the day:

Flash'd from his bed, the electric tidings came,
He is not better, he is much the same.

Yet at the time there was only unadulterated relief that another heir had not gone the way of Princess Charlotte half a century before. The thanksgiving service at St Paul's the following year sealed Bertie's rehabilitation. Thereafter, he was readmitted after a fashion into his mother's affections and into the nation's respect.

This same benediction never quite occurred for the two other men most markedly and in these latter days, famously, admitted into the Queen's presence during her long years of widowhood. The Balmoral ghillie John Brown and the 'Munshi', the 'teacher', Mohammed Abdul Karim.

What John Brown did for the Queen is not exactly known beyond the fact that he lifted her from her grieving gloom, a blessing evident to her family at the time and a reason why the gruff Highlander was readily accepted by them and the Royal Household. Deathbed confessions by Presbyterian ministers of illicit marriage ceremonies seem absurd and fanciful but they do underscore the existence of persistent gossip, at the time and since, that there was a good deal more to this very odd relationship than simply one of servant and mistress. Certainly it is the case that the friendship between these two ostensibly mismatched individuals was every bit as real as her love for Albert.

However, the clearest sign that Brown was no illicit Royal lover lies in the fact that Victoria's children were comfortable enough in his presence. There were jokes made about 'Mama's lover' and they spoke affectionately of Brown. Though Victoria finally retained a private secretary from 1861 on, Brown came to discharge many of the same essential functions as Albert had previously done, in terms of managing access to the Queen and conveying her wishes to others. His death in turn, in 1883, produced another paroxysm of high Victorian mourning, every bit as sincere as that Albert triggered. Why should the Queen not weep for her best friend and most trusted confidant?

On the supposedly overly familiar servant/mistress relationship, the portraits Victoria commissioned of them together were one thing but the biography Victoria proposed to write of Brown after his death was something else. It necessitated the Household stepping in to persuade the Dean of Windsor to dissuade her. As for the apparently telling signs of love, such as the fact that on her own death the Queen instructed that a photograph of John Brown be placed in her coffin in the fingers of her left hand, these, taken in isolation, can be read as a sign. However, they signal only that the Victorians treated death much as the Pharaohs of ancient Egypt had done, for their coffins were loaded with as many mementoes and trinkets as they could carry for their journey to the underworld. Into her coffin, for example, the Queen also asked to be placed plaster casts; a shawl knitted by Princess Alice, a daughter who had predeceased her; sundry rings and other curios, and locks of hair; and the Queen herself, arrayed in her wedding dress. Victoria, in short, was very Victorian. So her coffin was as cluttered as her office had been in life.

As for the 'Munshi', her next and last familiar, Karim was a private secretary brought into the Royal Household to help teach the Queen the languages of her Indian Empire. Like Albert and Brown before him, he in time became a mainstay of the ageing Victoria, as she dealt through him with the formal bureaucratic and courtly world round her. Unlike Brown, who was variously indulged, tolerated and even respected by her family and courtiers, the Munshi was simply loathed by all concerned. In this, the truth is that is it difficult to acquit them of racial prejudice. The Munshi's character may well not have been as flinty and upstandingly Presbyterian as that of John Brown. There were fabulous, positively Victorian tales of illustrious origins and siblings brought into the Household to make hay while the sun shone but these were petty and common vices in all Royal establishments. There were plenty of individuals eager to make hay and most of them were British.

One telling tale, as related by her biographer A. N. Wilson, is that at one point, revolted by having to sit with the Munshi and treat him as an equal, cowardly, older, male courtiers fixed on a Lady of the Bedchamber to tell the Queen that the Household would go on strike, should the Munshi accompany them on an upcoming holiday to the Riviera. Victoria was well able to handle such trifling opposition. She swept everything off the table in front of her, ornaments and state papers, as in her fury she faced down her petty-minded courtiers – and won, naturally. The Court ultimately had its revenge. The first thing Edward VII did on succeeding his mother was to dismiss the Munshi and seize and destroy all the letters between him and the Queen.

If the Munshi and John Brown were the two *private* men of Victoria's later reign, the two *public* men were undoubtedly two of her Prime Ministers and the Queen was certainly not shy about expressing her prejudices about both Benjamin Disraeli and William Gladstone.

*

Where Disraeli had the good sense to make Victoria an Empress, Gladstone drove the Queen, amazingly, to threaten abdication. These two men were not, in fact, utterly dissimilar, at least in background. Disraeli as Prime Minister was proof of the social and political progress on offer to talent in Victorian Britain while Gladstone, the Etonian descendant of slave owners and industrialists, was only slightly less so. The Queen was aware of the status and background of both men. Disraeli's father had been, as she noted, 'a mere man of letters' and occupying Number 10 was therefore a 'proud thing for a man "risen from the people"'.

Disraeli knew very well how to use a trowel to lay on his flattery with virtuosic skill. He was keen to tell the

Queen that in constitutional and foreign-policy matters in particular he was so fortunate to have her. 'How great is the power of the Sovereign in this country, if firm and faithfully served,' he assured her. Disraeli was exactly the Prime Minister any Queen would want. 'He repeatedly said *whatever I wished* SHOULD *be done*,' the Queen happily recorded of Disraeli. He proclaimed himself delighted to benefit from the Queen's stock of wisdom. She in her turn delighted in the coups he carried out in her name, from acquiring control of the Suez Canal to formally having her name Empress of India proclaimed by Act of Parliament, an innovation the *Daily Telegraph* called 'a sinister revolution'. Disraeli had '*very large ideas*, and *very lofty views* of the position this country should hold,' the Queen wrote. 'His mind is so much greater, larger, and his apprehension of things great and small so much quicker than that of Mr Gladstone.'

Unfortunately for the Queen, she was obliged to suffer Gladstone's company through four terms as Prime Minister and with her least favourite politician the Queen's manner was different. She was ever eager to remind him that while she had no opposition to constructive reform, 'she also thinks [that] the great *principles* of the *Constitution* of this *great* country ought to be maintained and preserved'. Gladstone paid little attention to this, indeed, he did little to endear himself to the Queen. She was sceptical of his campaign against the Bulgarian atrocities and was contemptuous of his Midlothian campaign, agreeing entirely with Disraeli that it was 'rhodomontade and rigmarole'. Even worse than his election rhetoric was what he did in office, which was to retreat where Disraeli had advanced. His actions in Afghanistan and South Africa were dreadful and his attitude to Gordon in the Sudan was regarded as indefensible.

Victoria even probed the limits of constitutionality, such was her dislike of Gladstone. She manoeuvred to avoid appointing him Prime Minister in 1880. Instead, she invited Lord Hartington, later the Duke of Devonshire, to form a government but the Liberal Party caused her to see the limits of her authority and Gladstone was summoned in the end. This 'half-crazy enthusiast ... ruining all the good of 6 years [of] peaceful, wise government' was the Queen's description of her new Prime Minister, as she mourned the departure of Disraeli into the political darkness.

When Salisbury, her last public favourite, lost office in 1892, forcing Gladstone upon her one final time, bitter were the Queen's lamentations. She wailed of 'a defect in our much famed Constitution, to have to part with an admirable Govt like Ld Salisbury's for no question of any importance, or any particular reason, merely on account of the number of votes'. How very differently things were done in the German Empire, when compared to the realms of our own dear Queen.

*

William of Prussia was the only grandchild Albert ever saw and this was not a fortuitous omen. In her later years, Victoria had become the 'Grandmother of Europe' but Europe did not constitute a happy family. It had begun so well, Albert and Victoria had built up high hopes of the marriage of their eldest child Vicky to the soon-to-be

Crown Prince of Prussia in 1858. In 1888, on his accession as Emperor Frederick III of a united Germany, her son-in-law told the Queen: 'My feelings of devoted affection to you prompt me ... to repeat to you my sincere and earnest desire for a close and lasting friendship between our two nations.' It was not to be, for even as he sent the telegram Frederick lay dying of cancer. His son and heir would blame Vicky for appointing an English doctor to treat her husband. In other words, he would blame her for the death of her husband.

It is impossible to overstate the tragedy which Frederick's death meant for Europe. Prince Albert, in contracting a marriage worthy of his wire-pulling Uncle Leopold, had sought to secure Prussia and then Germany for the cause of liberalism, constitutionalism and peace. Had, as almost happened in 1862, William I of Prussia abdicated in favour of his son, near thirty years of Anglo-German amity and German progress could have occurred. As it was, in stepped Bismarck and William ruled on until the age of ninety. More accurately, Bismarck ruled on, for it was the Iron Chancellor who truly ruled the united Germany he had forged. As part of his rule, he made the life of the Crown Prince and Princess as desperate as only he could.

Alienating their son William from his parents was hardly the least of Bismarck's crimes. William endured a still more suffocating childhood than Bertie, or Victoria come to that, and in addition he had been born with a withered arm. His iron will led him to master horsemanship regardless of this infirmity and this determination marched together with a deeply restless nature. He was a fiery, deeply temperamental and profoundly complicated individual. He oscillated wildly between idolising his grandmother, her country and its power – upon being made an admiral of the fleet, he gushed that he too was to 'wear the uniform of Nelson!' – and hating his British antecedents. Upon having a nosebleed, he wished famously that every drop of English blood in him would drain out. The contrast between cultured, thoughtful father and half-mad son was painful for Vicky and Victoria alike. Frederick William was a veritable second Albert, while William epitomised everything wrong and impulsive and weak about princes and kings.

Victoria felt the sufferings of her daughter, her brilliant Vicky, her brightest child, as sharp as her mother but without the security of her mother's position and all the more so when Vicky retreated into widowhood too after 1888, the traumatic 'year of the three emperors' in Germany. Even after William sacked Bismarck in 1890, Vicky's situation did not improve. Her son's treatment of his mother was wicked in its cruelty. Vicky and Victoria had been devoted correspondents. Their letters are the best guide to the minds of both and they open a window into the Victorian world and it is impossible to escape in the pages of correspondence the sorrow of Frederick William's brief reign. In so many senses, the only problem with the Victorian age is that it did not go on long enough, as it easily could have done, had Germany enjoyed a long and healthy reign under Frederick William and Vicky.

*

The closing years of Victoria's life were jubilees. Golden and diamond, they confirmed the Queen Empress's place in the heart of the nation and empire beyond the seas. Victoria, having had enough of the European royalties who swamped her palaces in the course of the Golden Jubilee year of 1887, insisted on having none in her Diamond year of 1897. This in turn gave Joseph Chamberlain, ever the innovator, a chance to organise something entirely novel. He summoned the first Colonial Conference, where eleven of her Prime Ministers, leaders of her self-governing colonies, from New Zealand, Newfoundland, Canada and the Australian and South African colonies, joined their Queen in London to celebrate the most powerful nation on earth.

In the face of these public celebrations, Victoria did not change. Although she privately exulted in the reaction of the crowds to her, she did not perform at the diktat of her ministers. 'She will not be teazed & bullied ab[ou]t the Jubilee', the Queen had her private secretary tell her ministers, 'w[hich] seems to be considered only for the *people* and their *convenience* & amusement while the Queen is to do the public and the newspaper bidding. She will do *nothing* if this goes on.' Indeed, she only agreed to the Golden Jubilee in the first place as a kind of *Jubilaeum*, the German 50th wedding anniversary she had been denied by Albert's death.

*

It is worth concluding on what the figure and idea of Victoria *meant*, both to those who were eminent in her time and to those who were not. It is right to dismiss the historians' myth that she was truly threatened by some 'surge' of republicanism. Such disquiet as manifested was only ever relative and fleeting. Victoria sat as securely on her throne as almost any British monarch ever has done and certainly any long-serving one. While sitting there, she did not spend her time reading Bagehot. This constitutional theorist may have formulated doctrines but there is no evidence the Queen either read them or subscribed to them. Yet she must have understood them, for Bagehot declared that public life is theatre and 'the climax of the play is the Queen' and Victoria understood her fame and understood her part in the play.

To understand the Victorian age, it is necessary to see it as they did. Their time was *not* the age of stolidity so many now imagine. The nineteenth century was rather a century of unparalleled, dynamic change. The world was made anew. Conditions which had, to a greater or lesser extent, prevailed since the dawn of civilisation gave way in the face of modernity to new modes of being. Amid this whirl, Victoria was a still, constant centre of the world which was being made and remade around her. She supplied the stability and the continuity. She provided the foundations, as the nation worked and grew during this extraordinary, revolutionary time of change.

It is easy to lose sight of the discontinuity that occurred in Victoria's time. It had its downsides which were visible at the time and not least to the Queen herself. While its great gains came slowly, they did come, and that they came down to this generation securely is in part a tribute to the country and empire over which Victoria ruled. For it would be a worse world today had she and the Victorians never existed.

Victoria inspired those over whom she ruled to do the best they could. This is a simple story but its extraordinary achievements built the world in which we still live today. There could so easily have been worse ones and terrible efforts were made after Victoria to bring them into being. The late Queen deserves gratitude for what she and her subjects did to hold off barbarism, decline and defeat. Victoria was the Queen for a great empire, who viewed all her subjects equally and allowed the Constitution to develop peacefully rather than clinging to the remnants of monarchical power. This was at the heart of her success and secures her place as a Great Victorian.

Acknowledgements

This book would not have been produced without a considerable amount of help. First from Adam Gauntlett, my agent who persuaded me to write and then Jamie Joseph the editor who agreed to take it on and proved patient as political events regularly overtook publisher deadlines.

Christopher Montgomery was a particular help on a number of chapters and provided me with many good ideas. It was my eldest son, Peter, who persuaded me to write the chapter on W. G. Grace and leant me his copy of *Wisden on Grace* to help with the research.

A particular debt is owed to those who typed up my words from either dictation or manuscript. Most of this fell on my private office, Elizabeth Davis and Yasmin Mostafa with help from Fiona Oldfield-Hodge, who can always decipher my scribbles, and Alice Rule, who assisted with some of the initial research.

P. G. Wodehouse dedicated *The Heart of a Goof* to his 'daughter Leonora without whose never-failing sympathy and encouragement this book would have been finished in half the time.' Fortunately, my troop did not delay this work, I managed that all by myself, as Peter, Mary, Thomas, Anselm, Alfred and Sixtus were kindly looked after by my wife Helena and, of course, nanny, and all deserve thanks.

Finally, it was *Heaven's Command* by Jan Morris that sparked my interest in history, and learning about Gordon and Sleeman aged fourteen has influenced two chapters in this book.

Bibliography

Aldous, Richard. *The Lion and the Unicorn: Gladstone vs Disraeli.* Pimlico, 2007.

Arnstein, Walter L. *Queen Victoria.* Palgrave Macmillan, 2003.

Beasley, Edward. *The Chartist General: Charles James Napier, the Conquest of Sind, and Imperial Liberalism.* Routledge, 2018.

Belcher, Margaret. *A.W.N. Pugin: An Annotated Critical Bibliography.* Mansell Publishing, 1987.

Bennett, Daphne. *King without a Crown: Albert, Prince Consort of England, 1819–1861.* Heinemann, 1977.

Blake, Robert. *The Conservative Party from Peel to Major.* Faber and Faber, 1997.

———. *Disraeli.* Faber and Faber, 1966.

Bogdanor, Vernon. *The Monarchy and the Constitution.* Oxford University Press, 1998.

Brown, David. *Palmerston: A Biography.* Yale University Press, 2011.

———. *Palmerston and the Politics of Foreign Policy 1846–55.* Manchester University Press, 2002.

Bruce, George. *The Stranglers: The Cult of Thuggee and Its Overthrow in British India.* Harcourt, Brace & World, 1969.

Cosgrove, Richard A. *The Rule of Law: Albert Venn Dicey, Victorian Jurist.* Macmillan, 1980.

Cowling, Maurice. *1867: Disraeli, Gladstone and Revolution. The Passing of the Second Reform Bill.* Cambridge University Press, 2005.

Dash, Mike. *Thug: The True Story of India's Murderous Cult.* Granta, 2005.

The Davies, Godfrey. *The Early Stuarts 1603–1660, 2nd edn. The Oxford History of England.* Clarendon Press, 1963.

Dennison, Matthew. *Queen Victoria*. HarperCollins, 2013.

Dicey, A. V. *Comparative Constitutionalism*. Edited by J. W. F. Allison, Oxford University Press, 2013.

——. *General Characteristics of English Constitutionalism: Six Unpublished Lectures*. Edited by Peter Raina, Peter Lang, 2009.

Ensor, R. C. K. *England 1870–1914*. The Oxford History of England. Clarendon Press, 1936.

Ferrey, Benjamin. *Recollections of A. N. Welby Pugin, and His Father, Augustus Pugin: With Notices of Their Works*. Forgotten books, 2017.

Foot, David. *From Grace to Botham: Profiles of 100 West Country Cricketers*. Redcliffe Press, 1980.

Francis, George Henry (ed). *Opinions and Policy of the Right Honourable Viscount Palmerston*. Adamant Media Corporation, 2002.

Gash, Norman. *Mr Secretary Peel: The Life of Sir Robert Peel to 1830*. Longmans, 1961.

——. *Politics in the Age of Peel: A Study in the Technique of Parliamentary Representation 1830–1850*. W. W. Norton & Company, 2012.

——. *Sir Robert Peel: The Life of Sir Robert Peel after 1830*. Longman, 1972.

Gordon, Charles George. *Letters of General C. G. Gordon to His Sister M. A. Gordon*. Adamant Media, 2001.

Helps, Arthur (ed). *The Principal Speeches and Addresses of His Royal Highness the Prince Consort*. Cambridge University Press, 2014.

Hill, Rosemary. *God's Architect*. Allen Lane, 2007.

Hobhouse, Hermione. *Prince Albert: His Life and Work*. Hamish Hamilton, 1983.

Hyland, G. J. *The Architectural Works of A. W. N Pugin*. Spire, 2014.

Jenkins, Roy. *Gladstone*. Macmillan, 1995.

Le May, G. H. L. *The Victorian Constitution*. Duckworth, 1979.

MacGregor-Hastie, Roy. *Never to be Taken Alive: A Biography of General Gordon*. St Martin's Press, 1985.

Magnus, Philip. *Gladstone*. John Murray, 1954.

Marsh, Kate (ed.). *Writers and Their Houses: A Guide to the Writers' Houses of England, Scotland, Wales and Ireland: Essays by Modern Writers*. Hamish Hamilton, 1993.

Morris, Jan. *Heaven's Command: An Imperial Progress*. Penguin, 1979.

BIBLIOGRAPHY

Napier, Charles James. *Colonization, Particularly in Southern Australia: With Some Remarks on Small Farms and Over Population (1835)* . Kessinger, 2010.

Napier, Priscilla. *I Have Sind: Charles Napier in India, 1841–1844*. Michael Russell, 1990.

Nutting, Anthony. *Gordon: Martyr and Misfit*. Constable, 1966.

Pollock, John. *Gordon: The Man Behind the Legend*. Lion, 1995.

———. *Gordon of Khartoum: An Extraordinary Soldier*. Christian Focus, 2005.

Prochaska, Frank. *Royal Bounty: The Making of the Welfare Monarchy*. Yale University Press, 1995.

Rae, Simon. *W. G. Grace: A Life*. Faber and Faber, 1999.

Read, Donald. *Peel and the Victorians*. Blackwell, 1987.

Rhodes James, Robert. *Albert, Prince Consort*. Hamish Hamilton, 1983.

Rice, Jonathan (ed.). *Wisden on Grace: An Anthology*. Wisden, 2015.

Ridley, Jasper. *Lord Palmerston*. Constable, 1970.

Roberts, David. 'Lord Palmerston at the Home Office', *The Historian*, Vol. 21, No. 1 (November 1958).

St Aubyn, Giles. *Queen Victoria: A Portrait*. Faber and Faber, 2011.

Shah, Giriraj. *The Life and Times of Major Genaral William Sleeman: Elimination of Thuggies in India*. Kalpaz, 2003.

Sleeman, William. *A Journey Through the Kingdom of Oude, Volumes I & II*. Krill Press, 2016.

———. *Rambles and Recollections of an Indian Official*. Qontro Classic Books, 2010.

Tomlinson, Richard. *Amazing Grace: The Man Who Was W.G.* Little, Brown, 2015.

Trappes-Lomax, Michael. *Pugin: A Mediaeval Victorian*. Sheed & Ward, 1932.

Turnbull, Patrick. *Gordon of Khartoum*. Bailey Bros. & Swinfen, 1975.

Twain, Mark. *Following the Equator*. Courier, 1989.

Wagner, Kim A. (ed). *Stranglers and Bandits: A Historical Anthology of Thuggee*. Oxford University Press, 2009.

Weintraub, Stanley. *Uncrowned King: The Life of Prince Albert*. Simon & Schuster, 1996.

Williams, Basil. *The Whig Supremacy 1714–1760*. The Oxford History of England. Clarendon Press, 1960.

Wilson, A. N. *Victoria: A Life*. Atlantic, 2015.

About the type

This book was set in Clarendon, a typeface created by Robert Besley in 1845 while working at Thorowgood and Co., a letter foundry often known as the Fann Street Foundry in the City of London. Clarendon was the first patented typeface in the world and became a very well-respected typeface of the Victorian era, and the first typeface to introduce bold into running copy.